IMAGES
of America

WINCHESTER

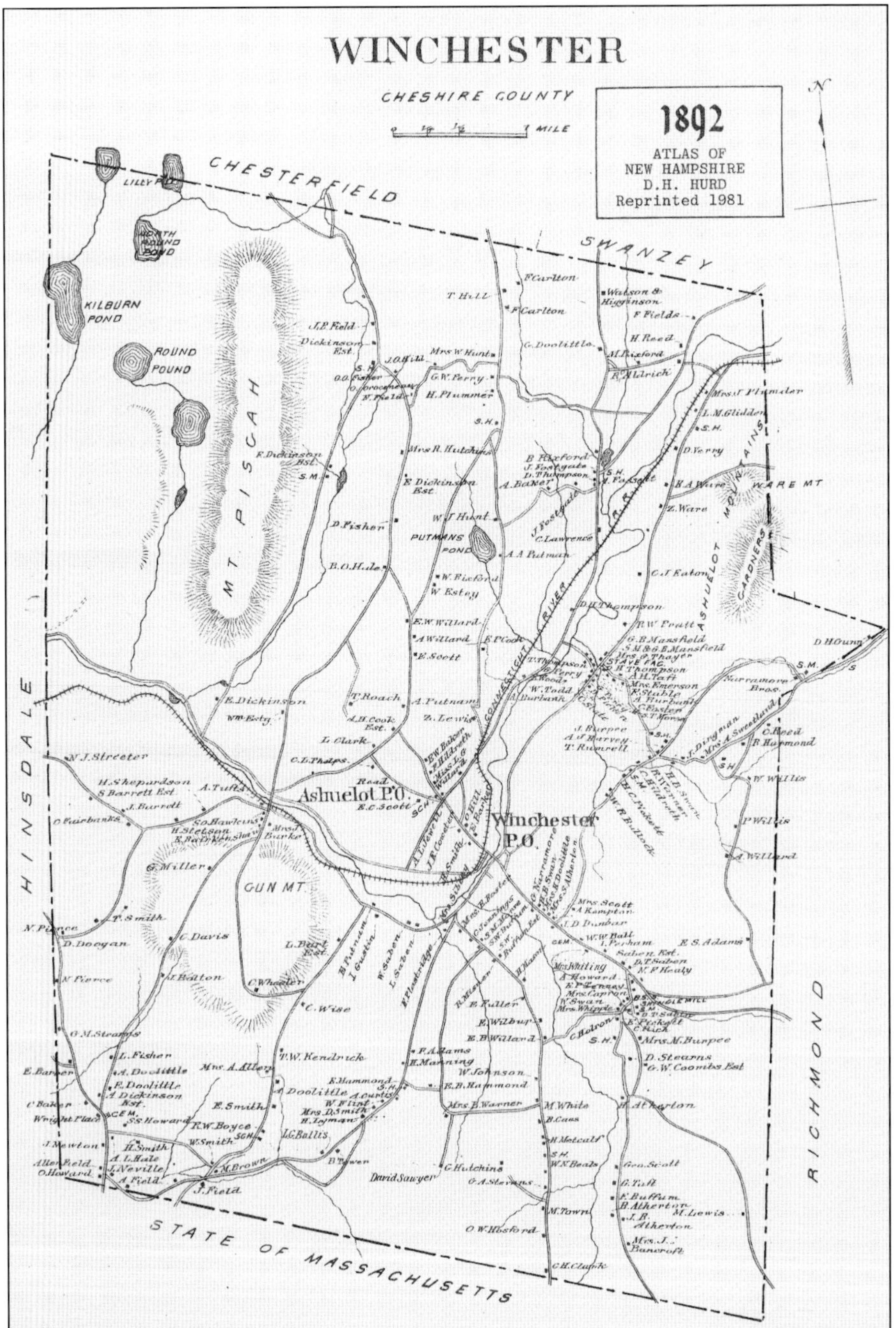

This 1892 map of Winchester identifies all the dwellings and shows the tidy, almost rectangular shape of Winchester. At 55 square miles, Winchester is the largest town in Cheshire County. In 1892, the town had approximately 2,600 residents. (Courtesy of Winchester Historical Society.)

On the Cover: This photograph shows the building formerly known as the Powers Block. It still stands north of the Elm Street intersection on Main Street. (Courtesy of Winchester Historical Society.)

IMAGES
of America

WINCHESTER

Carol Lamprey Poole
and Dorothy Doolittle Farnan

ARCADIA
PUBLISHING

ISBN 978-0-7385-9265-7

Published by Arcadia Publishing
Charleston, South Carolina

Printed in the United States of America

Library of Congress Control Number: 2012930266

For all general information, please contact Arcadia Publishing:
Telephone 843-853-2070
Fax 843-853-0044
E-mail sales@arcadiapublishing.com
For customer service and orders:
Toll-Free 1-888-313-2665

Visit us on the Internet at www.arcadiapublishing.com

We dedicate this book to all the volunteers who worked so hard for years to restore the Sheridan House to its former glory.

Contents

Acknowledgments		6
Introduction		7
1.	Downtown	9
2.	Ashuelot	35
3.	Institutions	45
4.	Famous Sons and Daughters	63
5.	Industry	71
6.	Farming	87
7.	Recreation	97
8.	Disasters	109
9.	Covered Bridges	123
Bibliography		127

ACKNOWLEDGMENTS

Unless otherwise noted, the photographs in this book are from the collections of the Winchester Historical Society and the Conant Library. We are grateful for the support of both of these organizations in creating this book. Their extensive collections made deciding what not to include the most difficult aspect of assembling the images.

There are too many people to identify here who contributed tidbits of knowledge that helped clarify, identify, or illuminate. We thank all of them for helping to make these pages as full of interesting information as they are of photographs. We particularly thank Eugene Piurkowski for sharing his extensive knowledge of Ashuelot. Though we have been careful to check facts and relay accurate information, we do not expect we have attained perfection, so we apologize for any errors we have made.

This book is not intended as a history of Winchester. These pages are instead intended to offer many windows into Winchester's rich history. We hope it whets your appetite for more, and if it does, we encourage you to check out the Conant Library's historical collection and the Winchester Historical Society's Sheridan House Museum.

INTRODUCTION

In 1733, Col. Josiah Willard and 63 other men from Lunenburg, Massachusetts, were granted a plantation by Gov. Jonathan Belcher of Massachusetts. Colonel Willard was, at that time, the commander of Fort Dummer on the Connecticut River at the south end of what is now Brattleboro, Vermont. The new grant was originally called Earlington; the "E" was soon dropped, and the settlement became Arlington.

The grant's western boundary was the Connecticut River, the southern boundary was the line of farms already established in Northfield, the eastern boundary was the western boundary of Richmond, and the northern boundary was the southern boundary of Swanzey. The list of grantees somehow gained three more names. Of the grantees, 27 chose to settle along the Connecticut River, and 40 chose to settle at "ye bow" on the Ashuelot River. Like all grants at the time, it came with the condition that it be settled and a house of worship be erected. Earlington had the additional condition that a road be cleared from it to Lunenburg. All of these conditions were satisfactorily met, and in 1739, Arlington was granted privileges of township and renamed Winchester.

By 1745, New Hampshire had claimed ownership of the territory that included Arlington, and the French and Indian War had begun. The settlers felt unprotected against the unrest and soon abandoned their land, retreating back to Massachusetts. It was not until 1753 that they started returning to their homesteads. France and England declared peace in 1748, but Native Americans continued the attacks on settlers. In 1756, they captured the Joseph Foster family, who lived near what is now Back Ashuelot Road and Ore Mountain Lane. The family was marched to Canada but within the year, they were able to secure their freedom and return to Boston via ship.

The return of the settlers in 1753 marked a major change. Boundaries had to be adjusted to accommodate surveying errors as well as the agreement about the state line between Massachusetts and New Hampshire. Settlers along the Connecticut River petitioned to break off from Winchester; their petition was granted, and the town of Hinsdale came into being. New Hampshire governor Benning Wentworth also re-granted Winchester to its original settlers, thus acknowledging it as a town of New Hampshire.

Colonel Willard had chosen his land well. Winchester included the Ashuelot River and several smaller streams active enough to harness, as well as the vast virgin forests of the area, which came to be called Pisgah. The land also included easily accessible iron ore deposits and a fertile valley created from an ancient lakebed. Early settlers soon started businesses. Significantly, two of the first included a tannery and a sawmill. The lumber industry would account for much of Winchester's future success, and the A.C. Lawrence Tannery was one of its biggest employers until near the end of the 20th century.

The 18th century was one of quiet growth in Winchester. By the beginning of the 19th century, it had taken on the characteristics of a settled town. Sawmills had sprung up in Scotland, Rabbit Hollow, and Pisgah. The available lumber led to the creation of pail and box shops. Three miles downriver, a furnace for smelting iron ore preceded the openings of blacksmith shops and kettle shops. Local craftsman Henry Pratt began producing organs. A musical instrument factory was located on the Ashuelot River. The tannery grew, and then grew again. Winchester became a manufacturing town, and Main Street began to look like a trading center. By 1820, there were almost 2,000 people living in Winchester.

Around 1850, the Ashuelot Railroad arrived, and with it came a few Irish immigrants. As the Ashuelot line was completed and connected with other lines, the market for goods expanded. Smart businessmen saw the potential of combining the waterpower of the Ashuelot River and the distribution power of the railroad. They invested in textile mills in the area that was then called West Winchester. These mills were huge (by the standards of the time), and the owners were soon actively recruiting Poles to immigrate to the area and work in the mills. The railroad also expanded the market for local agricultural products. A slaughterhouse and the Winchester Creamery were renowned for their excellent products. Winchester came into its heyday; by 1900, the town had 23 stores, 21 schools, and roughly the same number of mills.

The 20th century, however, was not as kind to Winchester. By the 1920s, the town's textile mills were losing the competition with South American mills. They were replaced by paper mills, but these also lost out to cheaper producers in other regions and closed one by one until the last mill was put out of business by the flash flood of 2005. The lumber industry faltered as well—box shops closed until only the New England Box Company remained, but then it closed and the Wood Flour Plant followed. By adapting to the market, the A.C. Lawrence Tannery stayed in business through most of the 20th century, but finally closed its doors in 1987.

The 21st century finds Winchester a much different place than it was 100 years ago. Most workers commute to jobs outside of town, yet Winchester remains a vibrant community. Its industrial past set Winchester up as a self-contained town. It is just large enough to support local businesses, which make it possible for townspeople to meet their needs locally, and Keene (New Hampshire), Brattleboro (Vermont), and Greenfield (Massachusetts), are only a short ride away when people want more options.

Today, Winchester's recreational activities attract outsiders. Pisgah State Park, now a state wilderness area, lures hikers, anglers, ATV users, and snowmobilers. Forest Lake continues to attract boaters and bathers who come for the day or the season. The now-clean Ashuelot River is drawing more and more kayakers and canoers. The biggest influx comes when there is racing at Winchester Speedpark or NASCAR's Monadnock Speedway.

For the people who live there, Winchester is a place where you always meet a friend when you go to the store, where you can catch up on a winter's worth of news on a "dump run" in April, where the librarian greets you by first name, where the principal greets your child by first name, and where your voice is heard in town government. Winchester inspires loyalty. The town's rich history helps roots grow deep. The assets of 21st-century Winchester are not mills and jobs, but nature and people. Winchester is a place where people can live healthy lives and feel that they belong.

One

Downtown

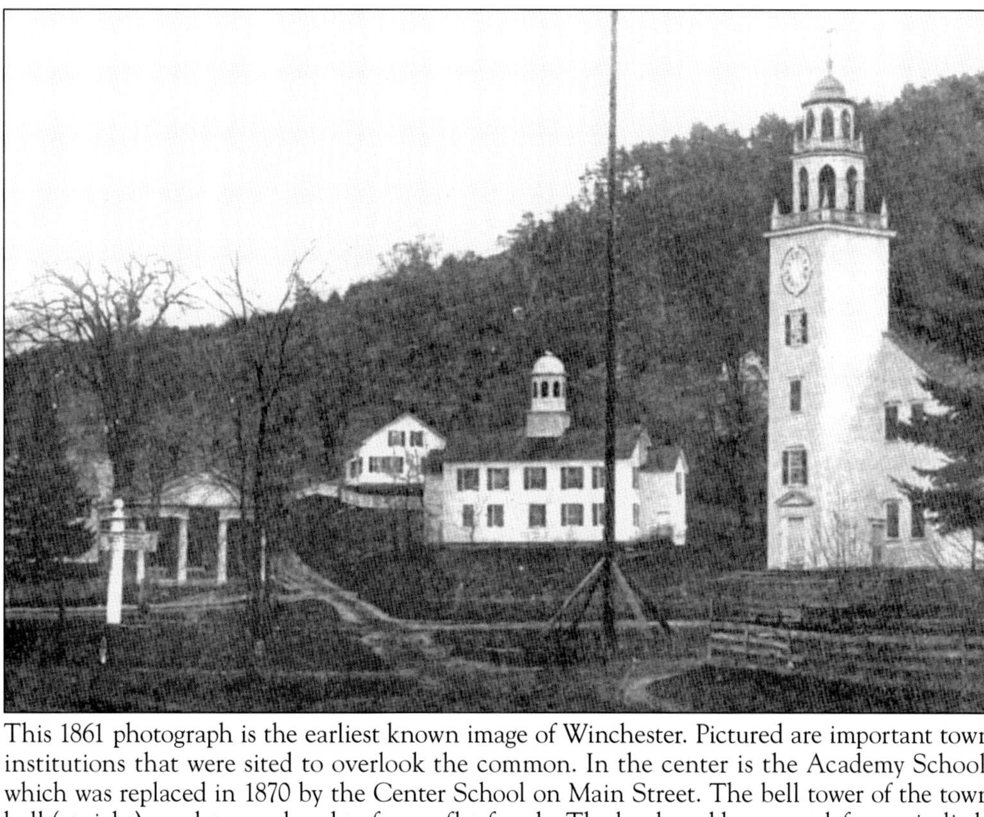

This 1861 photograph is the earliest known image of Winchester. Pictured are important town institutions that were sited to overlook the common. In the center is the Academy School, which was replaced in 1870 by the Center School on Main Street. The bell tower of the town hall (at right) was later enclosed to form a flat facade. The bank and houses at left remain little changed today.

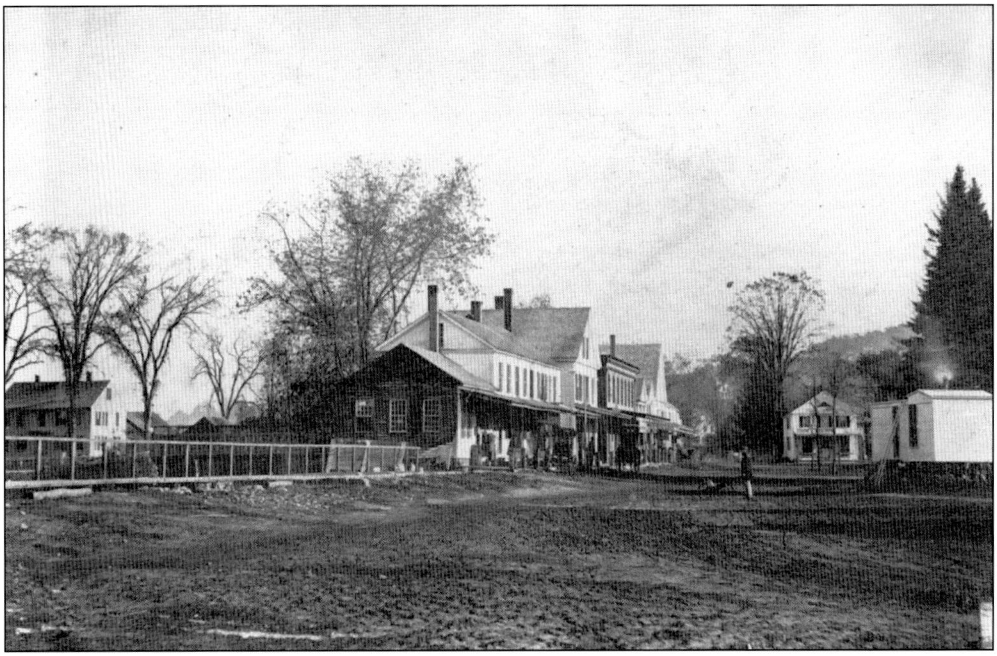

Although it is not possible to date this photograph, taken from the south looking towards Main Street, it predates electricity, automobiles, and a third story on the Burbank Block. At left, the Albee house is visible on the other side of the Ashuelot River. The structure on the right might be a construction office used during the building of the Conant Library.

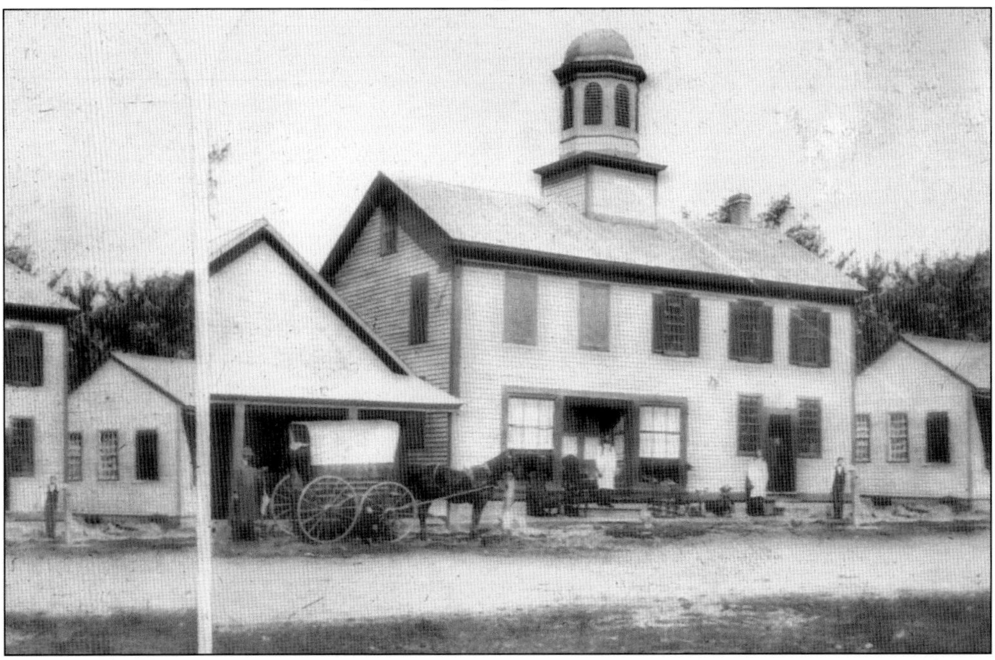

This photograph, taken from an old stereopticon card, is of the Academy School, which originally stood opposite the bank on Michigan Street. After the Center School was built, the Academy School building was moved down to Main Street and converted into a store. This building was lost in the fire of 1971.

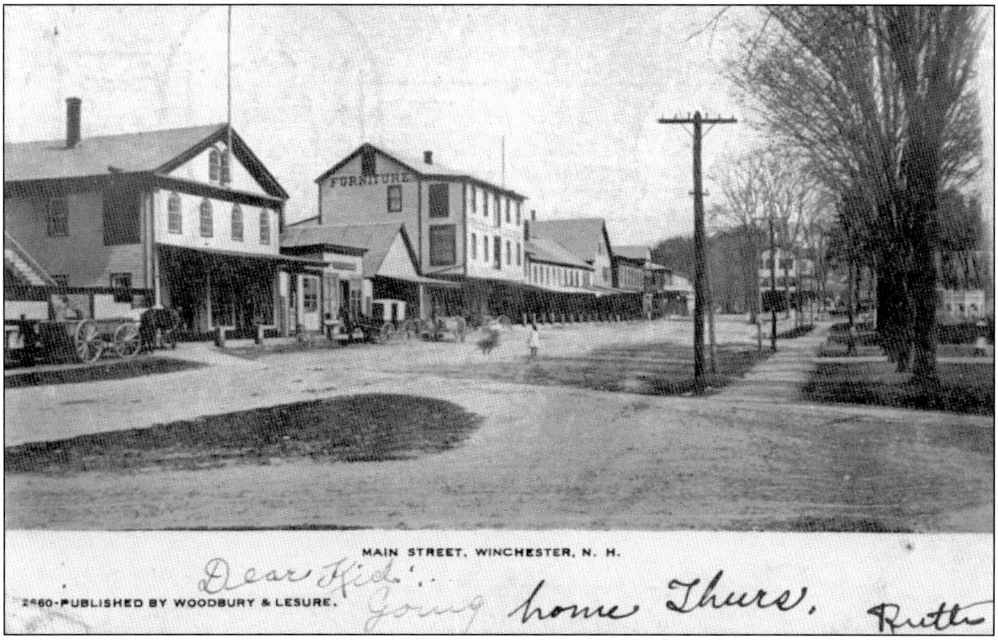

This view from the corner of Parker and Main Streets shows the addition of stores down Main Street. This image also predates automobiles, but electricity has arrived. The large building with "FURNITURE" written on the side was later destroyed by fire, but the peaked roof next to it is identifiable as the present-day location of Win Win Express.

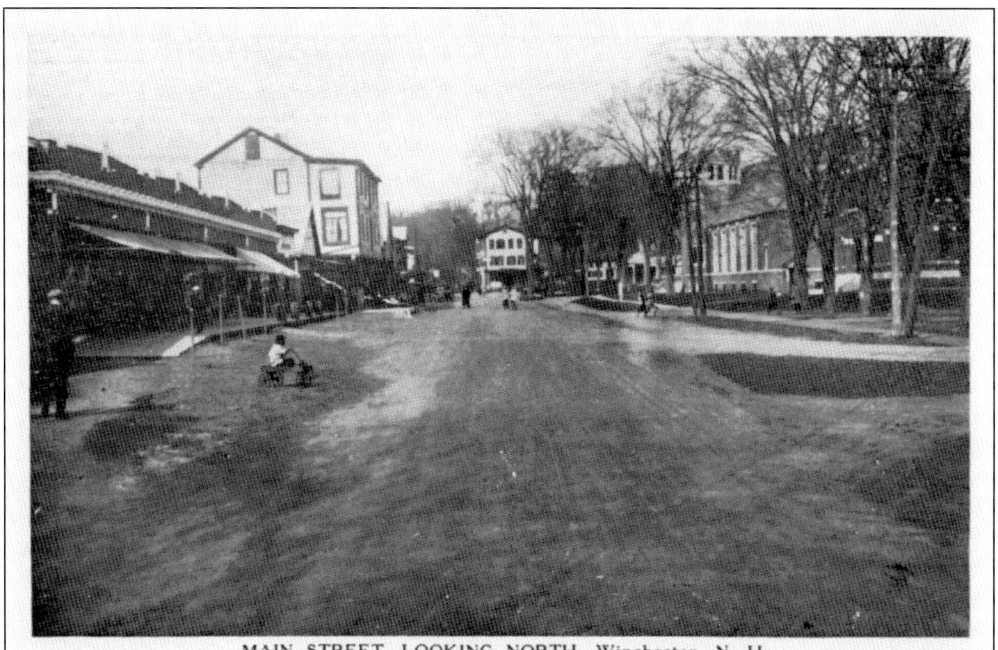

This photograph, looking north up Main Street, still predates pavement, but shows the addition of the brick building that replaced Goodnow's store after it was destroyed by fire in 1943. After Goodnow's closed, it was IGA Groceries, then Gomarlo's Store, and is now Mr. G's. The Conant Library and the town hall are visible at right. Straight ahead is the three-story Burbank Block.

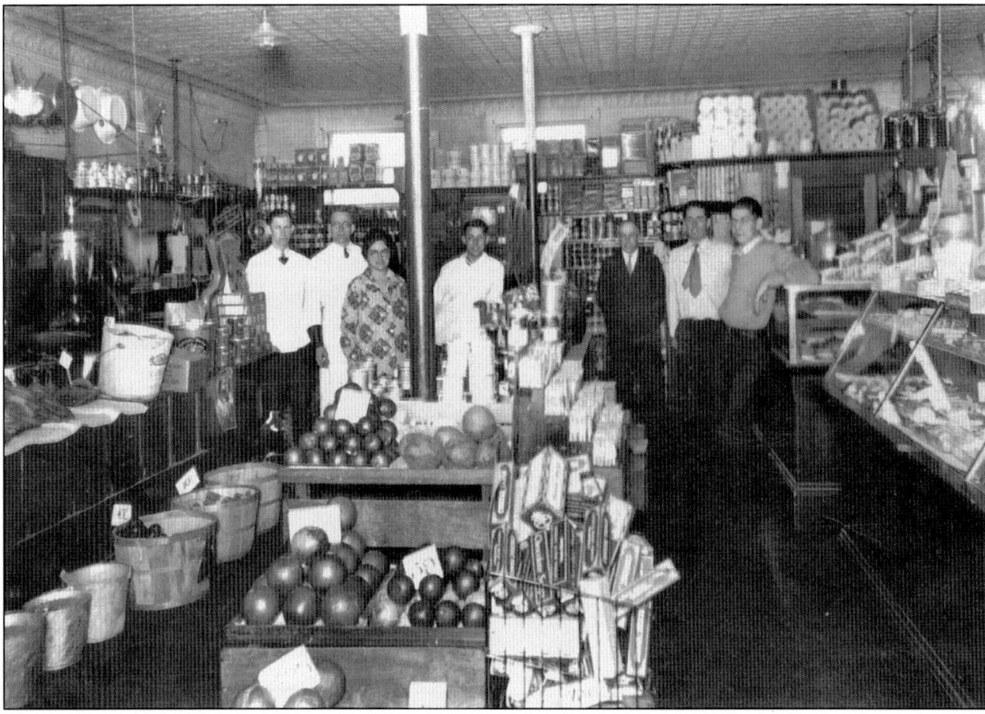

In this photograph of the interior of Goodnow's store, the man in the suit is Winfred Drugg, who became the manager in 1900. The staff members pictured are, from left to right, Steven Sosnoski, Bob Felch, Josephine Smofski, Donald Manning, Drugg, Eugene Allen, and Rodney Foster.

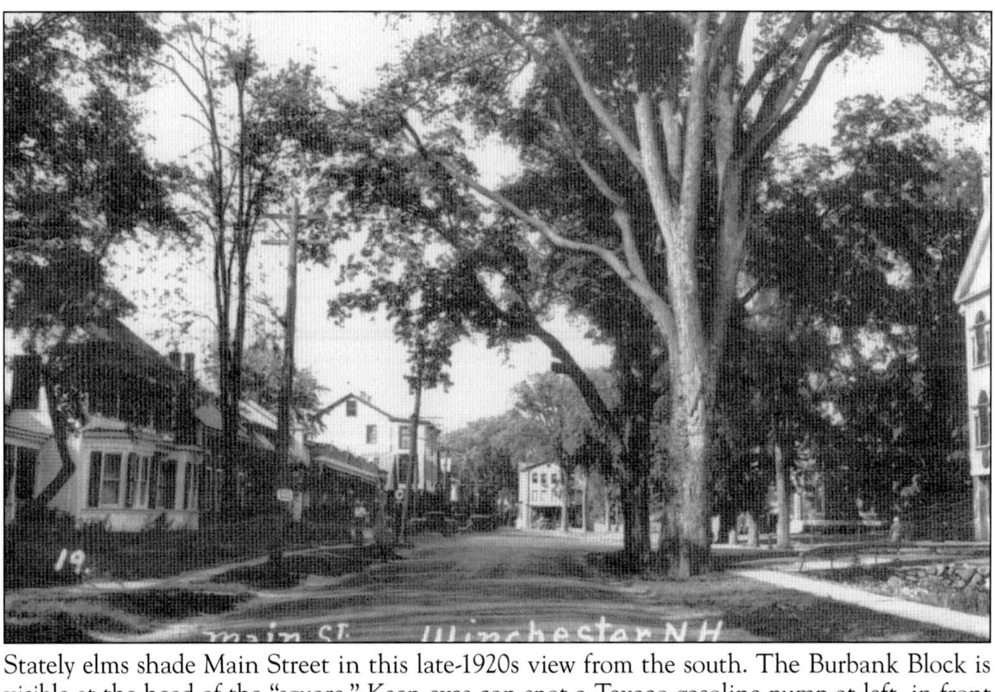

Stately elms shade Main Street in this late-1920s view from the south. The Burbank Block is visible at the head of the "square." Keen eyes can spot a Texaco gasoline pump at left, in front of the grocery store.

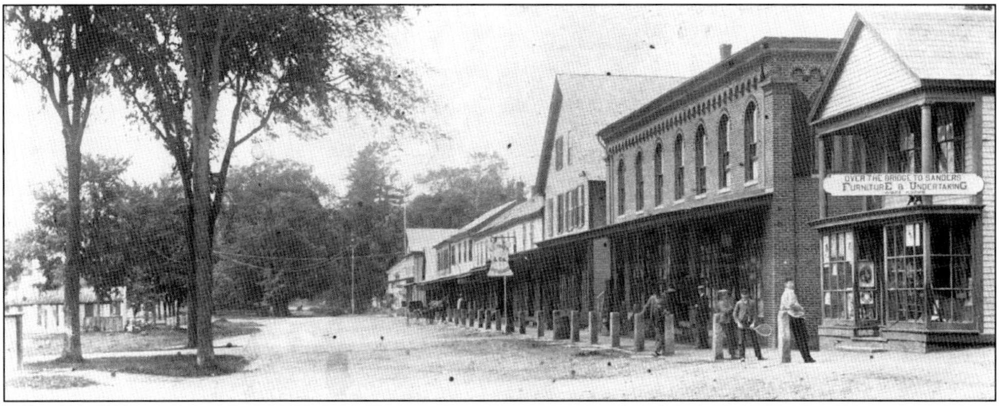

This view of Main Street from the north predates both the Conant Library and the town hall. Note that the building on the south corner of Elm Street has only two stories—it was later raised, and a lower story was added; that space became the post office. The post office was also located in the brick building to the left for a while before moving to a new building on Richmond Road in 1966.

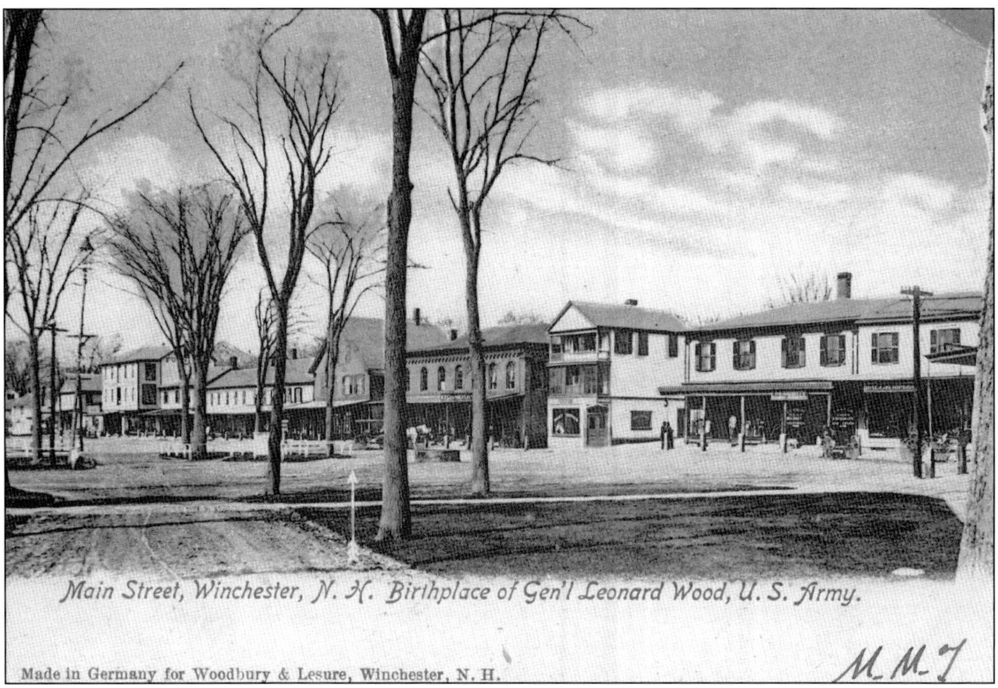

This postcard was mailed in 1905. Excepting the large frame building at left that extends over the sidewalk, the buildings remain much the same today. The three-story building on the corner of Elm Street (just right of center in the image) is marked "Post Office." It would later house a lunch counter for many years.

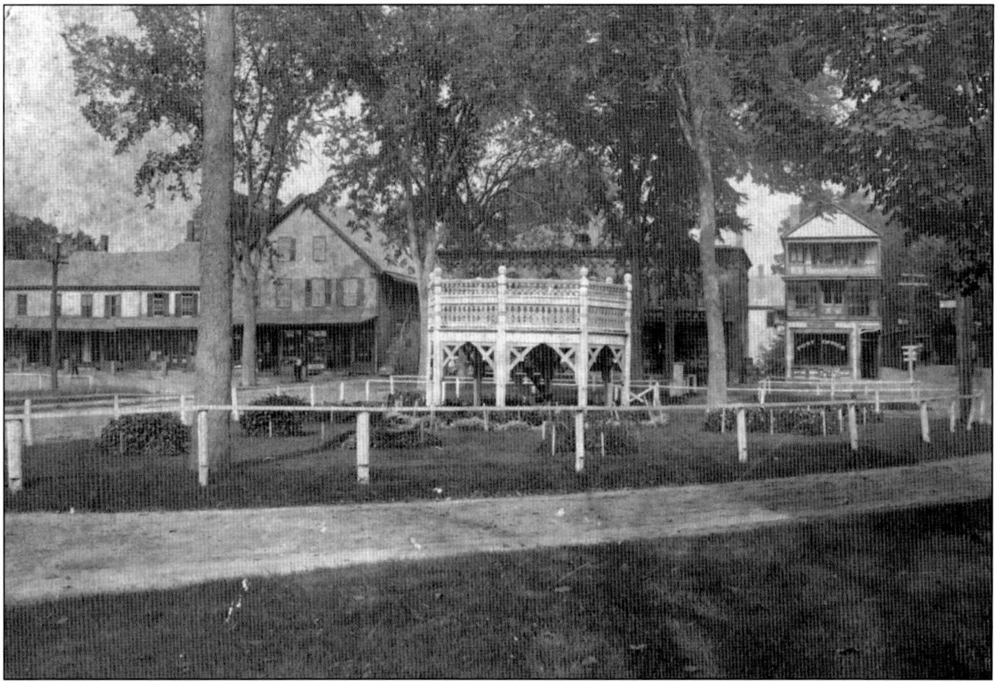

This early view shows the bandstand on the common near the present-day location of the Civil War statue. The common has been eroded over the years by changing traffic patterns. Today, most of it is covered by pavement; only a small part remains.

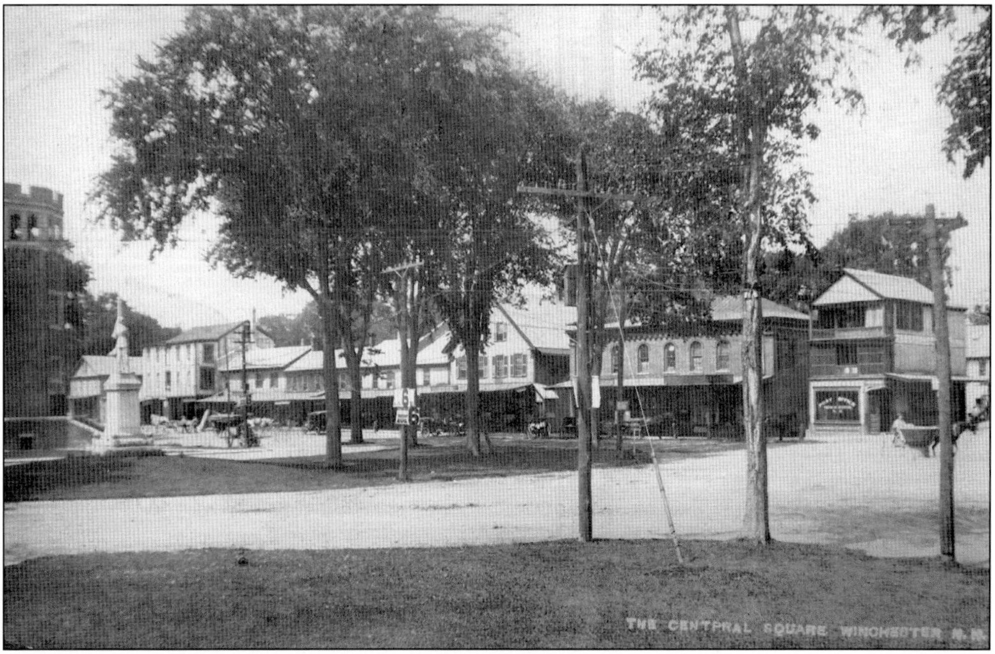

This postcard, identified as "Central Square" in Winchester, was mailed in August 1914. It is notable because the Civil War Memorial is facing south, the way all the monuments in the North were oriented when they were erected (those in the South faced north). At some point, the statue was turned to face Main Street, as it remains today.

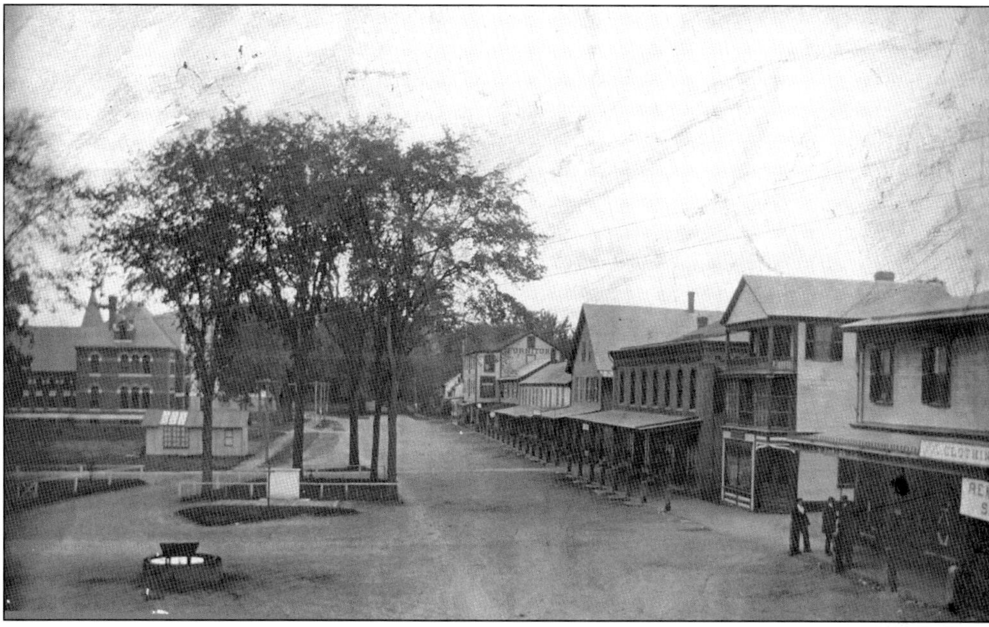

The photograph shows the "common," or "square," giving way to travel lanes. The town hall is not yet built, but electric wires are strung down the east side of Main Street. The elm trees seem to be standing guard to protect the shrinking green space.

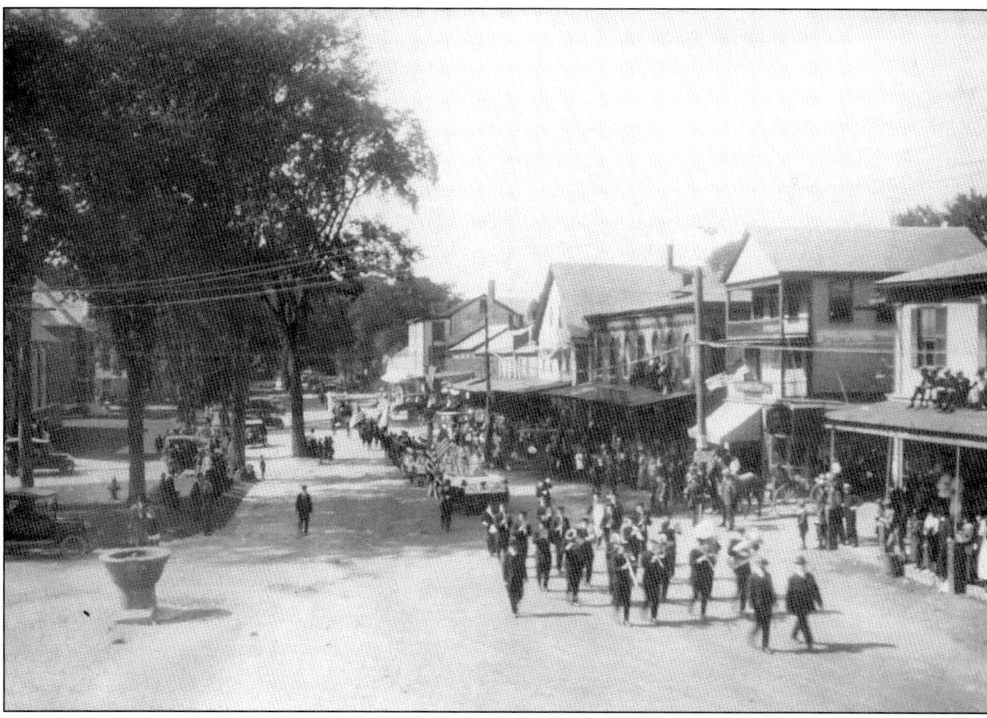

The occasion of this parade is not known, but it was held at a time when horse and buggies coexisted with automobiles. The band is a Polish band from Holyoke, Massachusetts. The two men walking at the head of the parade are Joseph Godleski (left), president of the Tadeusz Kosciuszko Society, and Carl Kulick.

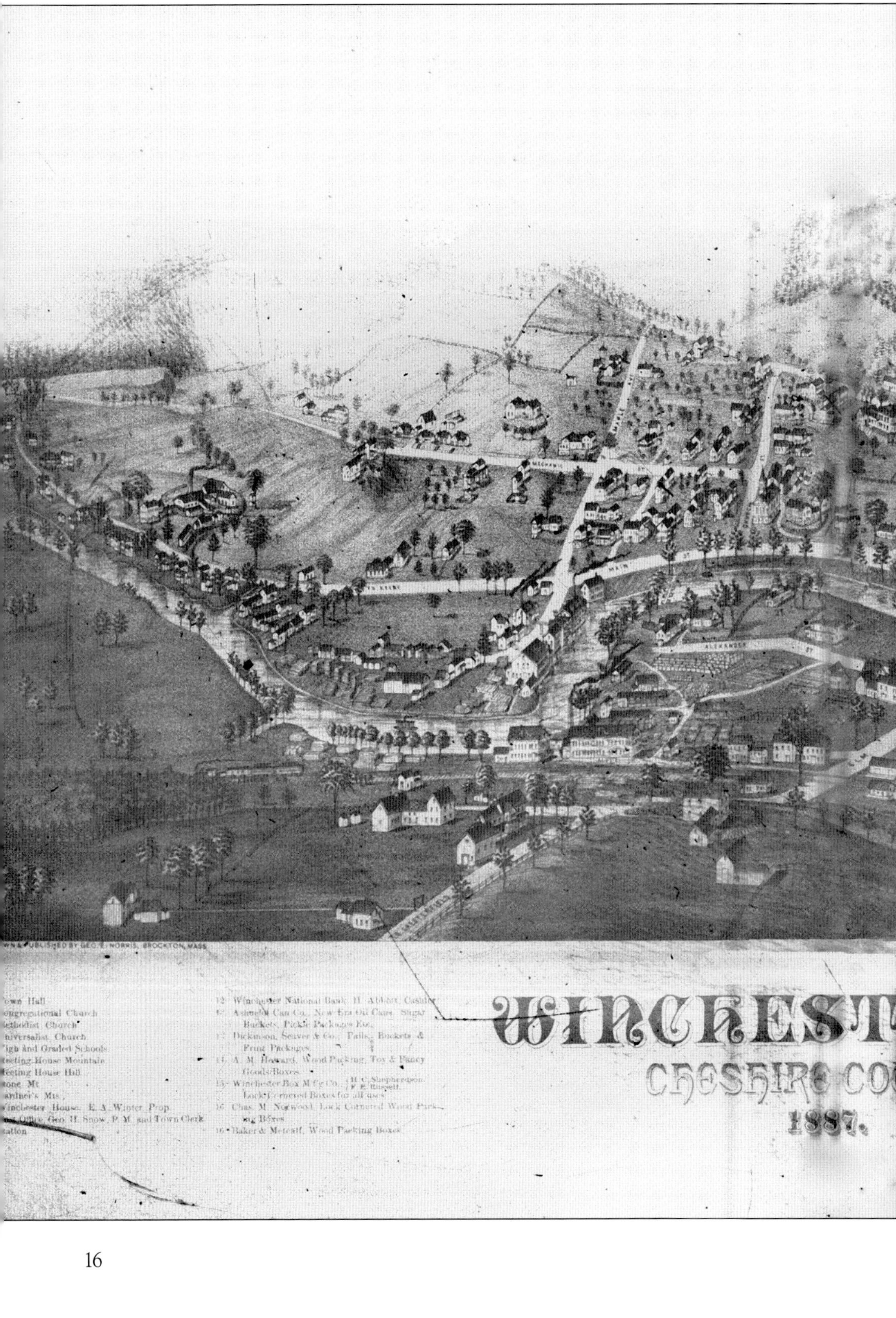
WINCHEST
CHESHIRE COU
1887.
own Hall
ongregational Church
ethodist Church
niversalist Church
igh and Graded Schools
eeting House Mountain
eeting House Hall
one Mt
ardner's Mts.
inchester House. E. A. Winter Prop.
Office, Geo. H. Snow, P. M. and Town Clerk
ation
12. Winchester National Bank, H. Abbott, Cashier
Ashuelot Can Co., New Era Oil Cans, Sugar Buckets, Pickle Packages Etc.
Dickinson, Seaver & Co., Pails, Buckets & Fruit Packages.
14. A. M. Howard, Wood Packing, Toy & Fancy Goods Boxes.
15. Winchester Box M'f'g Co. H. C. Shepherdson. F. E. Russell. Lock Cornered Boxes for all uses
16. Chas. M. Norwood, Lock Cornered Wood Packing Boxes
16. Baker & Metcalf, Wood Packing Boxes

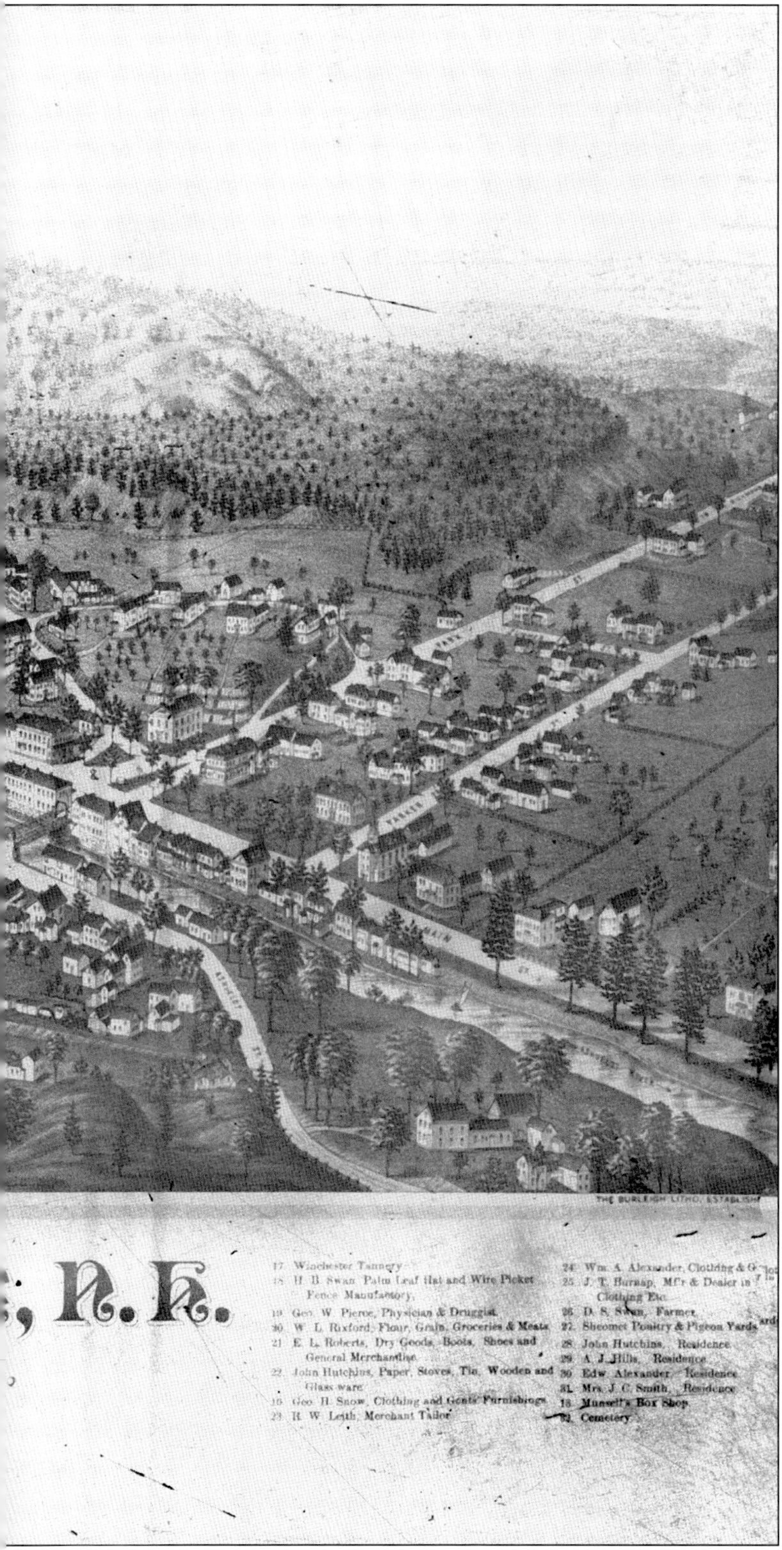

This bird's-eye view of Winchester was made in 1887. Panoramic maps, or bird's-eye views, were popular wall hangings in the Victorian era. The fact that one was done of Winchester is testimony to it being a thriving community, as cartographers only made panoramic maps of places where they could be assured a profit from enough people buying copies. This view is from the southwest, looking toward Meeting House Hill. Most of the houses depicted still exist today. Many commercial buildings, however, have disappeared. For a better view, the Conant Library has a large copy of this map under glass on their conference table.

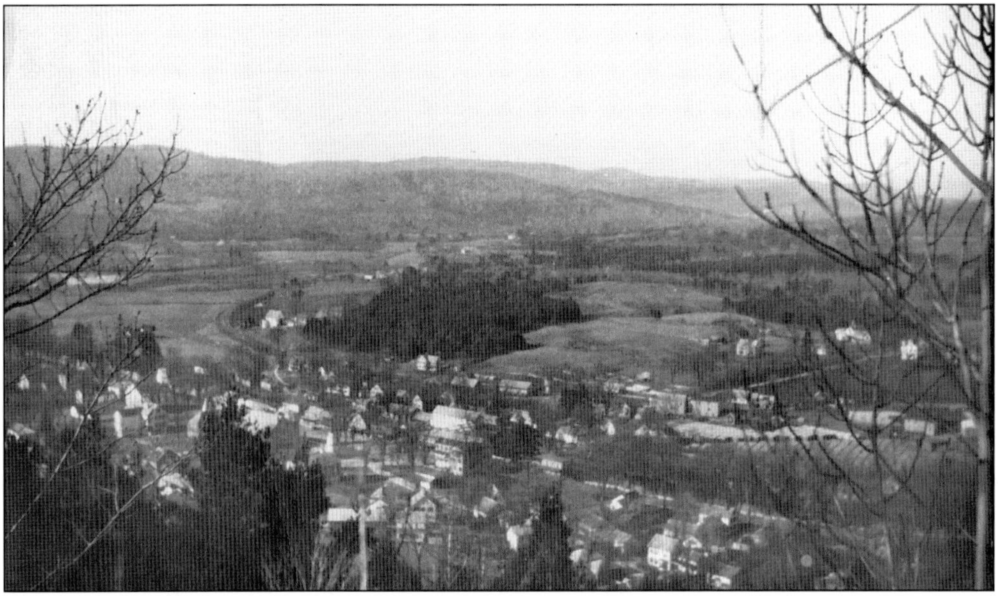

This photograph, which looks over downtown Winchester, was taken from Meeting House Hill. The churches, library, town hall, and Center School are all visible. The Burbank Block still stands, so the photograph predates the 1940s. A keen eye can spot the Smith farm on Ashuelot Street, Elm Hall atop Elm Street, and the Ryll house—with the Ammann house behind it—on Michigan Street. Noticeably absent are many trees and the sewage treatment facility.

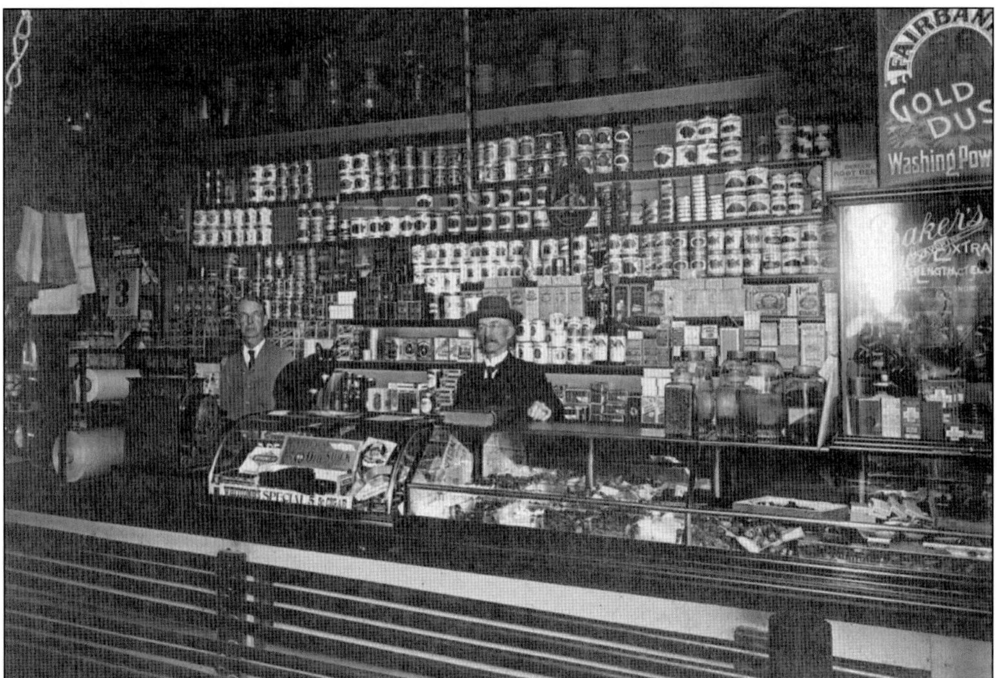

Though Ball and Ripley's store later became a hardware store, this interior photograph shows that they also sold groceries and 5¢ cigars. A lot of Main Street stores sold groceries alongside other products and evolved as the market changed.

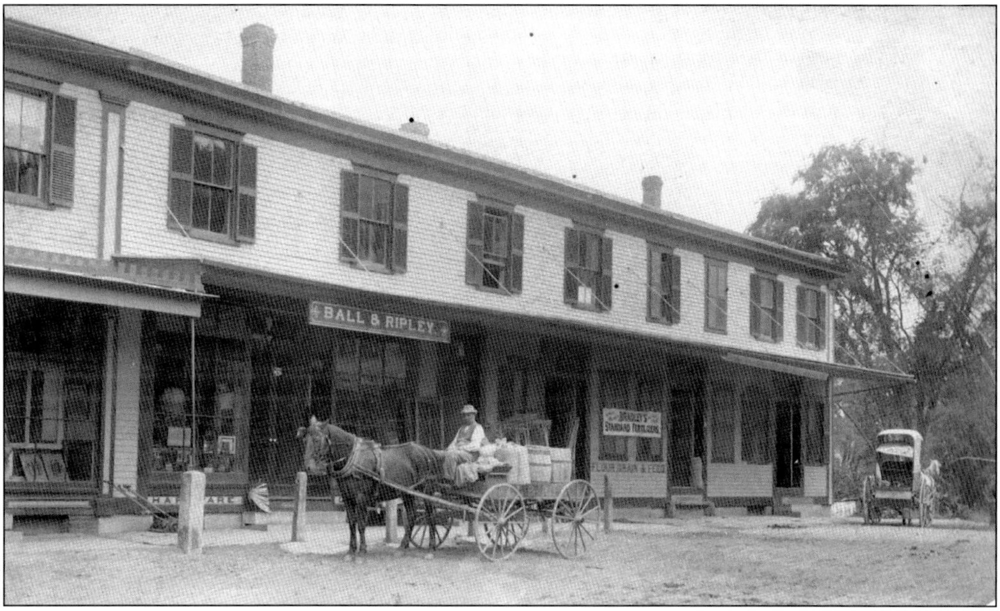

This photograph, which is also on the cover of the book, shows the Ball and Ripley Hardware Store, which was in the building sometimes known as the Power's Block or the Drugstore Block. Power's Drugstore was in the store to the left, on the corner of Main and Elm Streets; it later became the Winchester Pharmacy.

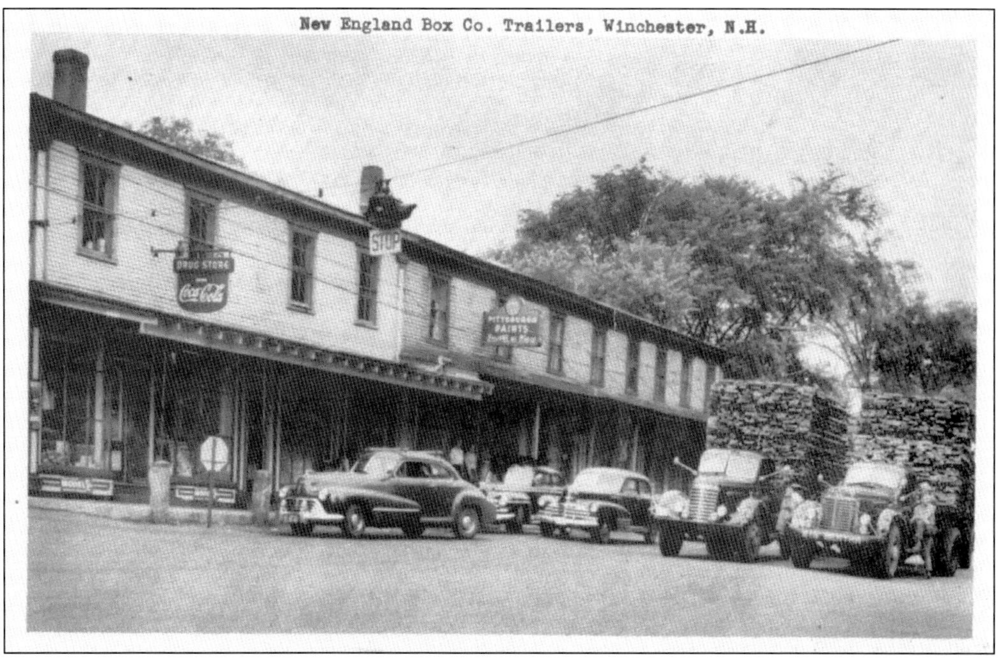

This photograph shows the same building, but at a later time. Truckloads of lumber from the New England Box Company have replaced the horse and wagon. As need declined for business space on Main Street, the block was gradually converted to apartments, which is how it remains today. (Courtesy of Dorothy Doolittle Farnan.)

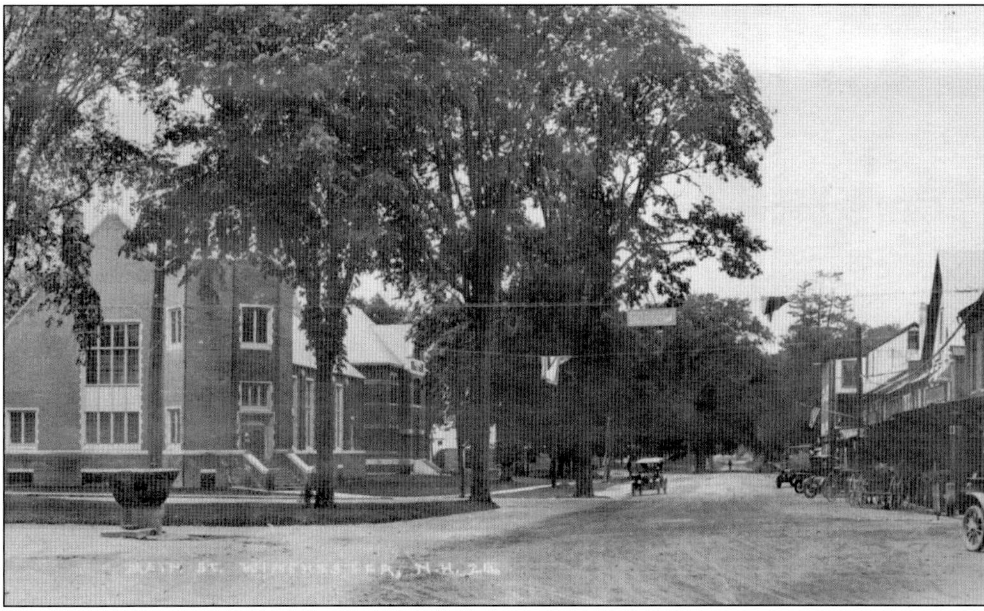

The postcard above was purchased in 1928. At right, a horse and wagon is visible, as well as several automobiles. The watering trough for horses is still in place in front of the town hall. The granite trough is now in Memorial Park, at the corner of Main and Parker Streets, and the Garden Club keeps it filled with flowers each summer. (Courtesy of Dorothy Doolittle Farnan.)

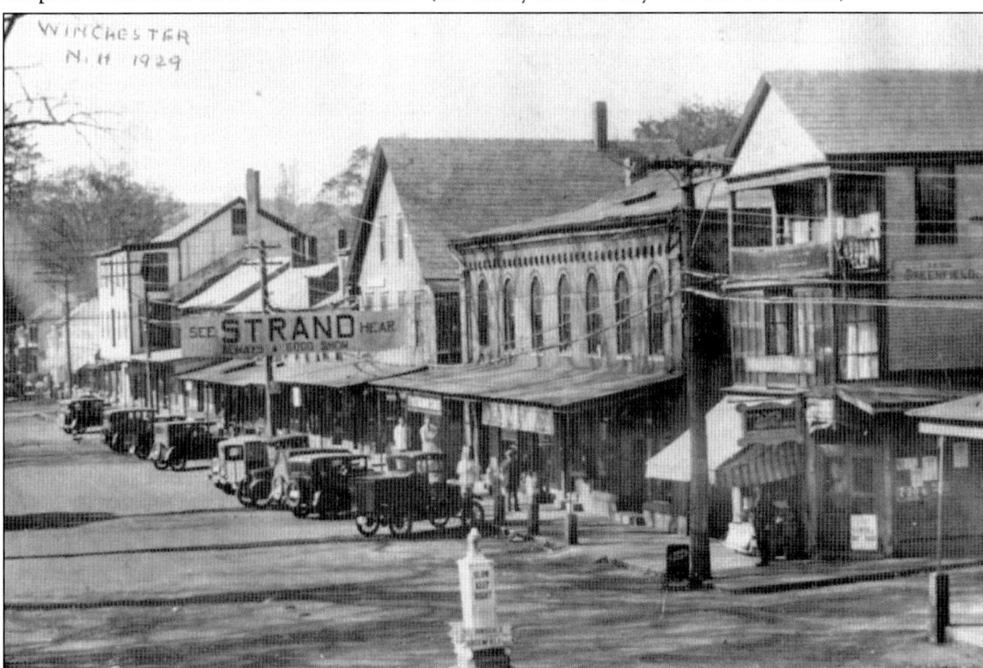

Automobiles have clearly taken over in this 1929 photograph. The Richmond Road/Main Street intersection now has a traffic monument instead of a horse trough. The banner strung across Main Street advertises Strand motion pictures, which were shown in the town hall. Note that one can not only "see" but also "hear" the show.

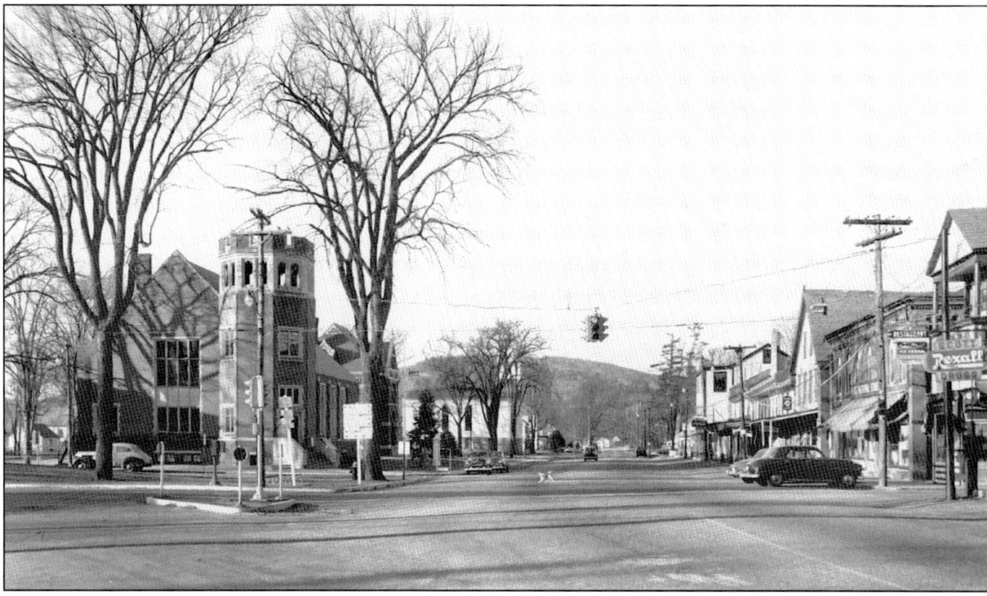

Though the buildings remain the same, this peaceful 1954 photograph of Main Street was clearly taken in the age of automobiles. In 1952, the town meeting voted to appropriate $1,300 toward the installation of traffic lights at the intersection of Richmond Road, Elm Street, and Main Street.

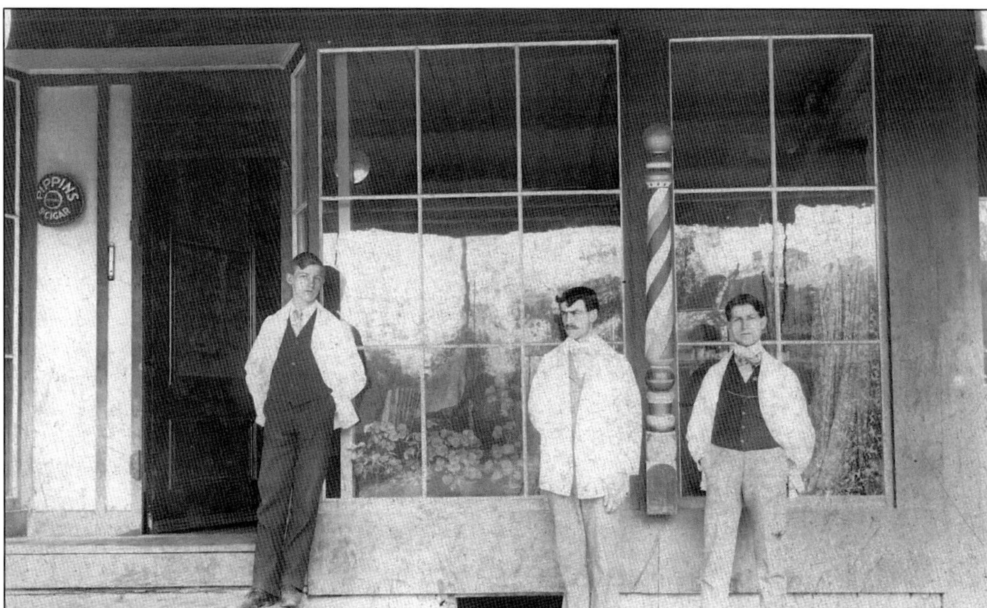

This photograph shows Lumen Nelson (center) outside his barbershop, which was located on Main Street in a building that was lost in the fire of 1971. Nelson's shop was next door to the barbershop currently owned by Don Hubbard. At one time, there were three active barbershops on Main Street. Businessmen would come in two or three times a week for a shave. Verne Stetson is at right, and the other man is unidentified.

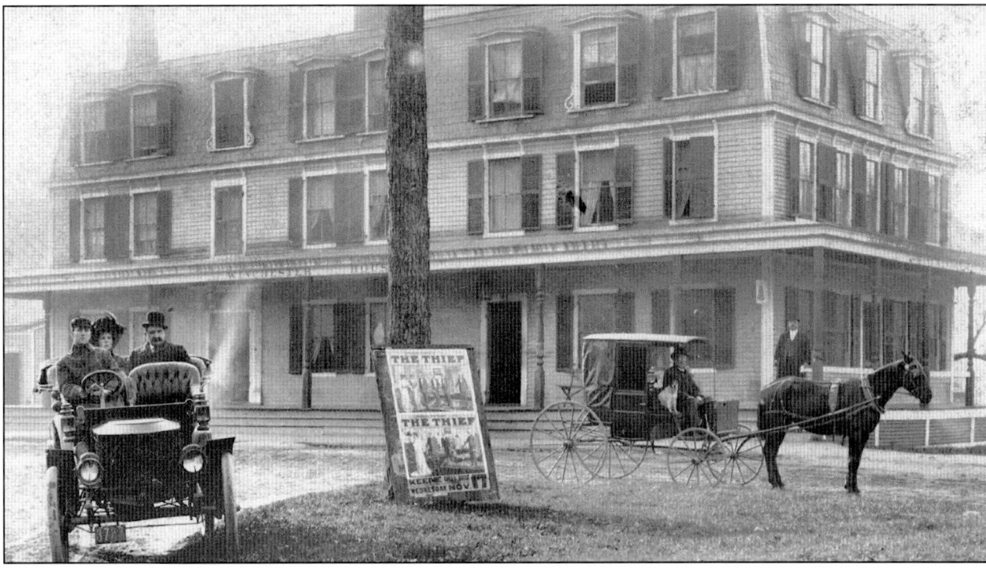

The Winchester Hotel graced the common until 1983. It began life as a home for a few members of the Alexander family, original grantees in Earlington. It was added to over the years, but the major renovations started in 1872 by then-owner Ebenezer Richards turned it into this beautiful Victorian building. It now had 28 bedrooms, plus a bridal suite, a reading room, sitting rooms, a bar room, and two rooms in the attic.

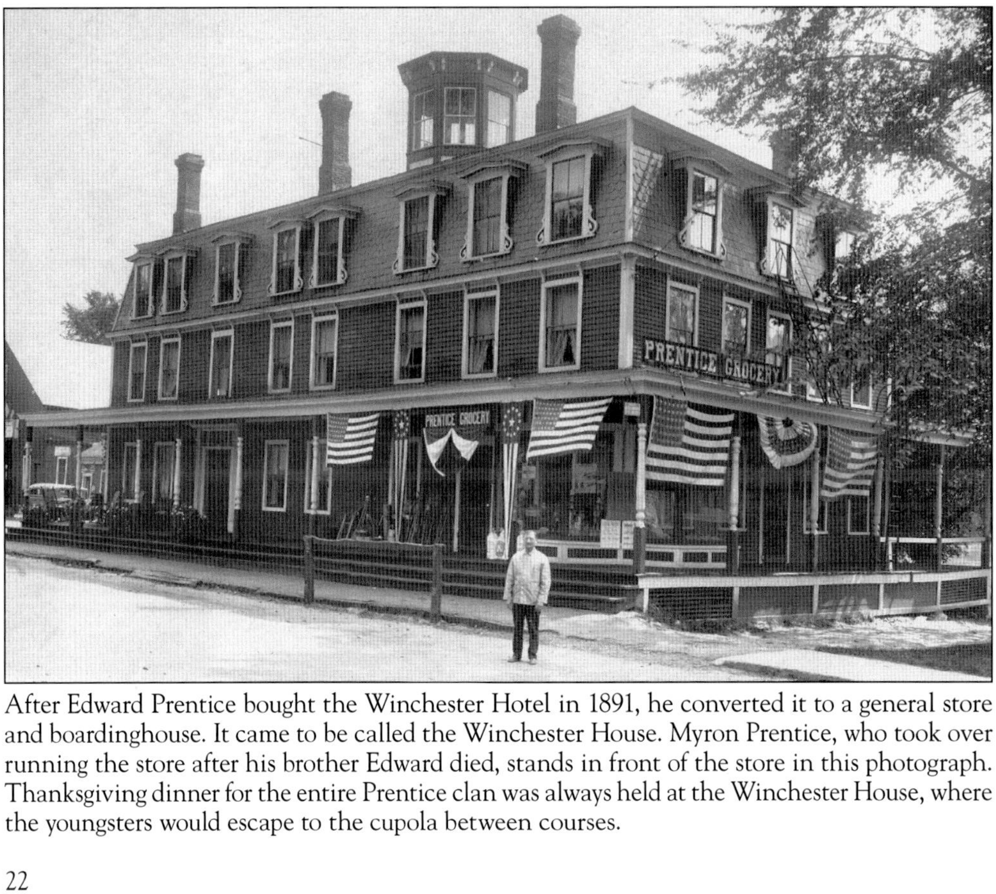

After Edward Prentice bought the Winchester Hotel in 1891, he converted it to a general store and boardinghouse. It came to be called the Winchester House. Myron Prentice, who took over running the store after his brother Edward died, stands in front of the store in this photograph. Thanksgiving dinner for the entire Prentice clan was always held at the Winchester House, where the youngsters would escape to the cupola between courses.

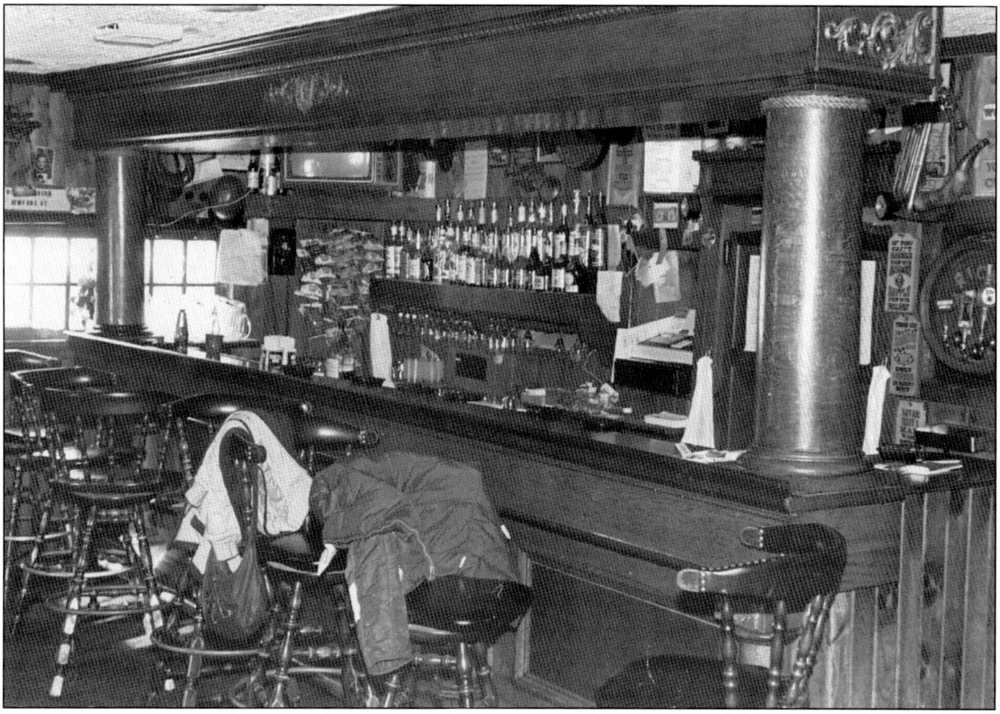

After the death of Mrs. Prentice in 1945, the Winchester House was bought by Clyde Struthers, who installed an 1890 bar he had found. The handsome bar served patrons for nearly 40 years, through several owners. The last owners to operate the Winchester House as a restaurant, bar, and boardinghouse were Mr. and Mrs. Henry Lehrman.

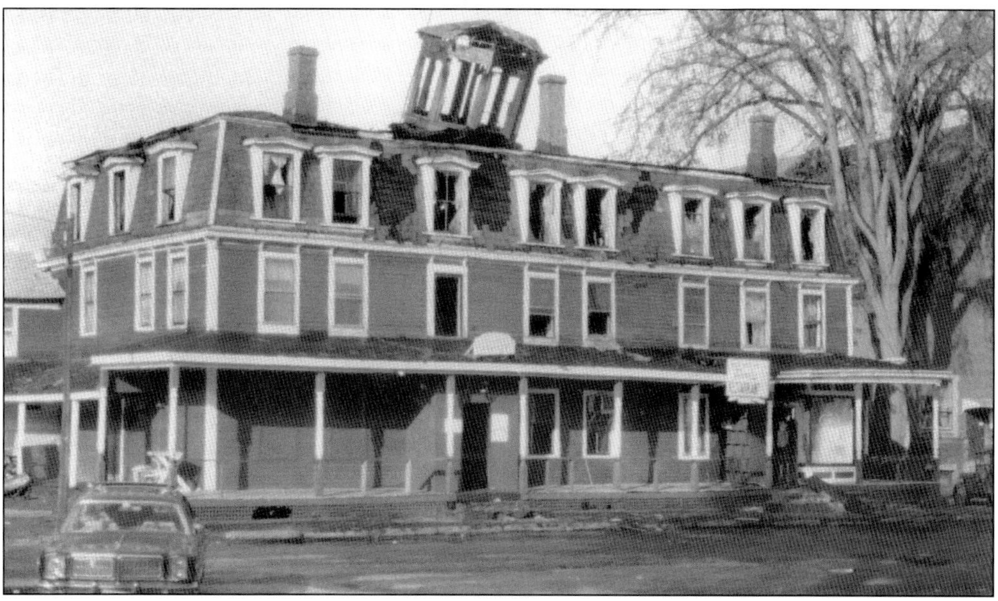

In May 1983, a fire destroyed the Winchester House. Though arson was the cause of the fire, no one has ever been charged with the crime. After it was determined that the building could not be saved, it was leveled in 1986. A parking lot now fills the space, between the town hall and post office, where the proud Winchester Hotel once stood.

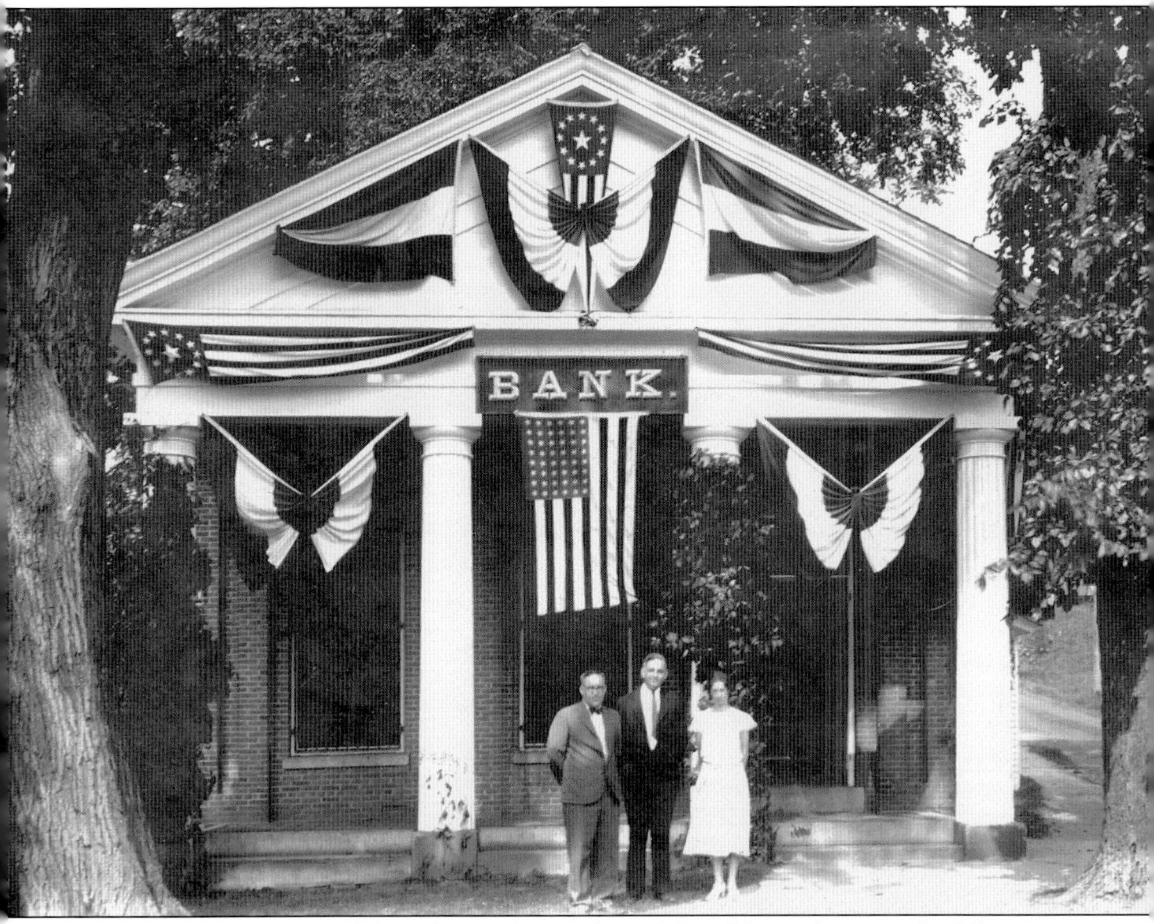

The Winchester National Bank was chartered in 1847 and began business the following year in this beautiful little Greek Revival building on Michigan Street, facing the common. In 1881, the Security Savings Bank was chartered and shared space with what was then the Winchester National Bank, opening during times when the Winchester National Bank was closed. Pictured in front of the bank are James Kellom (left), Franklin Kellom (center), and Dorothy Gee Walker. The bunting was probably for Winchester's 200th birthday celebration, which was celebrated a year early (in 1932) possibly because the date of filing for the grant was used instead of the date it was granted. The Winchester National Bank merged with the Cheshire National Bank in 1964 and did business under that name. It was later called the First Cheshire Bank, which was swallowed up by the First New Hampshire Bank. In 1997, it closed its doors as a bank; the building is now used as storage space for a convenience store.

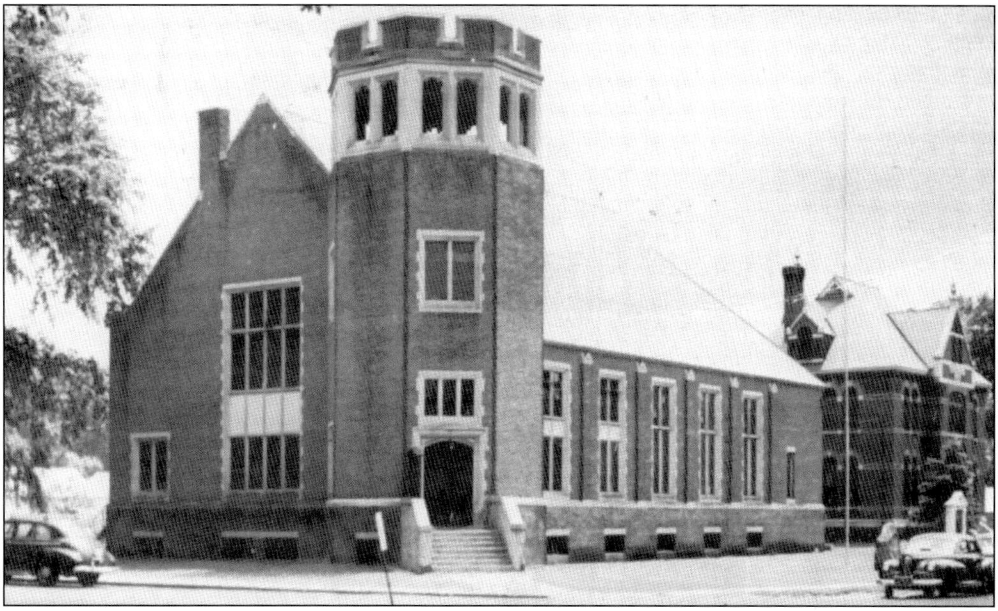

There had been talk of building a new town hall, but when the old town hall burned to the ground in 1909, it became a necessity. At the 1911 town meeting, $20,000 was appropriated to construct a new building. Four architects submitted plans, and the townspeople chose the design of S.W. St. Clair of Boston, who was a former resident of Winchester. The $20,000 could not complete the project, so a special town meeting was called to appropriate another $5,000.

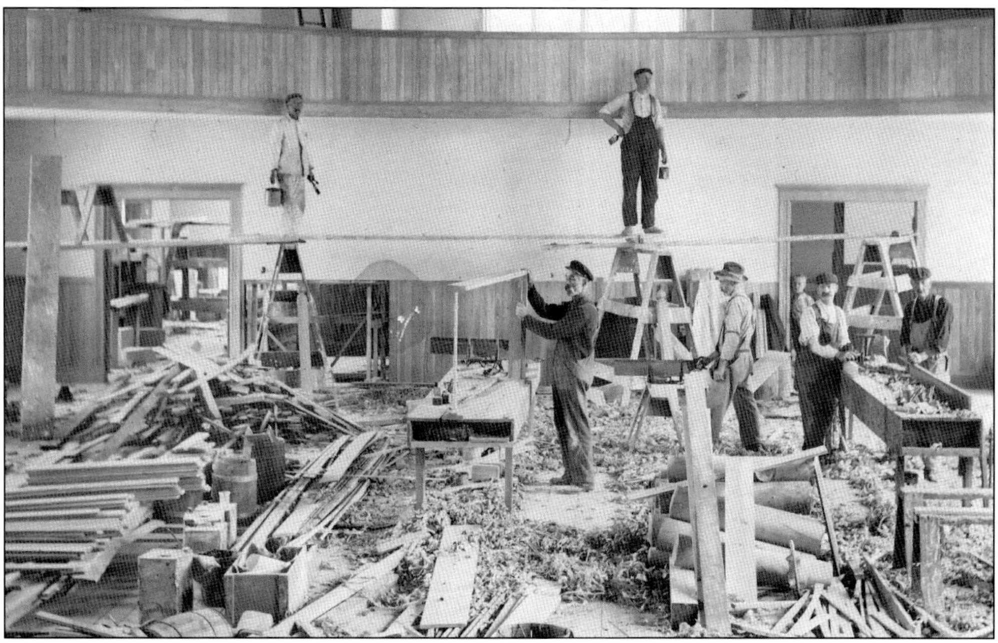

The town hall officially opened in October 1912. It originally had a balcony that could seat 250 people. Over the years, the building has been renovated to accommodate modern needs. In 1956, the balcony was cut back, and a corridor was incorporated into the auditorium to allow room for basketball games. The basement, which originally housed a banquet hall and kitchen as well as dressing rooms for the stage, is now used for offices. (Courtesy of Dorothy Doolittle Farnan.)

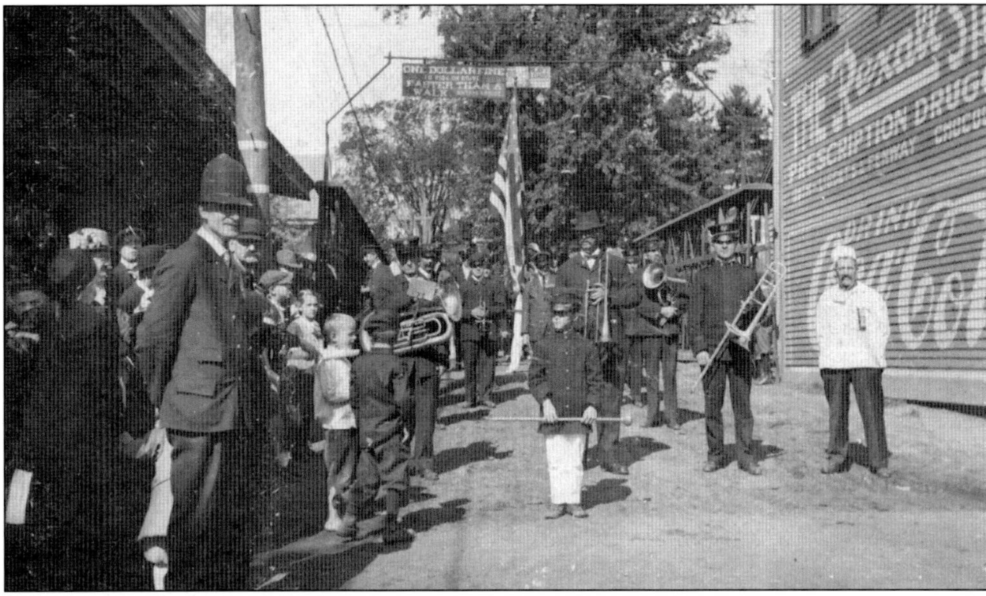

Here, a parade makes its way across the Elm Street Bridge. Note the Coca-Cola advertisement on the side of the drugstore. The sign overhead says there is a $1 fine for proceeding faster than a walk; the man at left looks like a "bobby" ready to enforce it.

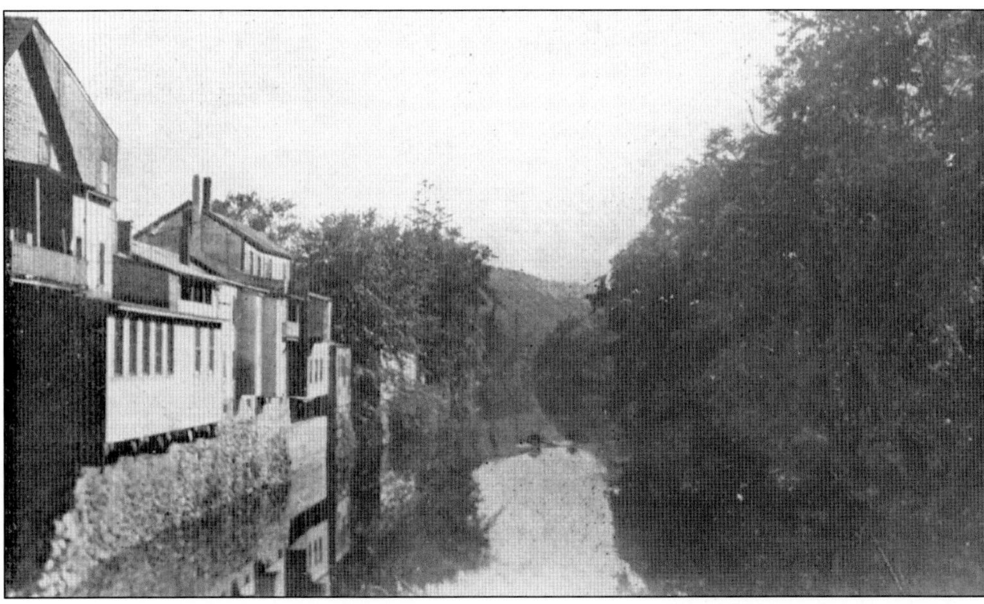

If anyone ever wondered why businesses were built on the little strip of land between the street and the Ashuelot River instead of on the other side of Main Street, where there is plenty of room, the answer is visible in this view from the Elm Street Bridge. Note the long vertical additions that project out over the river; those contained the "privies."

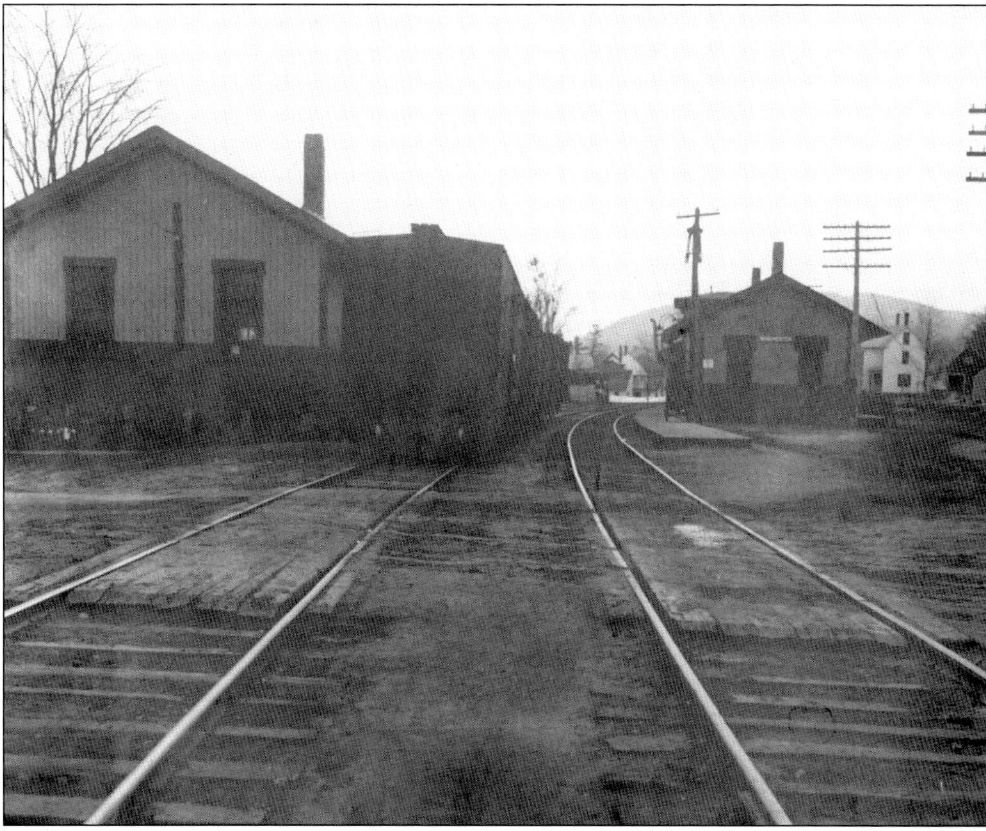

This photograph of the Winchester railroad depot is dated November 1913. In March 1914, it burned to the ground when boxes of millinery piled near the stove caught on fire. Station agent H.T. Coombs saved some of the money and part of the mileage books. George Poizer, the telegraph agent, saved most of his records and the freight records. The building's loss was put at $2,500, plus an additional loss of $1,200 from the tank house, which also burned.

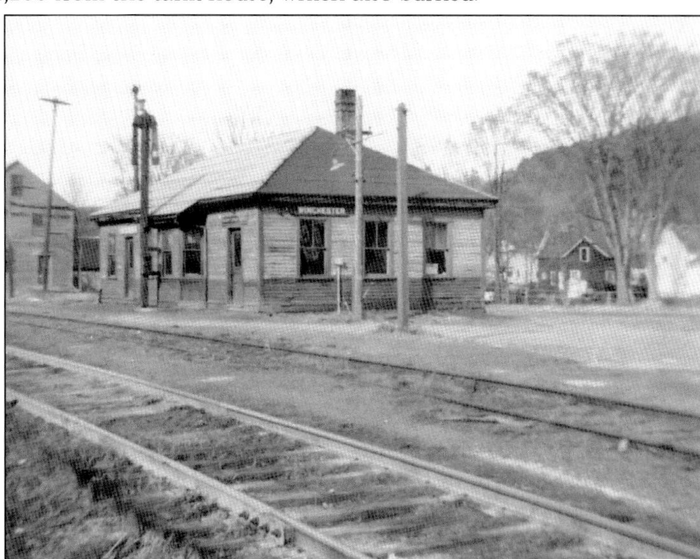

The rebuilt station had a different roof line. In this 1960 image, it sits all but abandoned. Passenger service had ended some years back, and only a daily freight train remained on the Ashuelot line. The trains stopped for good in December 1982, when there was no longer enough freight to make it profitable.

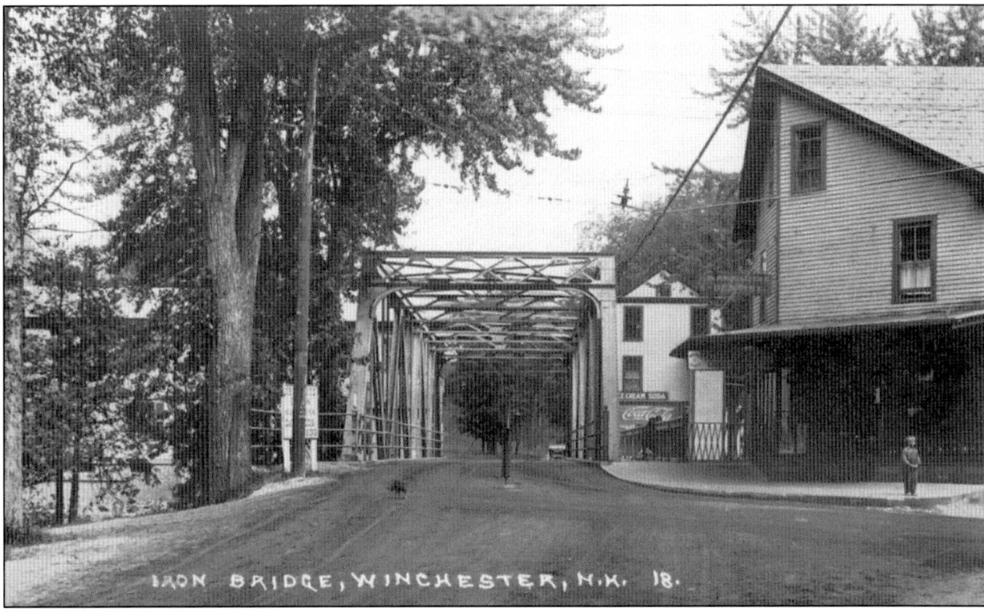

The Cook Block (far right) was wedged between the Ashuelot River and Ashuelot Street, next to what was then the Depot Street Bridge. It housed the office of Dr. D.M. Qualters, a dentist, as well as a grocery store that not only sold retail, but also bought and bartered wholesale directly from local farmers. After sitting empty for many years, it was razed in the early 1990s. The space is now vacant.

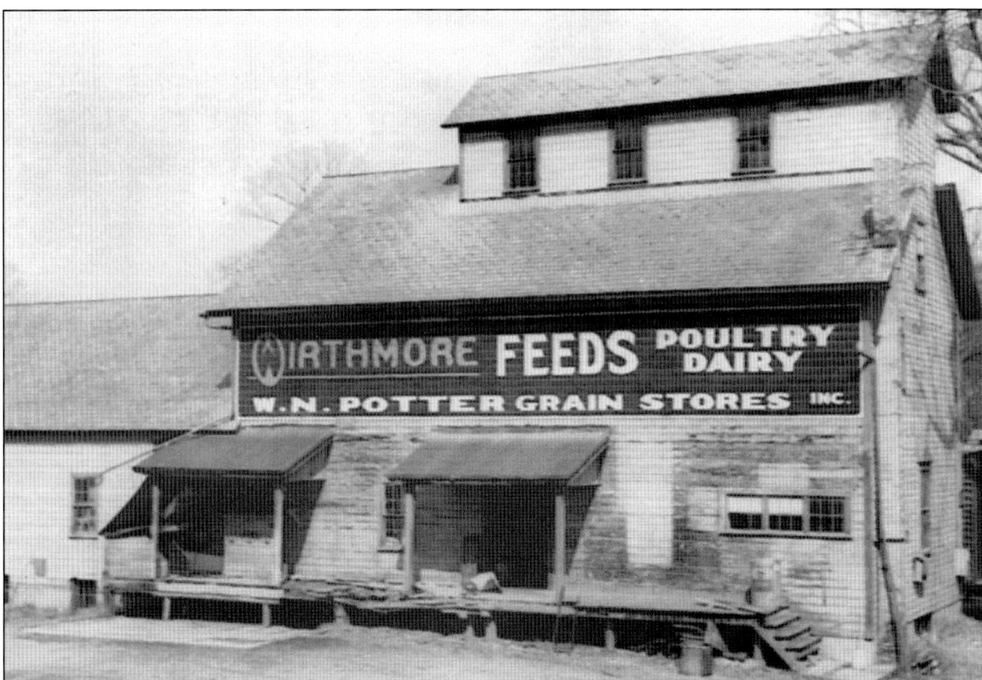

This photograph shows one of the Ashuelot Railroad buildings that was adapted for commercial use. Wirthmore's Feed was a gristmill that processed grain for local farmers; it also sold feed and farming supplies. This was an active store into the 1960s.

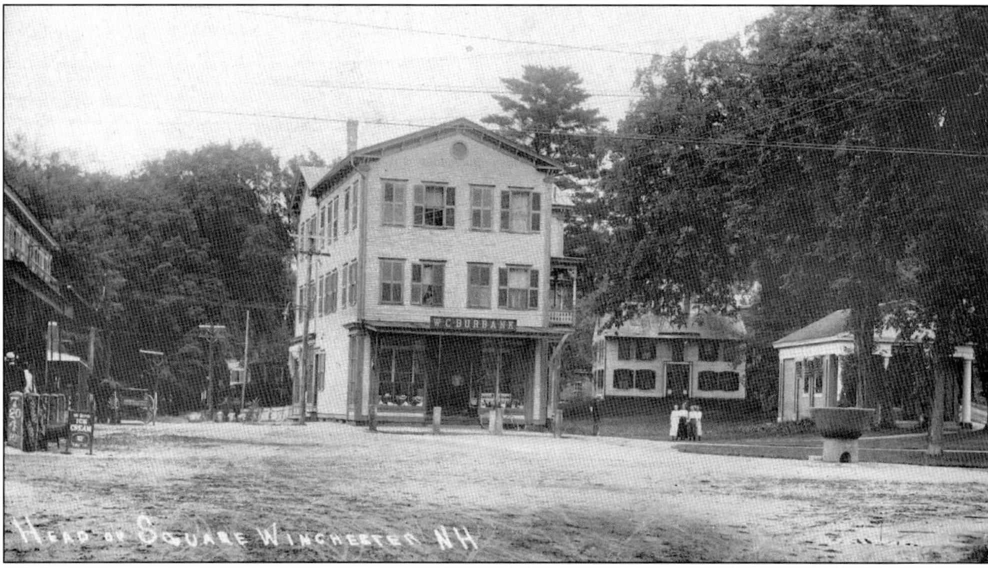

This postcard, which was sent all the way to Oklahoma City, shows the Burbank Block. It was an extensive building that stood roughly where a convenience store and gas pumps are now located. The house next to the Burbank Block—one of Winchester's oldest—and the bank building still stand.

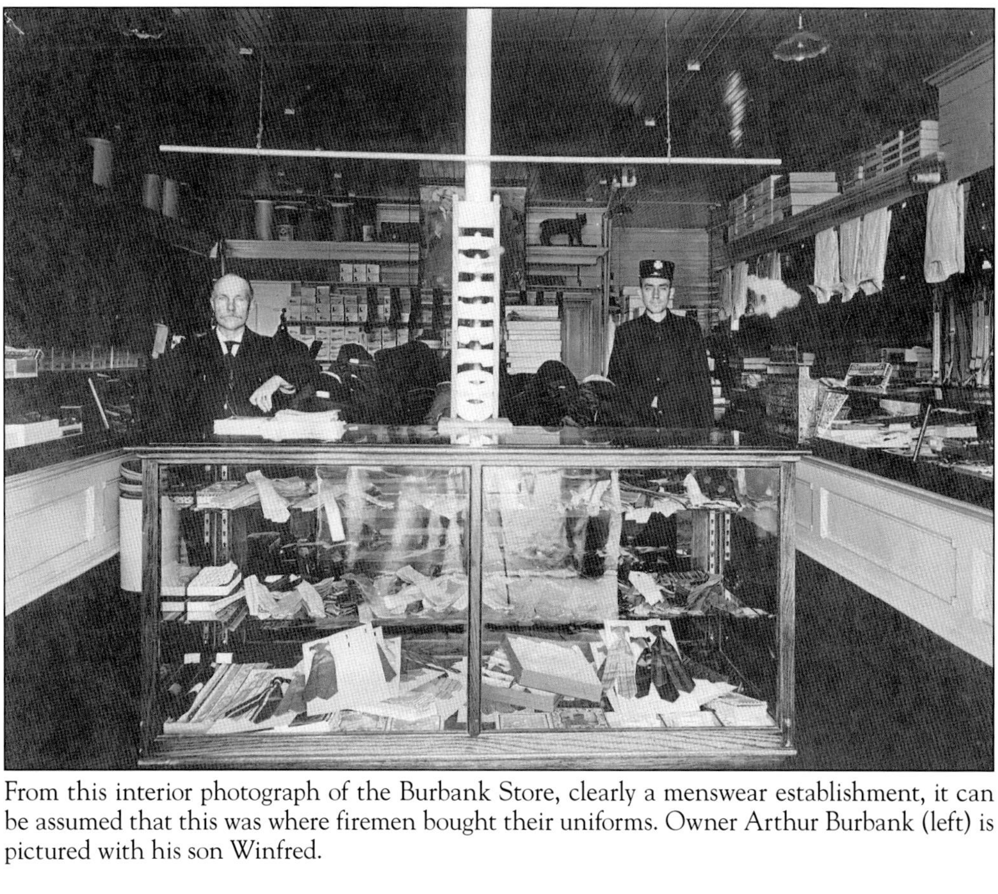
From this interior photograph of the Burbank Store, clearly a menswear establishment, it can be assumed that this was where firemen bought their uniforms. Owner Arthur Burbank (left) is pictured with his son Winfred.

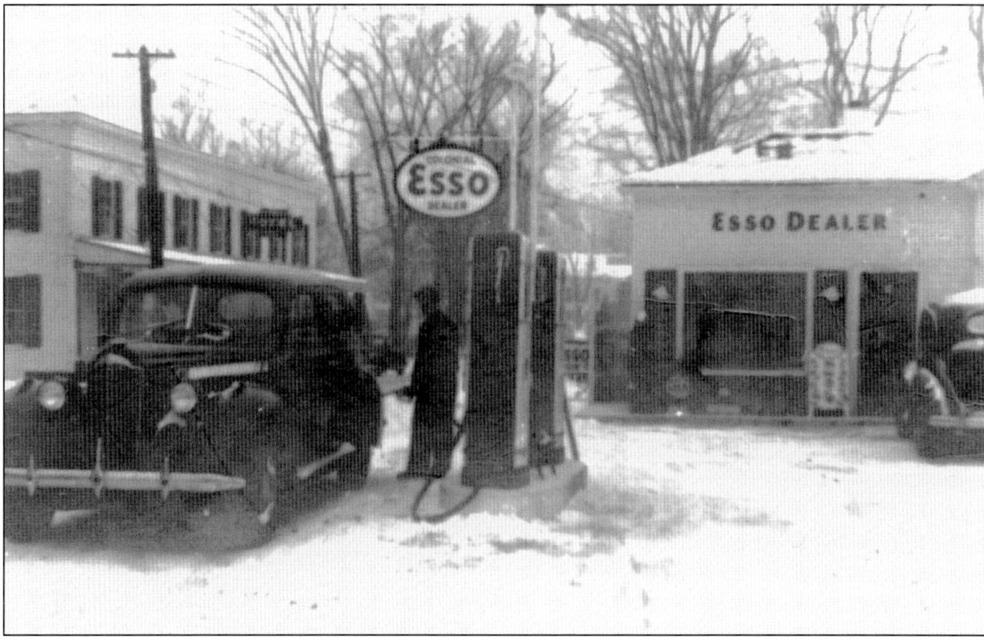

By 1943, the Burbank Block had been replaced by this Esso service station. It was later Earl Swett's Exxon station before becoming Mr. Mike's convenience store, as it remains today. At left is the old Strand Hotel, located along the Ashuelot riverbank.

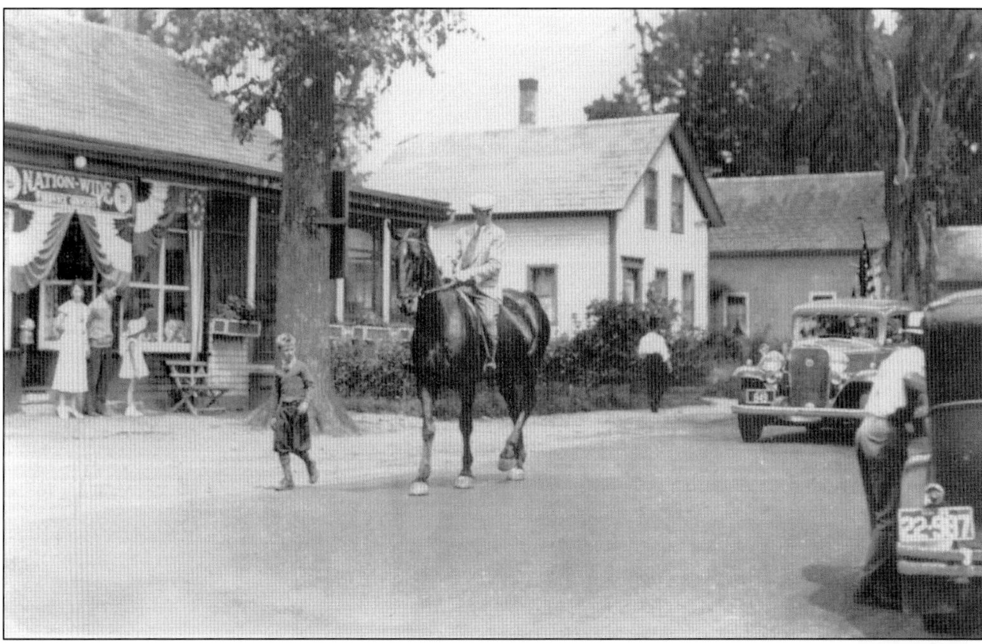

Here, a parade marches past the original Kulick's store on Keene Road (then North Main Street). The bunting suggests the parade was for the town's 200th birthday celebration. Kulick's moved into its current store, on Warwick Road, in 1972. Shortly after moving, the old store became Fat Chance Antiques, which remains in the space today.

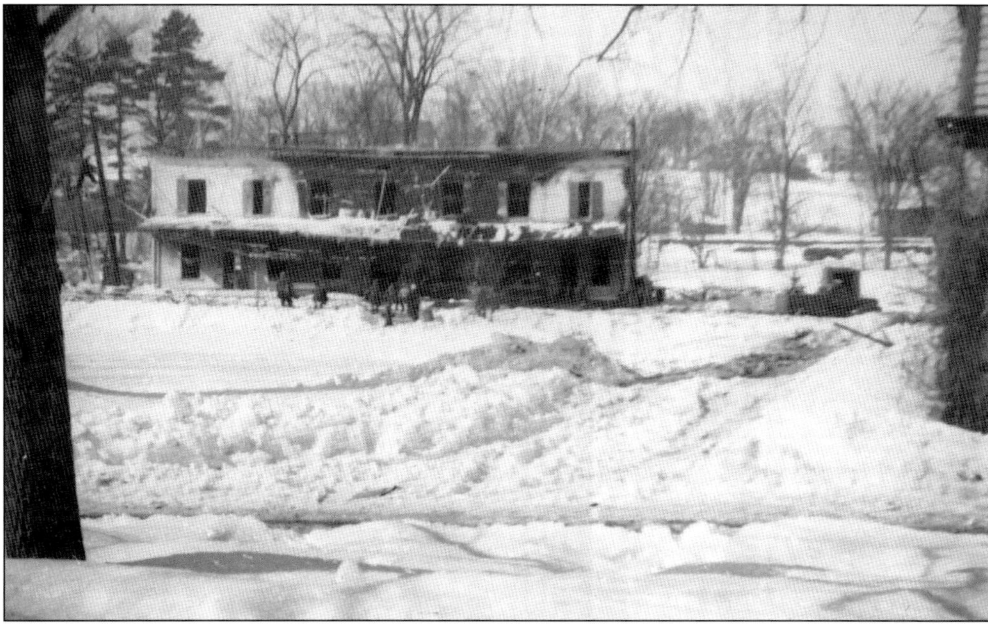

The Strand Hotel, once a busy stopping place for businessmen and tourists, burned down in the winter of 1943. One man died, and a woman had to be rescued through a second-story window. Many firefighters were away, serving in World War II, so teenagers as young as 14-year-old Tom Magee helped fight the fire. The building was a total loss. The photograph below shows the Thayer High School band passing by the site during a parade in 1960, after the Strand was rebuilt as a single-story Dairy Bar. It later housed the Riverside Restaurant and then Dino's. This building is now empty.

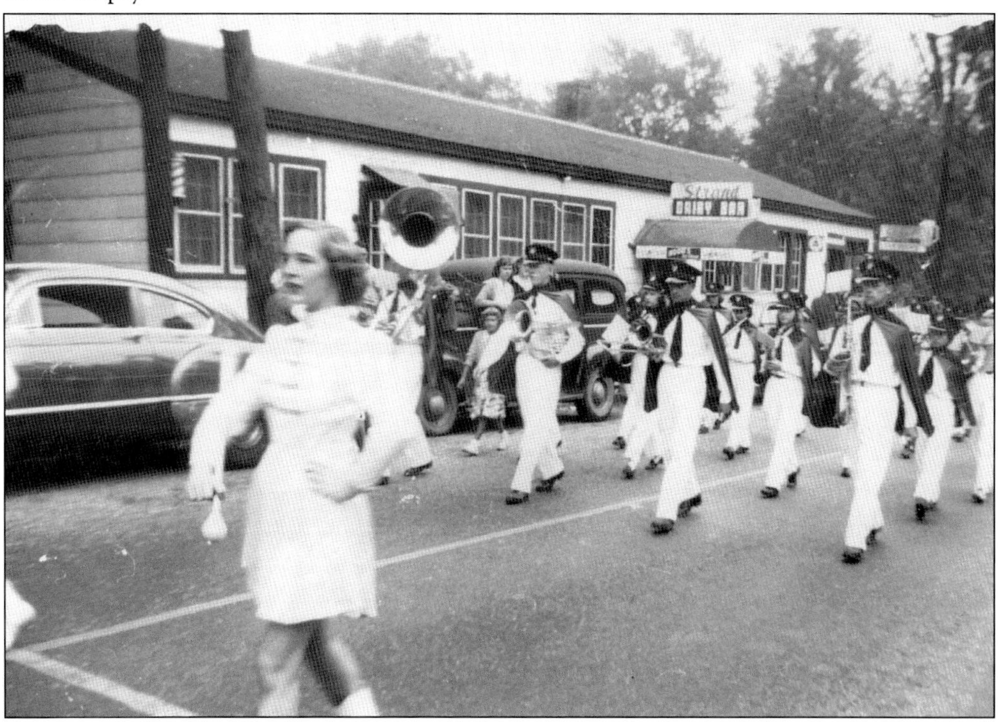

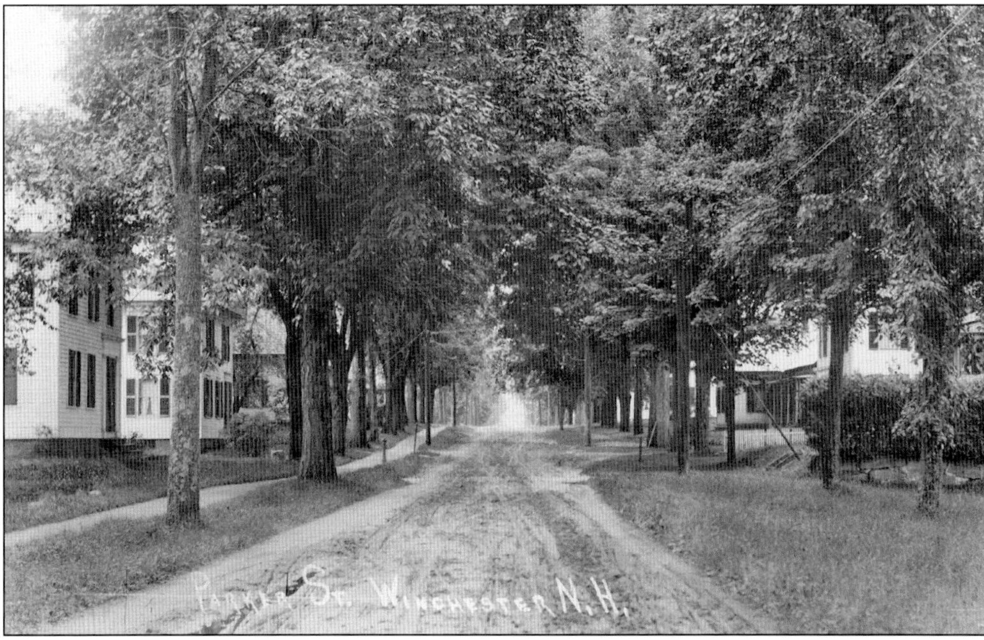

Trees shaded both sides of Parker Street in this pre-pavement photograph. The houses are still clearly recognizable today. Durkee Street now turns off to the right in front of the first house and leads to the Ellen Lambert Murphy Memorial Community Center.

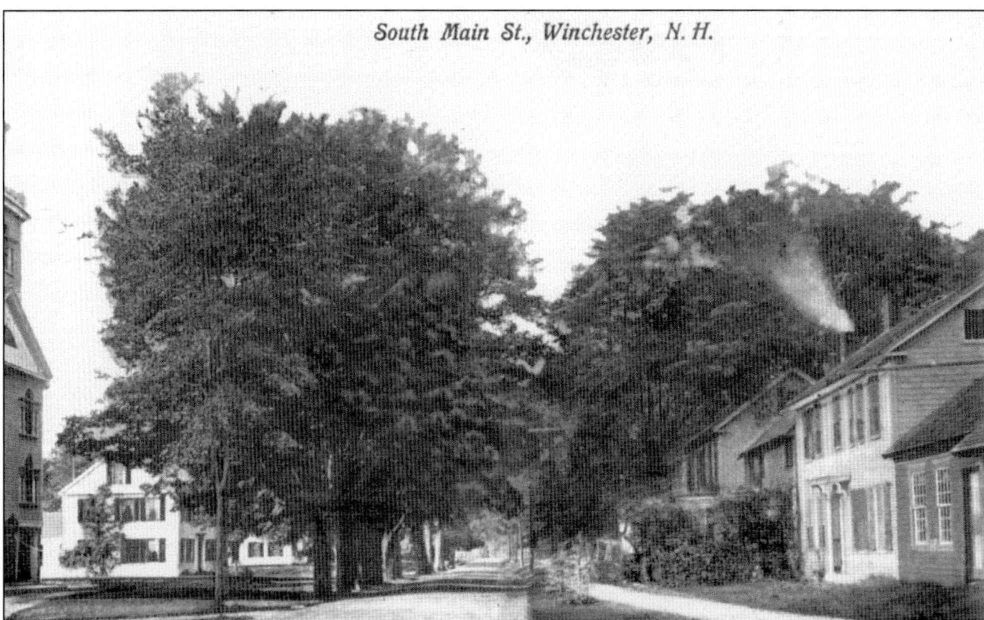

This view down South Main Street in this undated photograph remains much the same today. The shady maples are gone, and the sidewalk now goes down the east side of the road, but the buildings remain the same.

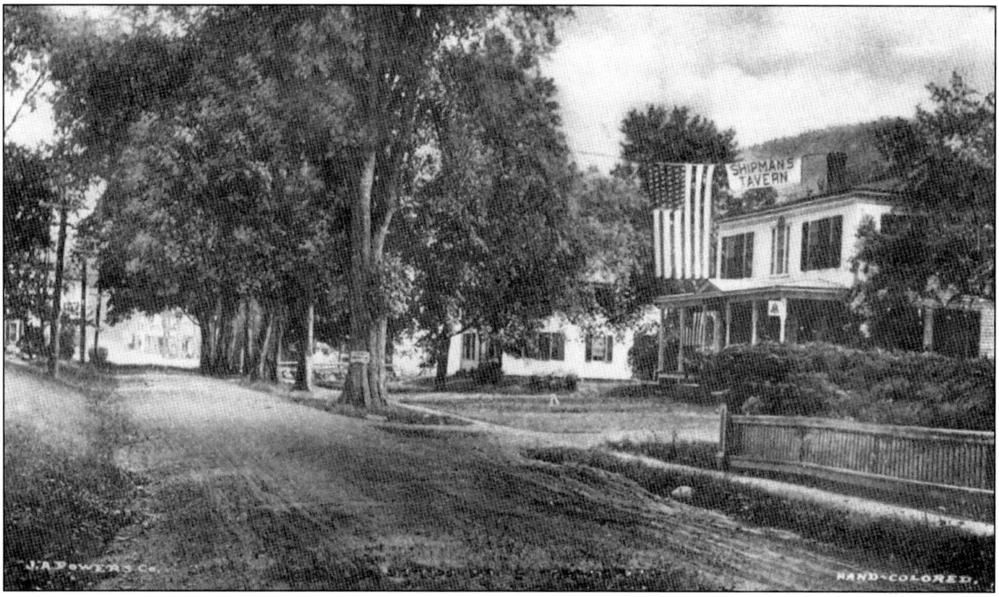

The origins of Shipman's tavern can be traced back to 1858, when Elisha Rich operated a tavern in the location. In 1882, it became the private home of the Jennings family. By 1914, it was owned by former circus performers Ada and James Shipman. Ada outlasted three husbands, dying at the age of 85. The tavern was always a clean, respectable place. The old registers list visitors such as Ty Cobb and Tris Speaker. Sometime during the Shipman years, the building acquired a third story. The barn became a garage for some years. From 1949 until 1965, Mable and George Brown used the building as a nursing home. It was then a building supply company, housed mainly in the barn, until 1970, when Velma and William Sawyer bought it and ran it as a boardinghouse. Josie Marsh took over after the Sawyers and kept the boardinghouse open until 2004.

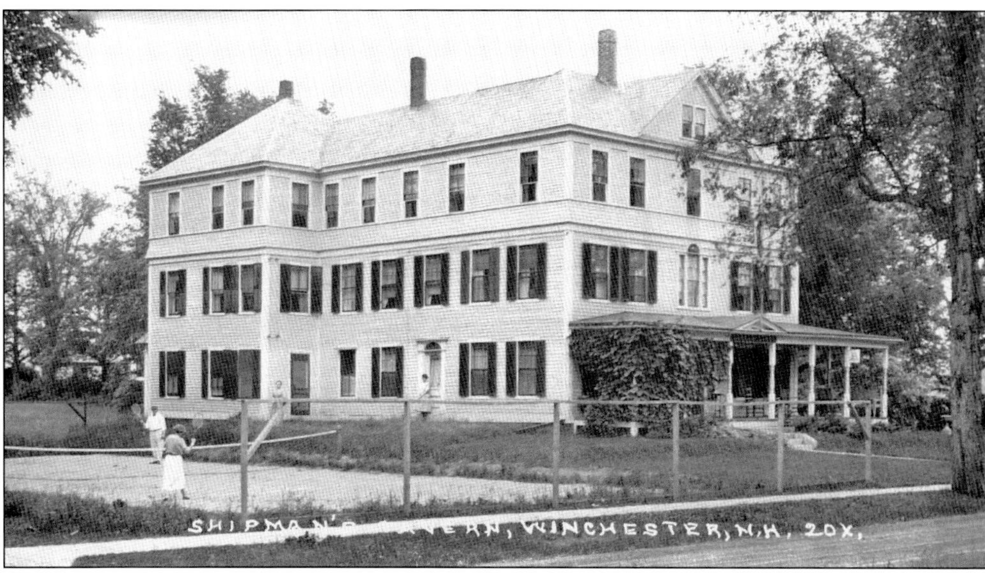

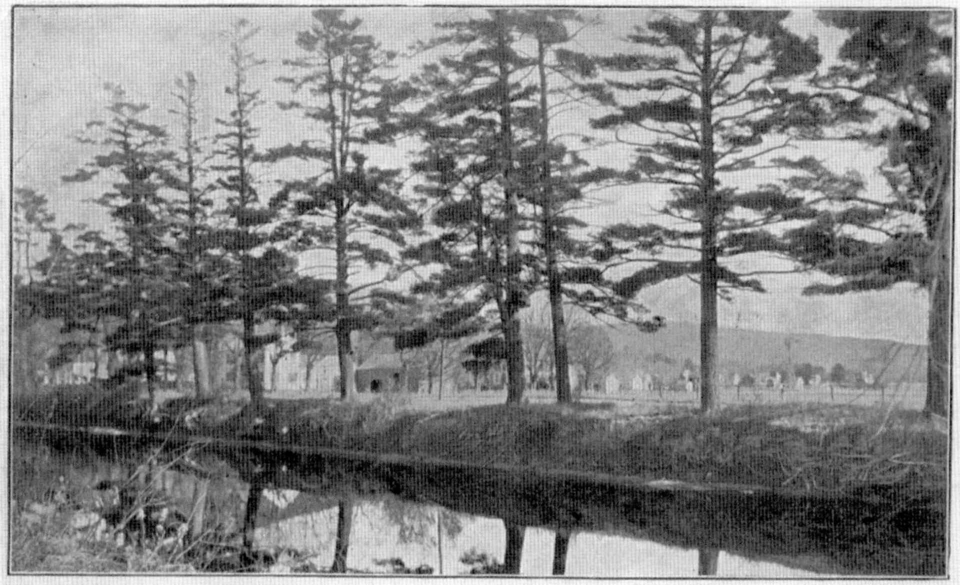

6 The Pines, Winchester, N. H.

There are so many different picture postcards of the pines along South Main Street that they must have been quite a beautiful sight. The pine trees, which stretched along the bank of the Ashuelot River from the end of the houses to the Middle Bridge, were lost in the hurricane of 1938.

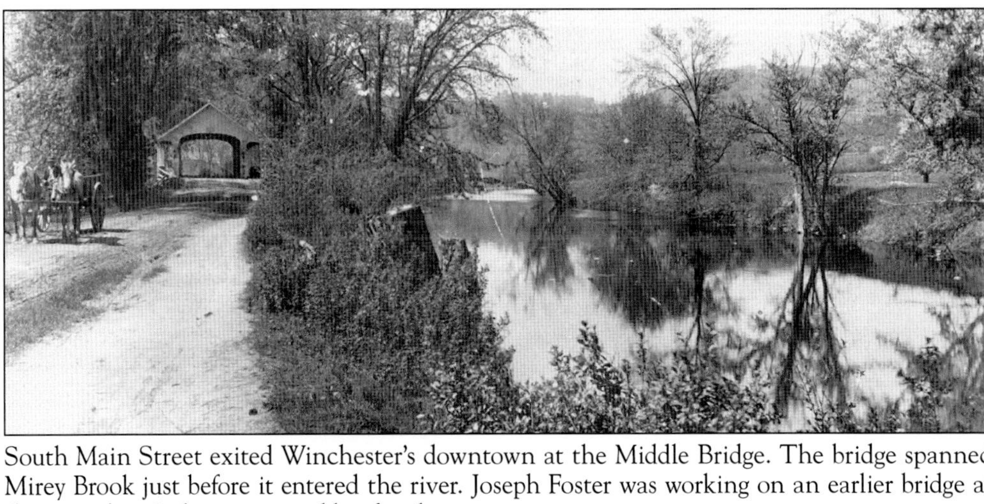

South Main Street exited Winchester's downtown at the Middle Bridge. The bridge spanned Mirey Brook just before it entered the river. Joseph Foster was working on an earlier bridge at this site when Indians captured his family.

Two

ASHUELOT

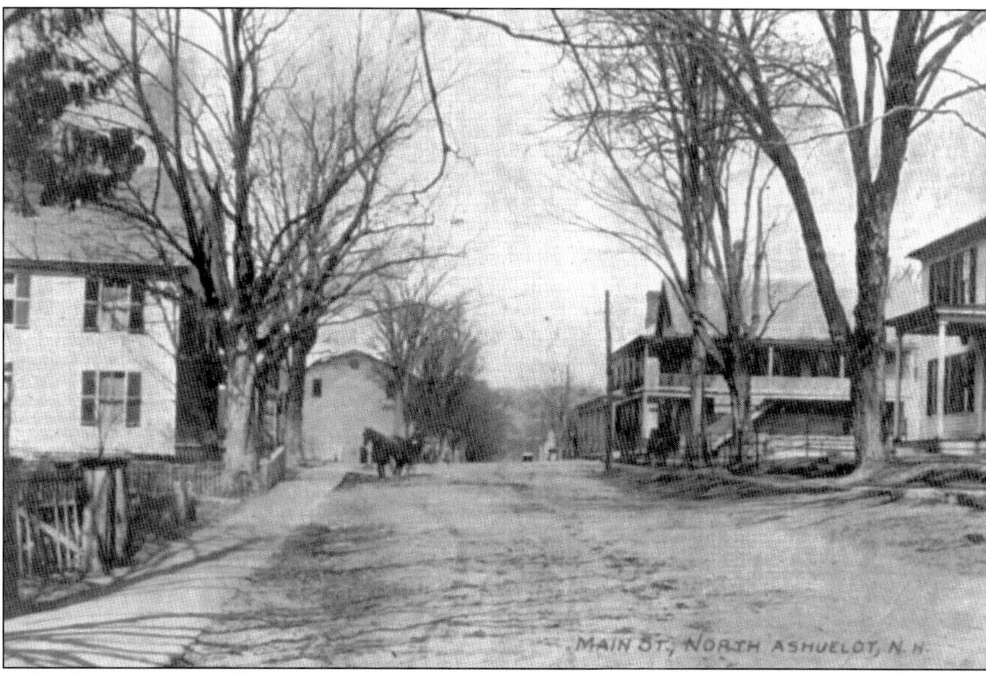

Ashuelot was originally called Furnace Village because the iron ore from Ore Mountain was smelted there. For a while, it was called West Winchester. In 1852, the name was officially changed to Ashuelot. It is divided into the Upper (upriver) and Lower villages. This view shows the Upper Village, with the building that was to become the Thayer Library cut off at the far right edge of the photograph.

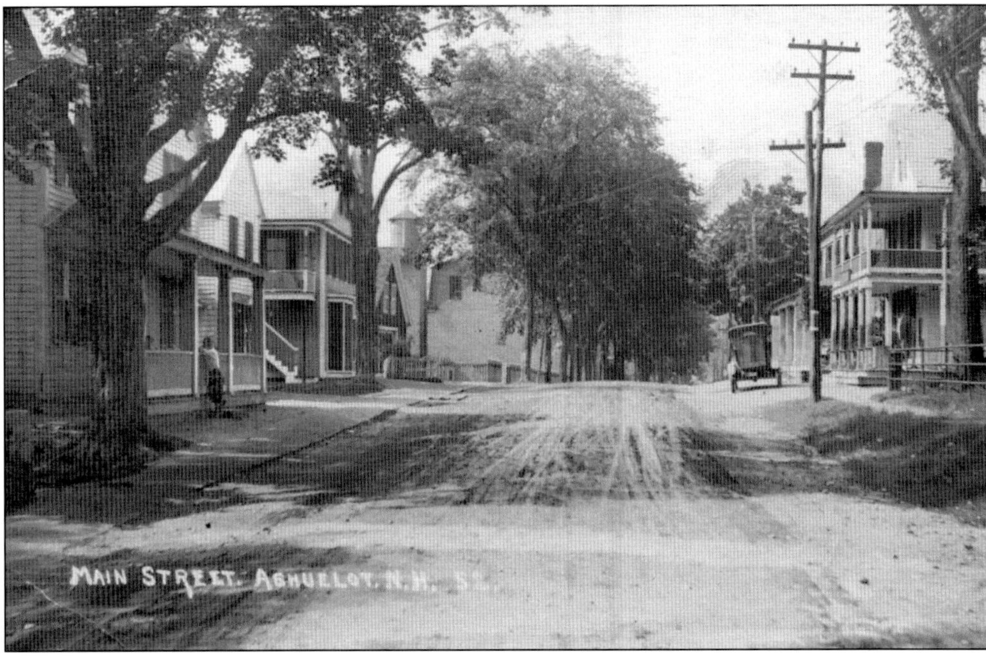

The vehicle in the photograph suggests that this view of Main Street in the Upper Village is from the 1920s. The building that now houses the post office is pictured second from the left. On the right, the fence defines the common, and the hotel can be seen beyond the double-decker porch of Wood's store. (Courtesy of Dorothy Doolittle Farnan.)

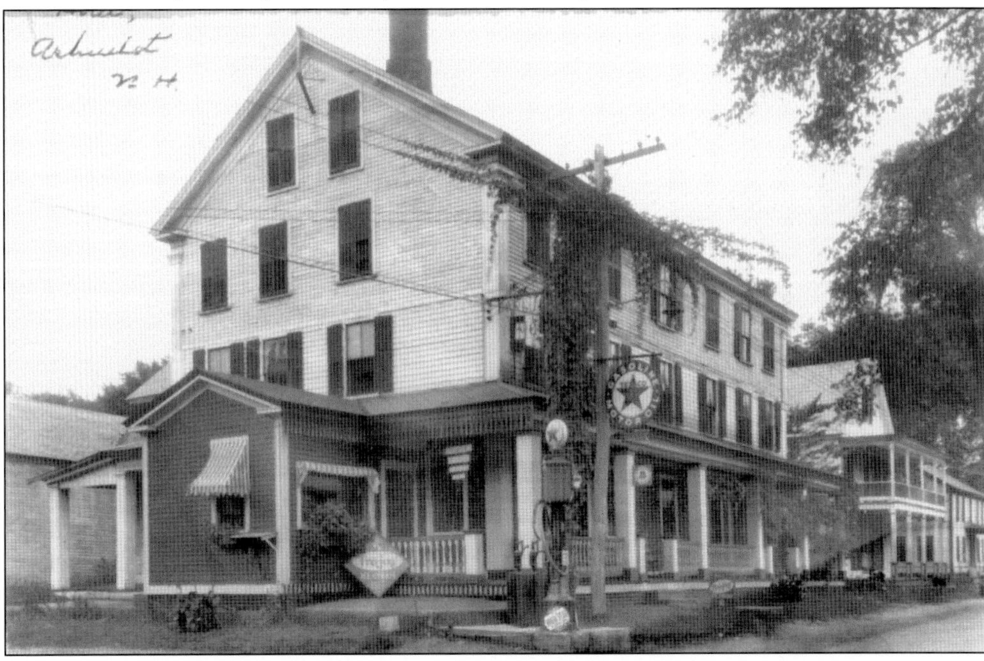

This view of the Ashuelot Hotel is probably from the 1940s. It remained a popular restaurant for many years after the hotel no longer hosted overnight guests. The building was recently renovated as apartments. The building between the hotel and the Thayer Library, which once housed a store, was removed many years ago.

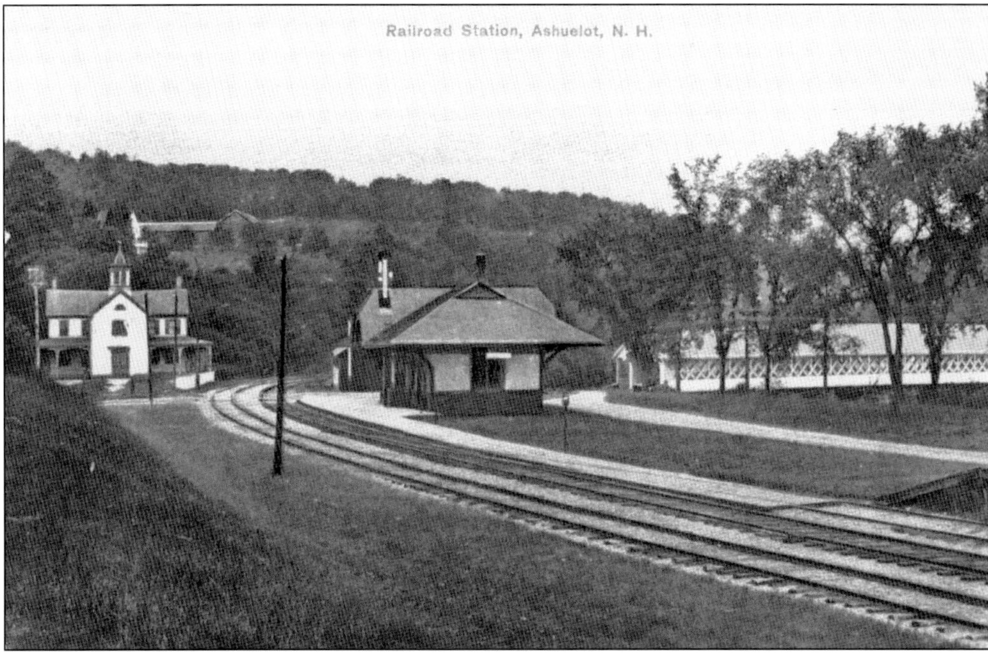

Looking west along the tracks reveals the old Upper Village School, the Ashuelot Railroad depot, and the covered bridge. In the 19th century, Winchester was less forested than it is today, allowing the viewer of this postcard the sight of a farm up on the hill that is now obscured by trees. (Courtesy of Dorothy Doolittle Farnan.)

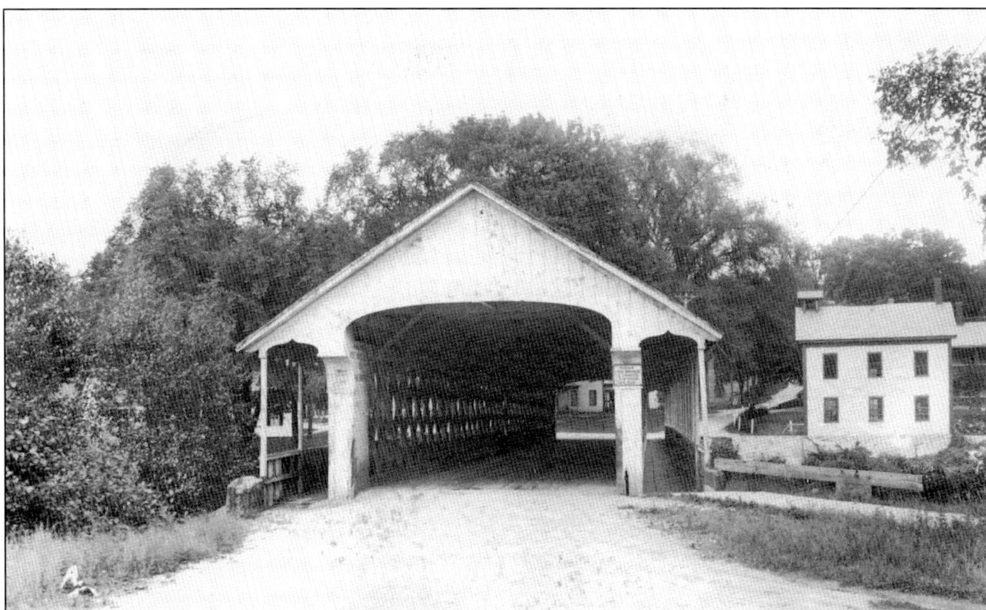

This view from the south side of the Ashuelot covered bridge shows the old firehouse on the opposite bank. A pumper was kept there to quickly respond to fires in the Upper Village. The danger of fire was ever-present in the days of wood-burning stoves and kerosene lamps. (Courtesy of Dorothy Doolittle Farnan.)

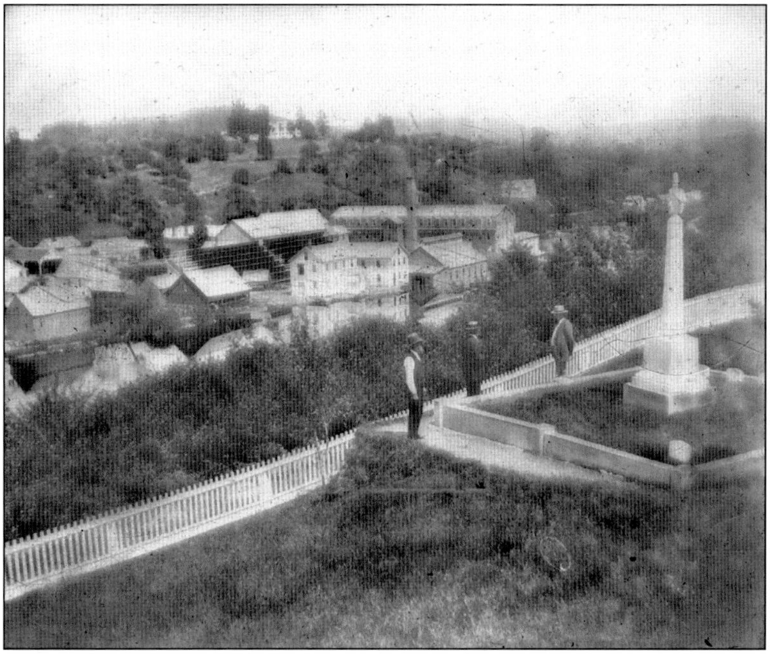

From Tuft's Cemetery on Old Hinsdale Road, the extent of the Sheridan Woolen Mill, with its drying racks, is evident. Besides the factory buildings, the mill owned most of the houses and stores in the Upper Village. Note the open land on Fenton Hill, above the mill.

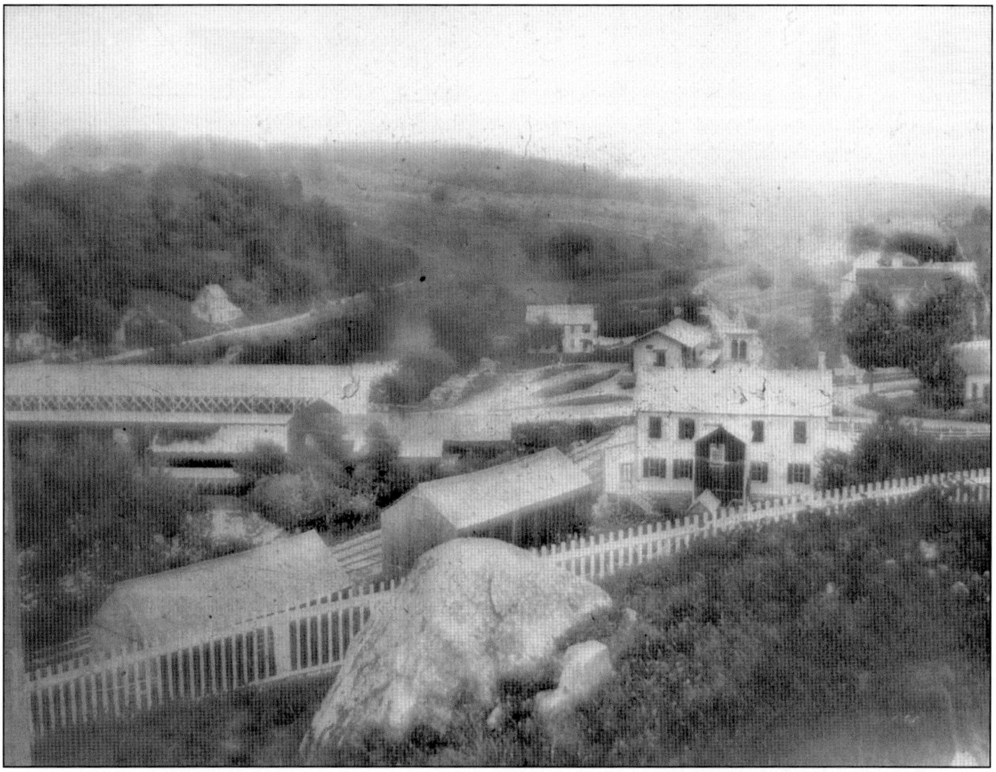

This view from Tuft's Cemetery shows Route 119 going toward Winchester, the covered bridge, and the back of the Ashuelot Upper Village School. The roof of the Sheridan House is visible at right. The house in the center, along the Ashuelot River, was torn down in 2010. The school and shed mark the site where the iron smelting furnace was once located.

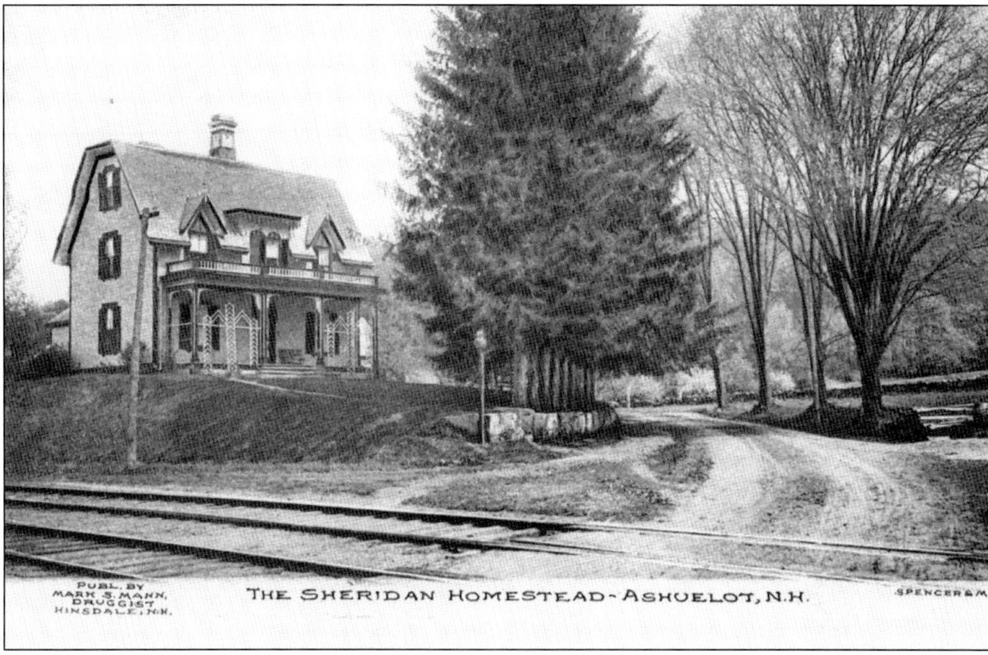

These two views of the Sheridan House in Ashuelot show it before (above) and after the improvements made by Hugh Sheridan. The house was originally built around 1870 by Charles Norton and sold to the owner of the woolen mill. When Sheridan bought the mill in 1901, the house was included in the property. Comparing the earlier image above to the postcard below, one can see that the porch was extended to wrap around the house, the front wall was replaced, and hydrangea bushes were planted along the banking. Not visible are the parquet floors, fireplace, and servant's room that were added inside. The house now serves as the Winchester Historical Society Museum.

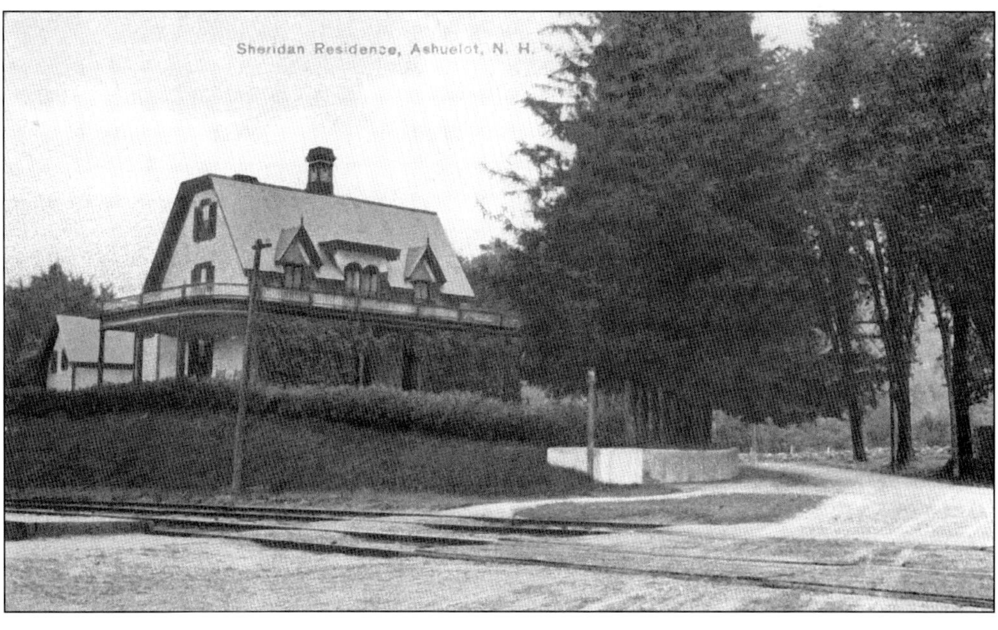

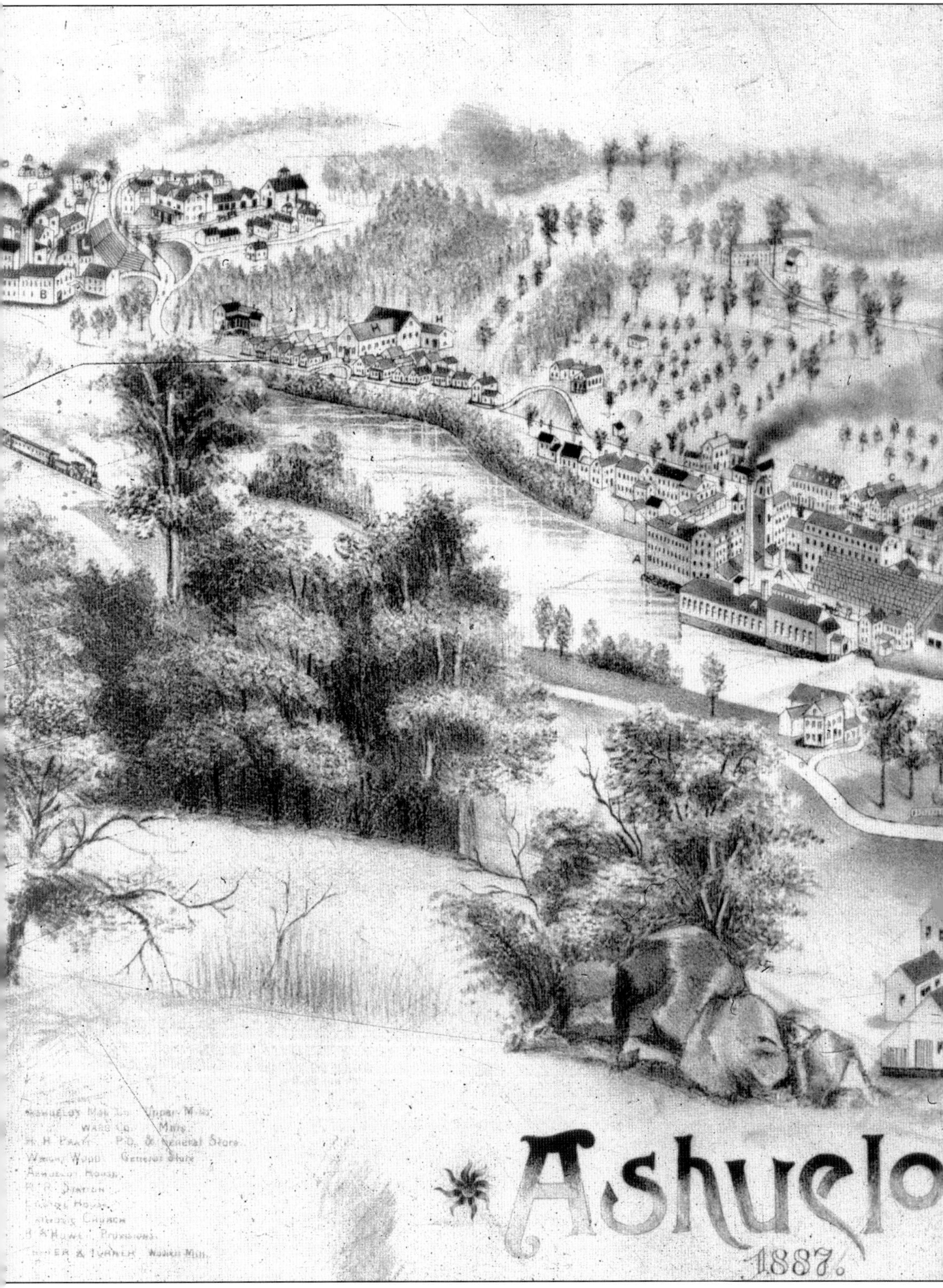
P.O. & General Store
General Store
Station
Church
Provisions
Ashuelo
1887.

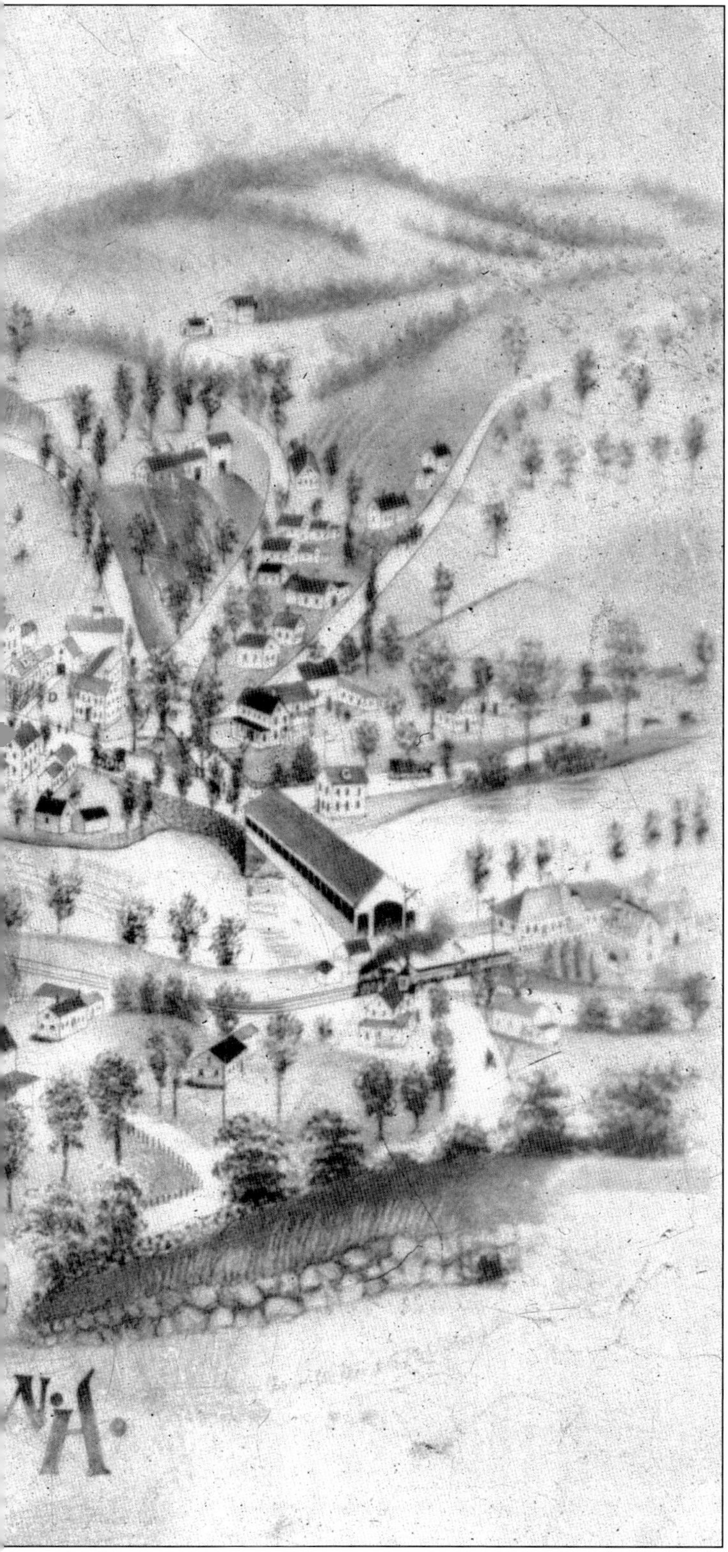

This bird's-eye view of Ashuelot depicts the village in 1887. At that time, Ashuelot rivaled Winchester for industry. The view shows the Upper Village from a vantage point on Gunn Mountain. Today, most of the woolen mill buildings are gone, but many of the houses remain. The artistic rendering is mostly faithful, except for the scale of St. Michael's Church, which is located among the houses on the river (perhaps the cartographer was trying to make a point). Fiddle Hill and the old cotton mill are visible at left. A full-size version of this map can be viewed at the Sheridan House Museum.

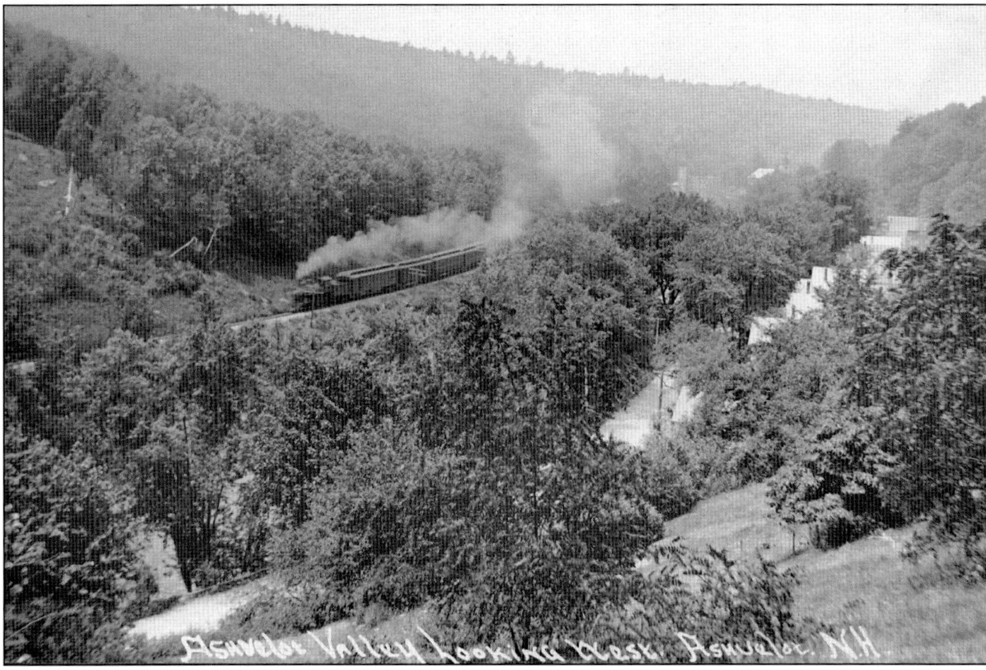

This photograph of a passenger train in Ashuelot was probably taken from a vantage point on Fenton Hill. The Ashuelot River runs between River Street (now called Route 119) and the Ashuelot Railroad tracks. Before everyone had automobiles, passenger trains ran five times per day along the Ashuelot line. Note the string of houses overlooking the river; these still stand. (Courtesy of Dorothy Doolittle Farnan.)

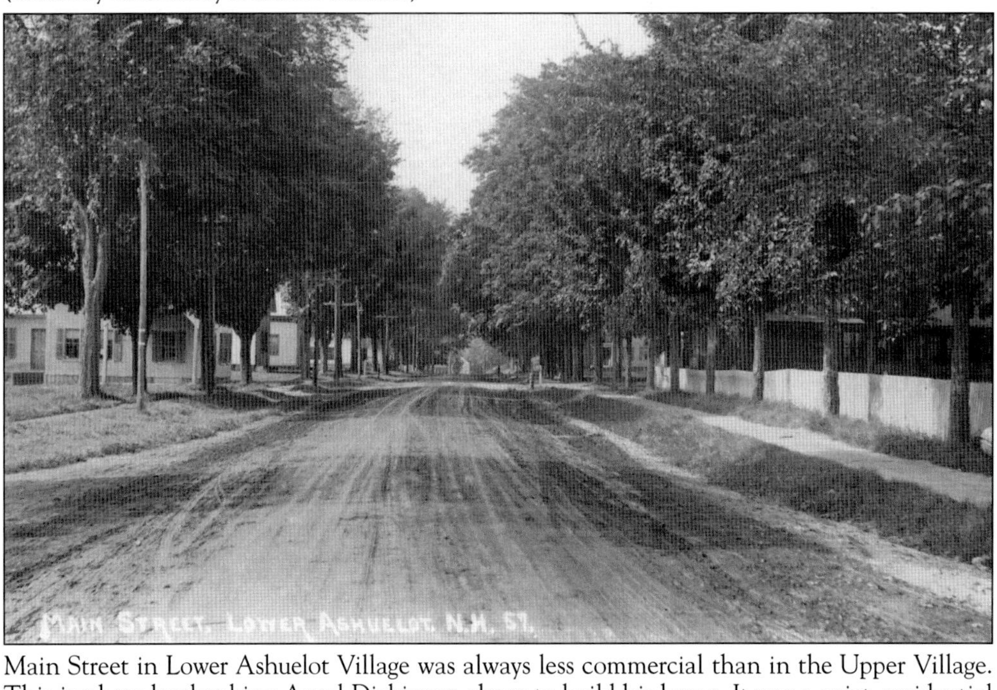

Main Street in Lower Ashuelot Village was always less commercial than in the Upper Village. This is where lumber king Ansel Dickinson chose to build his home. It was a quiet, residential area lined with nice homes and beautiful trees. This view looks west.

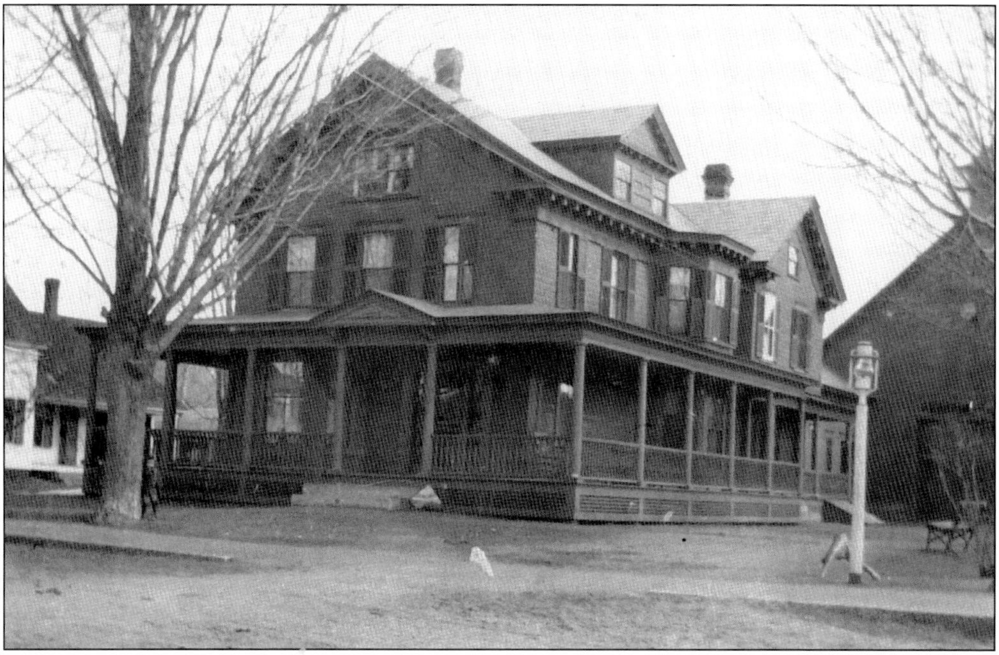

The Ansel Dickinson homestead in Lower Ashuelot Village was a grand home befitting a grand man. Ansel Dickinson, known as the "Lumber King," owned a large sawmill operation in Pisgah, wooden box shops in Ashuelot and Winchester, and several other businesses. This building now houses a Head Start program.

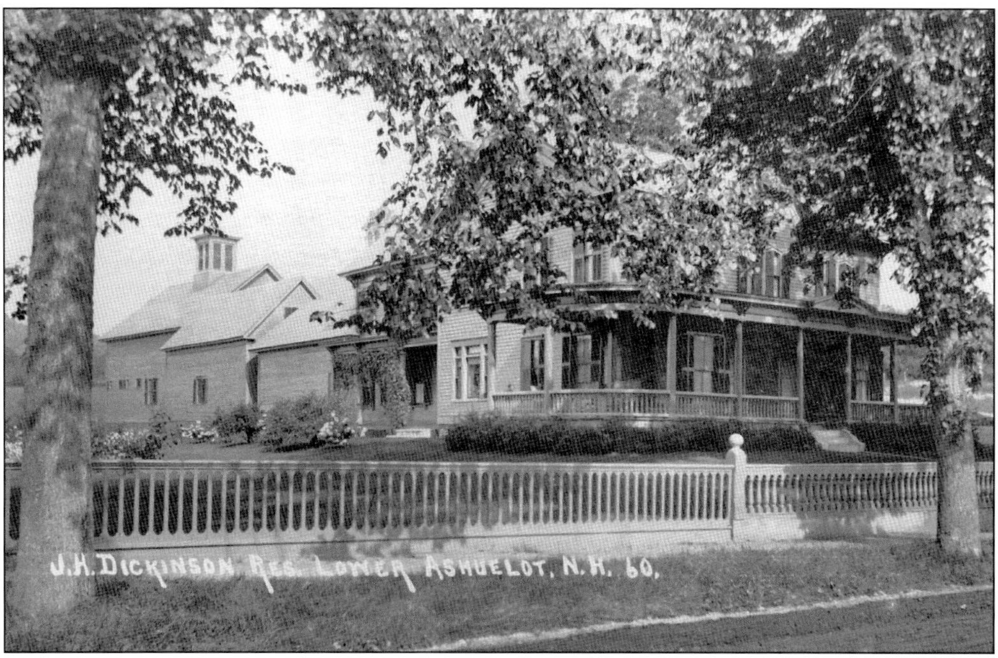

This substantial house is just down Main Street from the Ansel Dickinson house. It was the home of Ansel's son John and more recently known as the Doolittle home. John and his brother Lafell managed the Dickinson businesses after Ansel's death. (Courtesy of Dorothy Doolittle Farnan.)

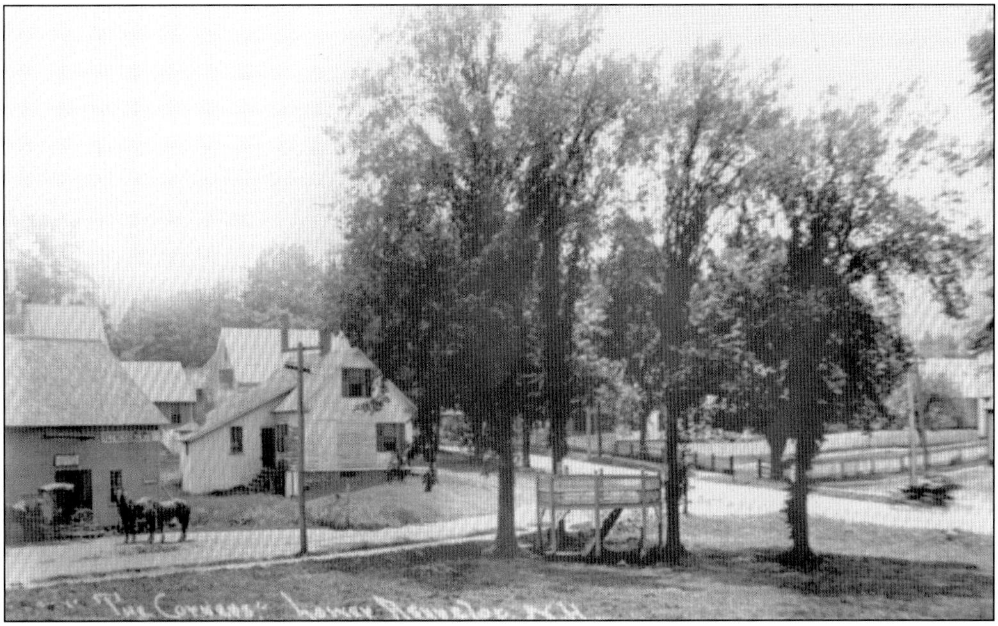

The Ashuelot bandstand was located at the intersection of Main Street and Broad Brook Road. The building at left, advertising "refreshments," has been replaced with an automobile repair shop. The house to its right was a store for many years, but has been returned to a private residence.

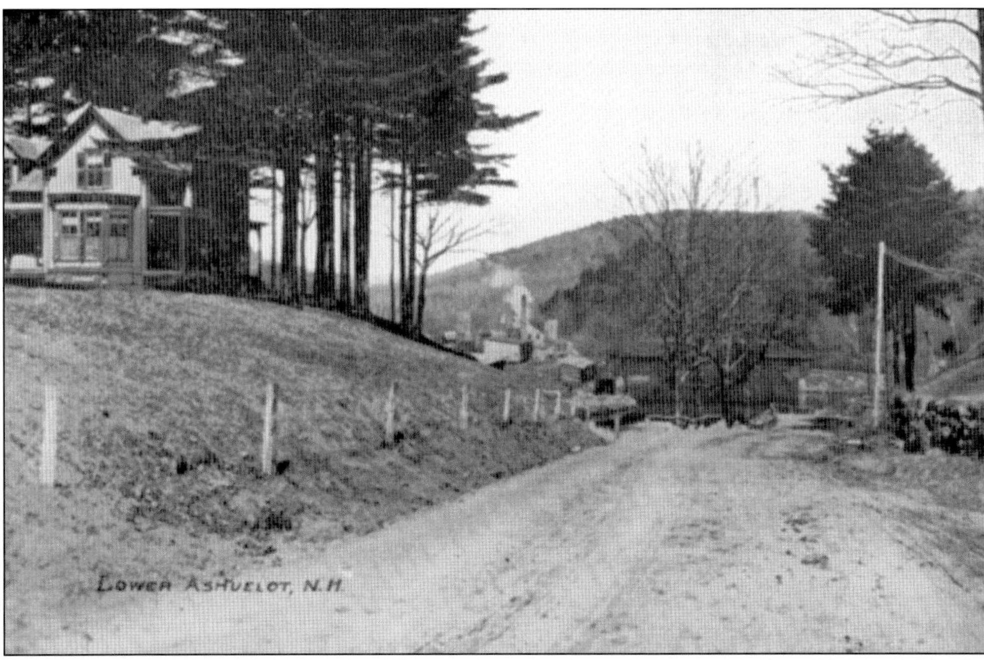

Looking down what is now Route 119 in the Lower Village, one can see the old covered bridge that allowed access to the mills and the Ashuelot Railroad on the south side of the Ashuelot River. The mill site was later home to the Paper Service Limited factory, which was damaged beyond salvation in the flash flood of 2005. (Courtesy of Dorothy Doolittle Farnan.)

Three

INSTITUTIONS

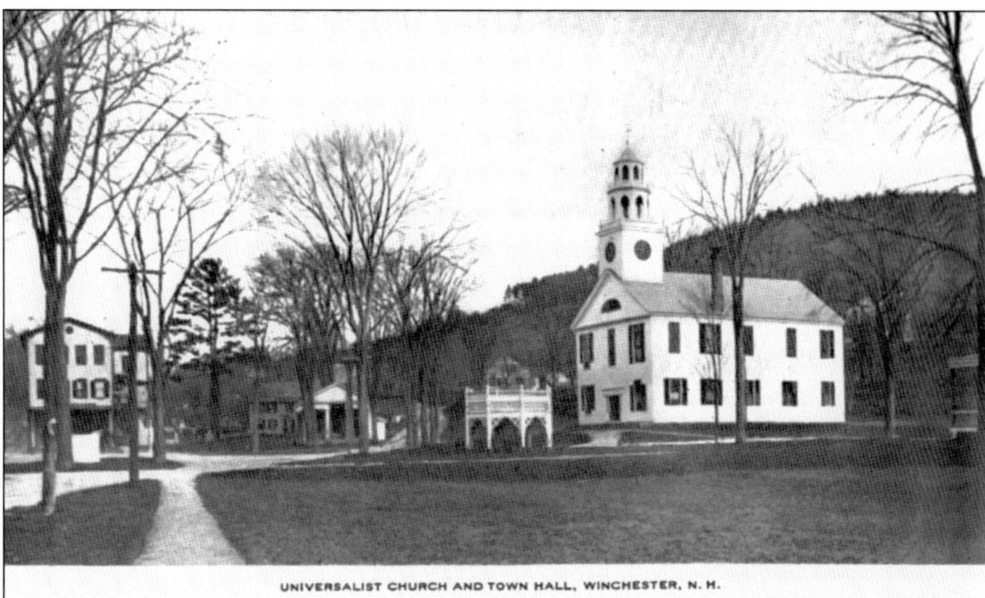

The town's meetinghouse was also a church. After 1834, when the Congregationalists built their own church, it came to be called the Universalist Church and town hall. The meetinghouse experienced several renovations. By 1903, when the Universalists celebrated their 100th anniversary, it looked like the picture above. Just six years later, it burned to the ground.

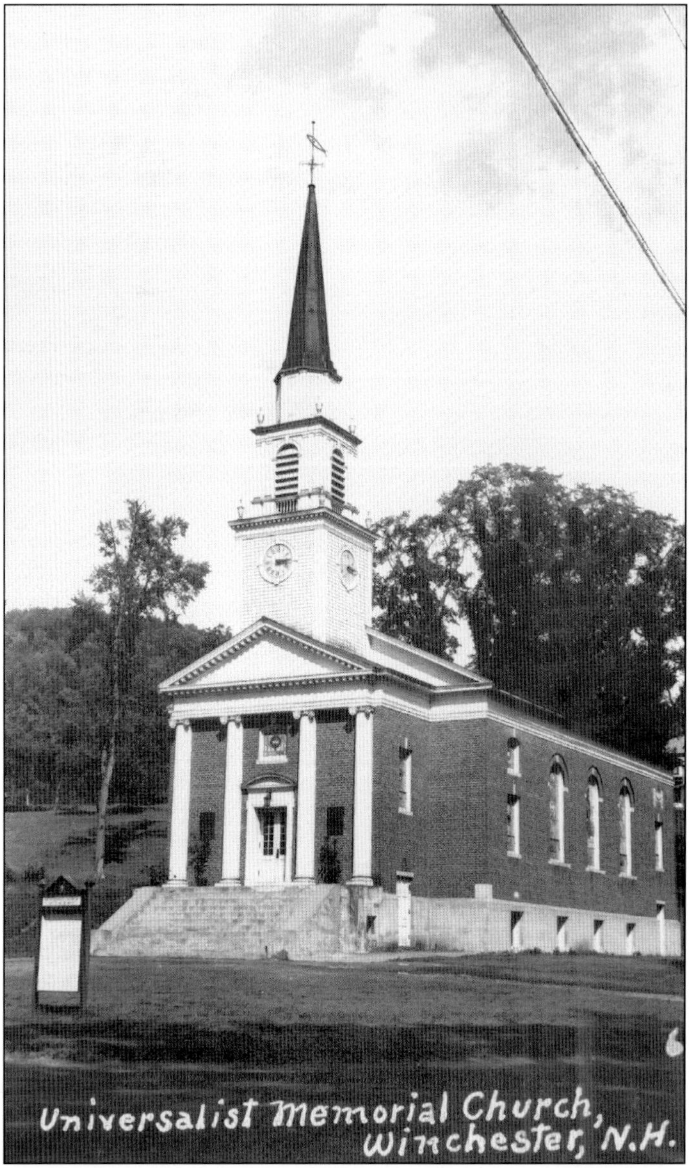

The brick church in the center of town, now known as the Universalist Heritage Center, rose from the ashes of the old town hall and Universalist Church. This marks the place where the General Convention of Universalists adopted their Profession of Belief in 1803. The Profession of Belief came to be known as the Winchester Confession and clearly delineated the Universalists from the Congregationalists. This was a significant part of efforts to truly establish freedom of religion in the young United States. The profession eventually became part of the Universalists' constitution and was enacted as a condition of fellowship. When the white clapboard building (pictured on page 45) went up in flames, there was a national campaign among Universalists to rebuild what they called their "mother church." The town donated the land, and by 1912, the architectural gem—which still stands—was completed. In 1935, the Universalists joined with other Protestant churches to form the Federated Church. In 1976, the Federated Church became the United Church of Winchester, and the decision was made to give up the old Universalist Church, which reverted back to the Universalist Society.

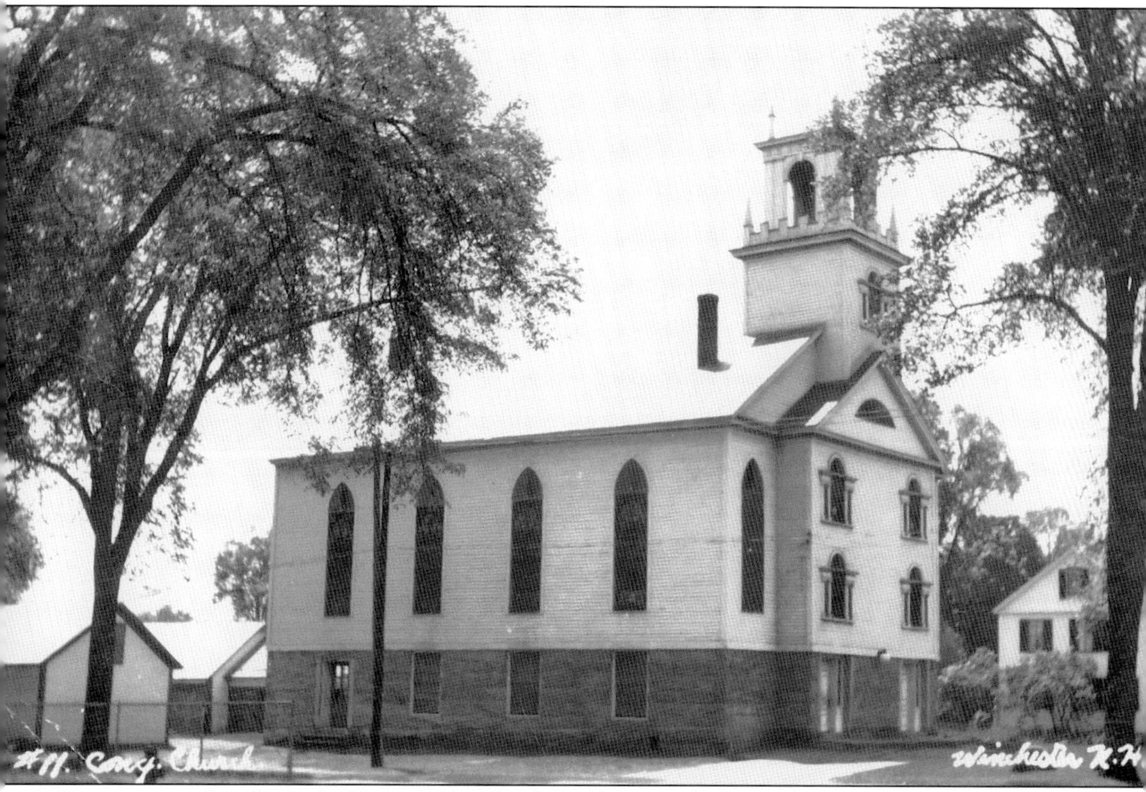

Congregationalists built the United Church of Winchester, which stands on the corner of Main and Parker Streets. The Congregationalists, who once offered the only religion in Winchester, held services at the town meetinghouse. After the Toleration Act of 1819, however, the Congregationalists found themselves sharing the building with the Universalists. In 1834, they built their own church. In 1849, the building was raised and the granite block foundation seen above was installed under it. In 1931, in response to dwindling attendance at the Protestant churches, the Congregationalists, Methodists, and Universalists joined to form the Federated Church. Then, in 1976, the individual denominations dissolved their governing committees and the Federated Church became the United Church of Winchester. For many years, they maintained both this church, on the corner of Parker Street, and the former Universalist Church at the corner of Richmond and Michigan Streets.

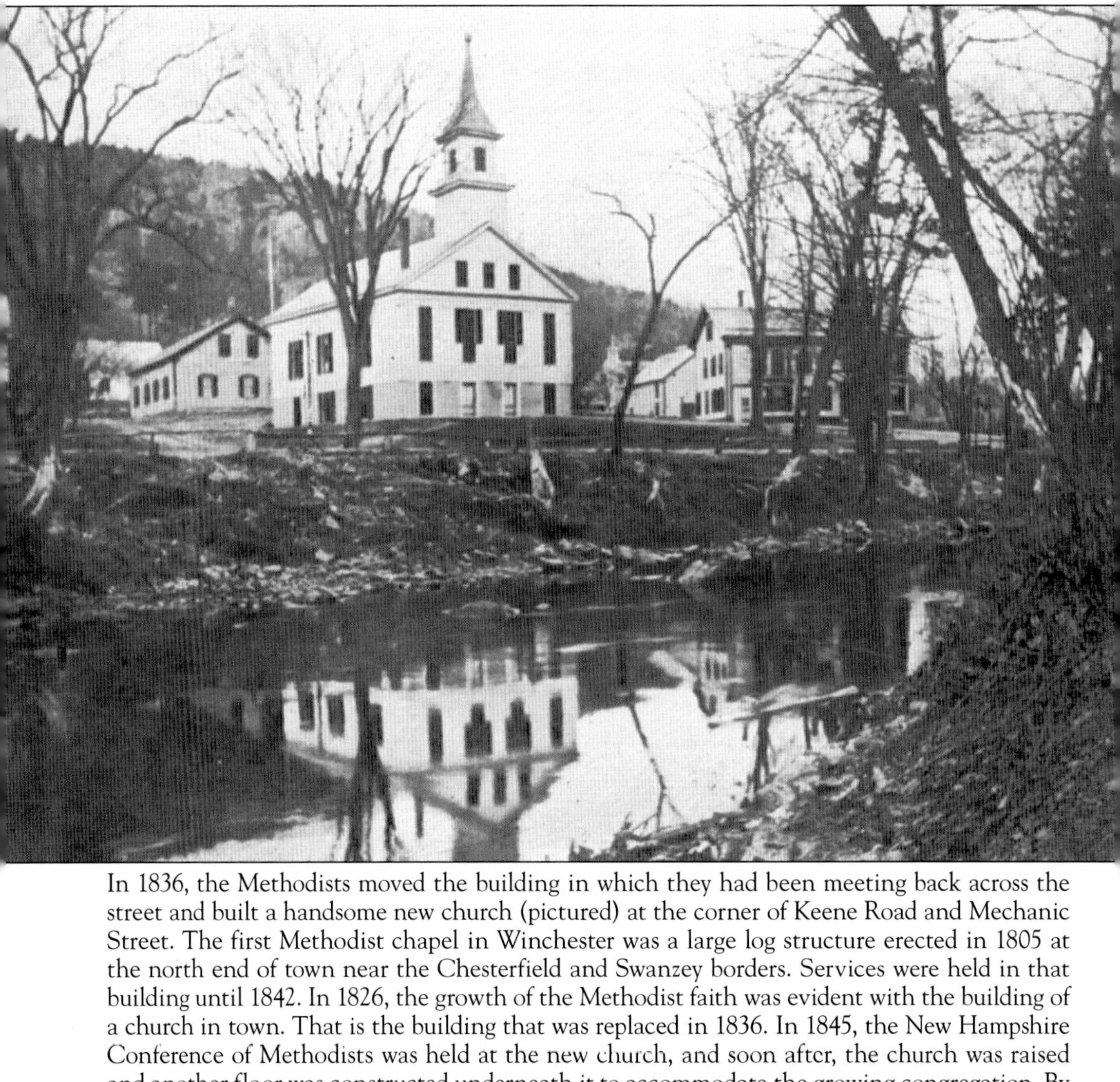

In 1836, the Methodists moved the building in which they had been meeting back across the street and built a handsome new church (pictured) at the corner of Keene Road and Mechanic Street. The first Methodist chapel in Winchester was a large log structure erected in 1805 at the north end of town near the Chesterfield and Swanzey borders. Services were held in that building until 1842. In 1826, the growth of the Methodist faith was evident with the building of a church in town. That is the building that was replaced in 1836. In 1845, the New Hampshire Conference of Methodists was held at the new church, and soon after, the church was raised and another floor was constructed underneath it to accommodate the growing congregation. By the early 20th century, Protestant church membership was declining and it was difficult for the smaller parishes to afford the upkeep of their beautiful buildings. In 1931, the Methodists joined with the Congregationalists and Universalists to form the Federated Church. The Methodist church was sold to the Masonic Order and served as their temple for many years. It served as the home of the Grace Christian Fellowship until the spring of 2012.

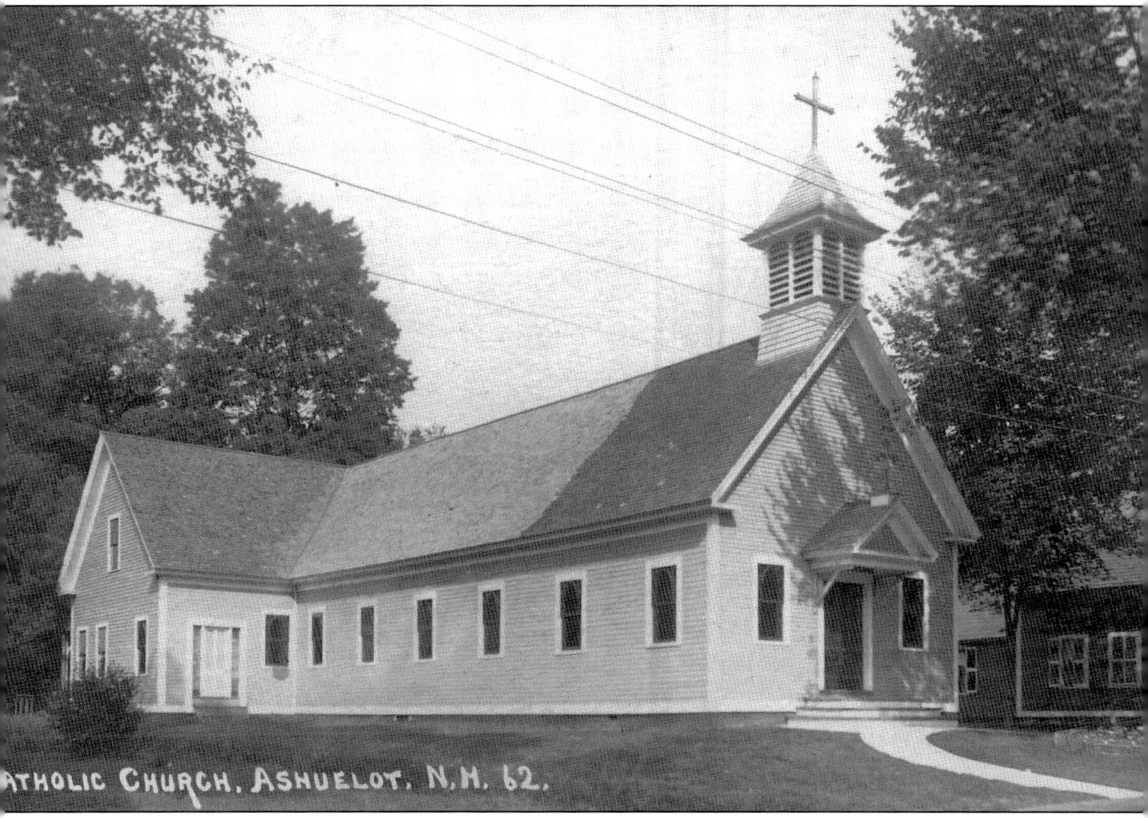

Traveling missionaries conducted Mass for immigrant Catholics in Ashuelot as early as 1845. St. Michael's Church was organized in 1856 as a mission of St. Mary's Parish in Claremont, New Hampshire. For a while, services were held in the Upper Village School. In 1873, local businessman Ansel Dickinson, though a Methodist himself, felt that Catholics should have a home of their own and gave St. Michael's a cottage on land along River Street (now Main Street) between the Upper and Lower Ashuelot Villages for use as a church. The building was renovated and became a very active church for many years. In 1958, St. Michael's Parish Hall, better known as the bingo hall, was opened in a building constructed next to the Ashuelot School. Besides parish functions, the hall hosted regular bingo games that attracted busloads of players from Massachusetts. The hall was sold in October 1986, when it was no longer in use. The Catholic church experienced declining attendance toward the end of the 20th century, and St. Michael's Church closed. In 2009, this building was razed.

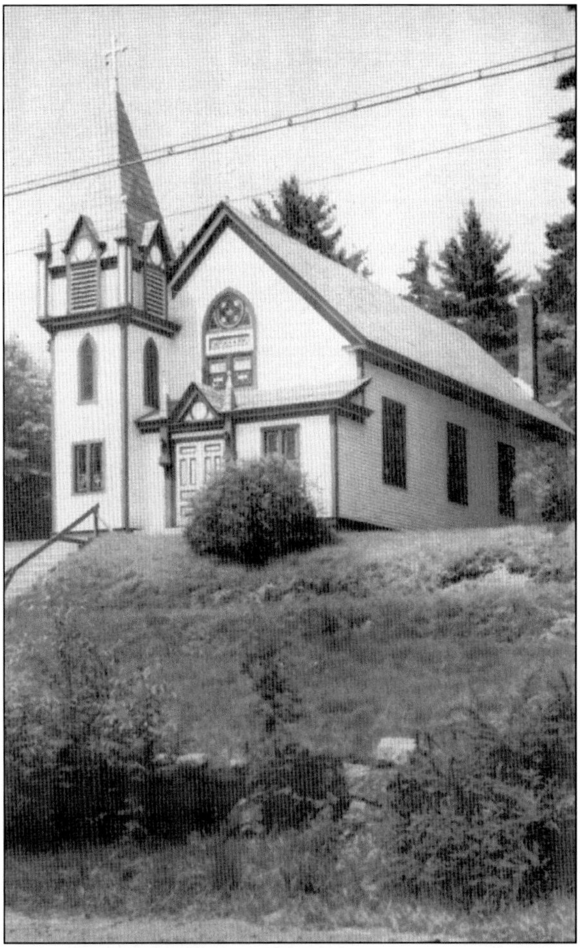

Though Ashuelot had St. Michael's, downtown Winchester had no Catholic church until 1911, when the Polish workers decided to build their own. They moved a barn from Ashuelot (behind the Thayer Library) to the hillside on Richmond Street and rehabilitated it as a church. The church, pictured at left, was named for St. Stanislaus and was literally built upon a rock. It had no foundation but sat on a granite ledge out of which enough room had been chipped to accommodate the furnace. By the 1950s, it was bursting at the seams, and a campaign was started to build a larger church. In 1961, a spacious new church (below) was opened a short way up Richmond Street. Today, it is part of the Mary Queen of Peace parish. The original St. Stanislaus church is now a private residence. (Courtesy Dorothy Doolittle Farnan.)

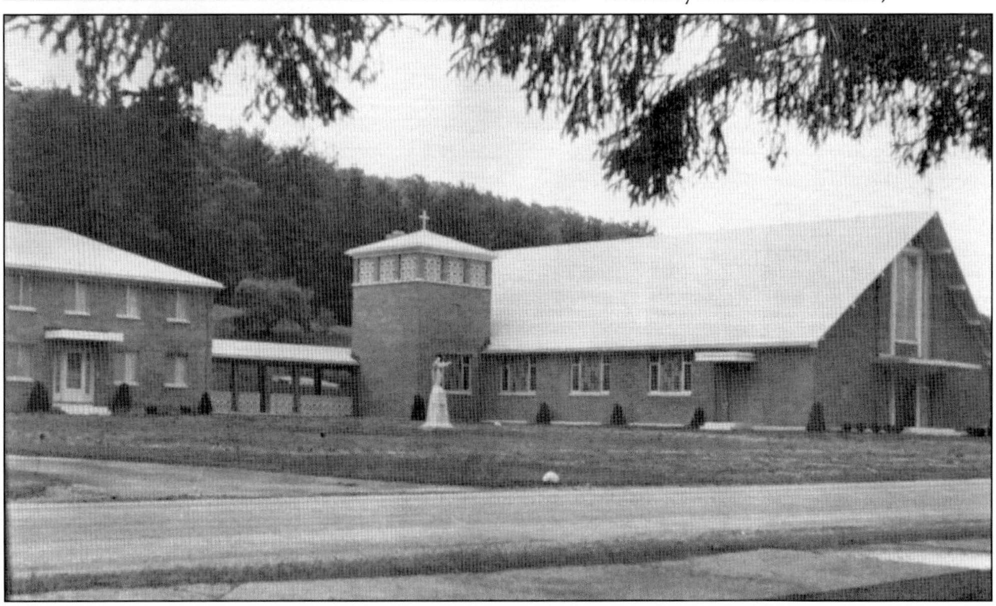

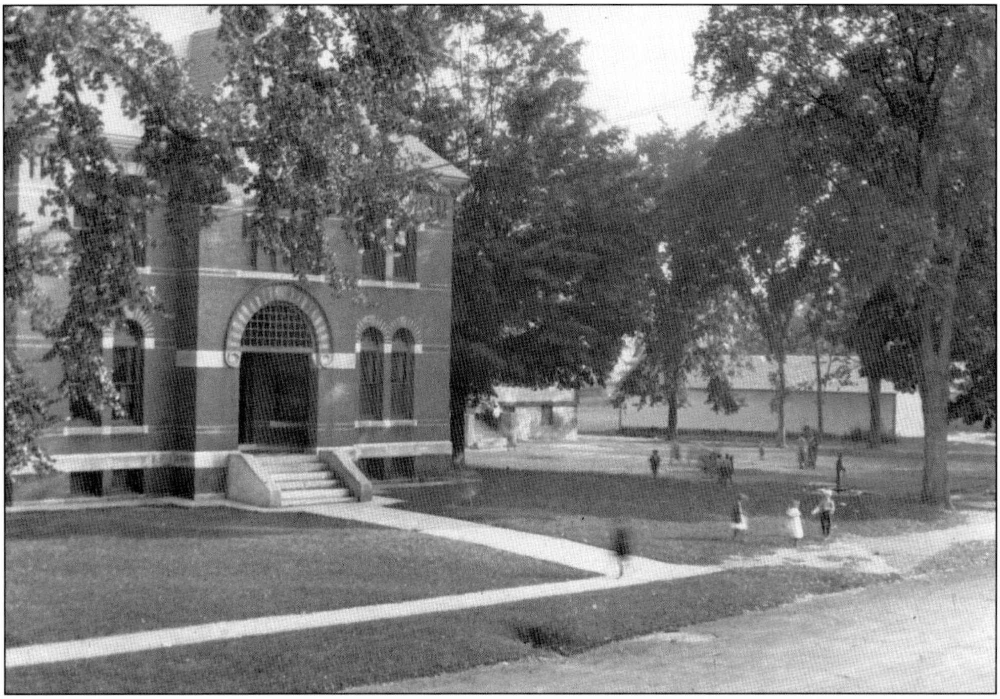

The Conant Public Library was built in 1890 with a bequest left to the town by Ezra Conant. The son of a minister of the Congregational church, Conant grew up in Winchester, left town at age 18 to make his fortune, and became a wealthy man. The town built a beautiful Victorian structure that is now listed in the National Register of Historic Places. When the above photograph was taken, the Center School was next door. Children can be seen playing on the front lawn, which is now a park. Below, the side view of the library shows the back wing that was not originally open to the public. In 1965, the main desk was moved to the side, allowing public access to the "stacks." A later addition on the back allows for handicapped access to the building.

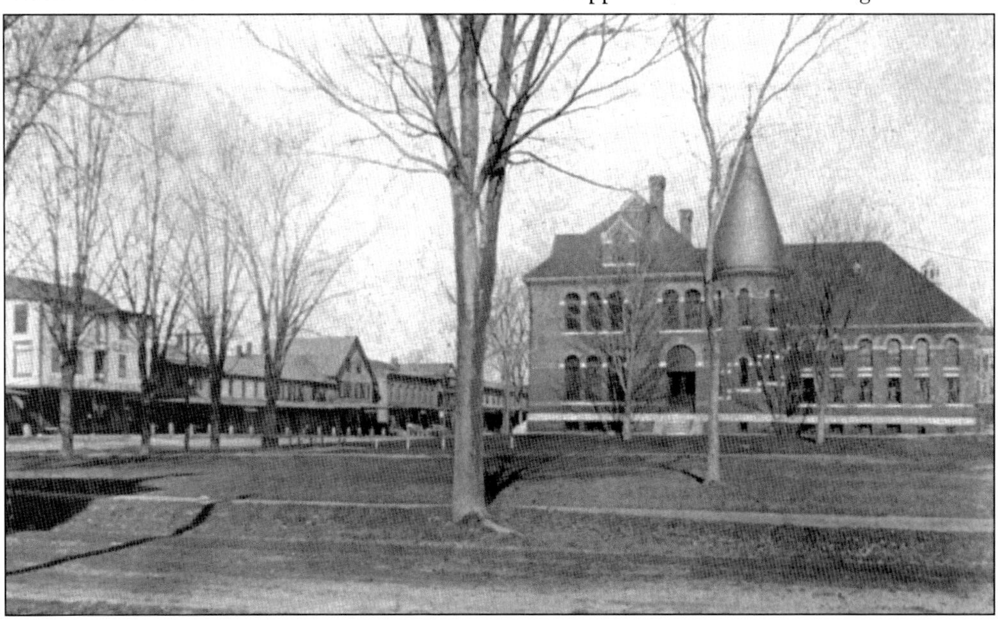

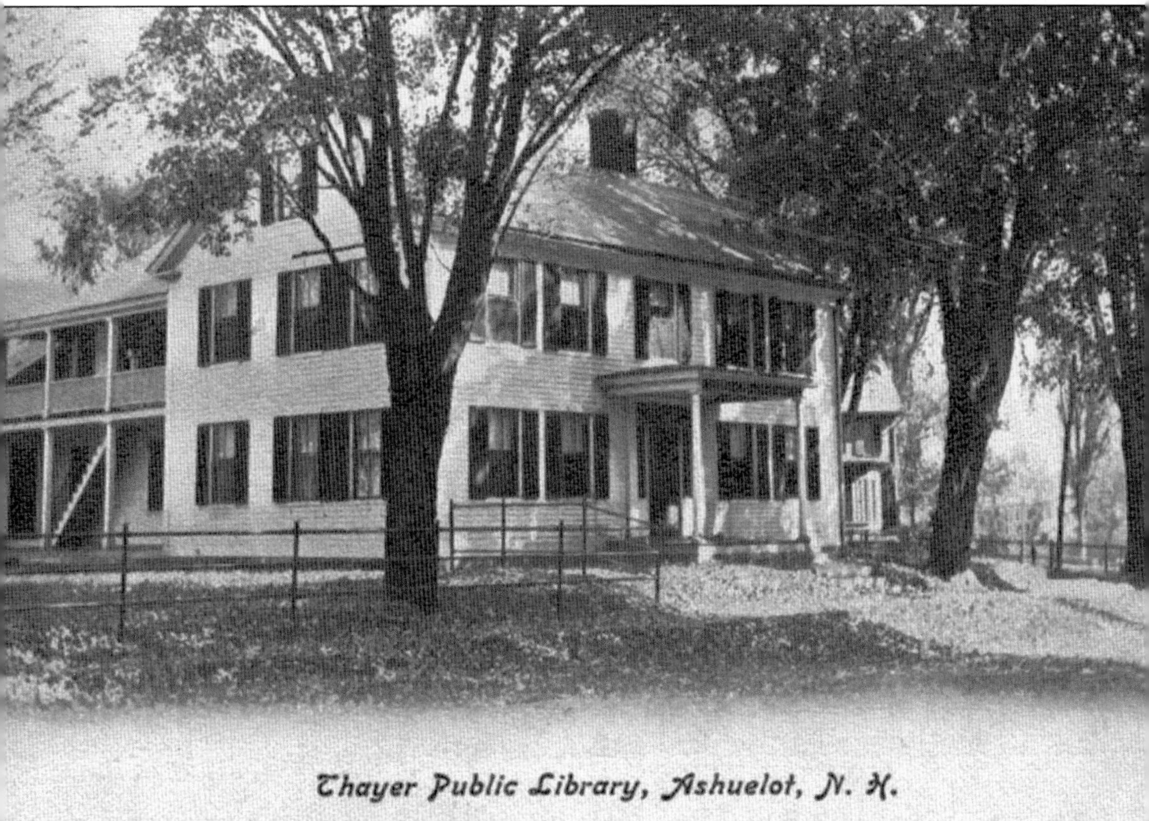

Julia Ball grew up in Ashuelot. Although she later married Edward Thayer of Keene and became quite wealthy, she did not forget her hometown. In 1902, she donated the house that had belonged to her mother, Persis Capron, to the town for use as a library. It was named the Thayer Public Library. The Federal-style building sits opposite the north end of the Ashuelot Covered Bridge, next to the common. It has remained a library ever since, with the interior unchanged. The second floor is a spacious apartment for the librarian's use. Minnie Ball, Alice Burdette, and Joyce Gregory were three favorite librarians throughout the years. The building, constructed in 1823, is now listed in the New Hampshire State Register of Historic Places.

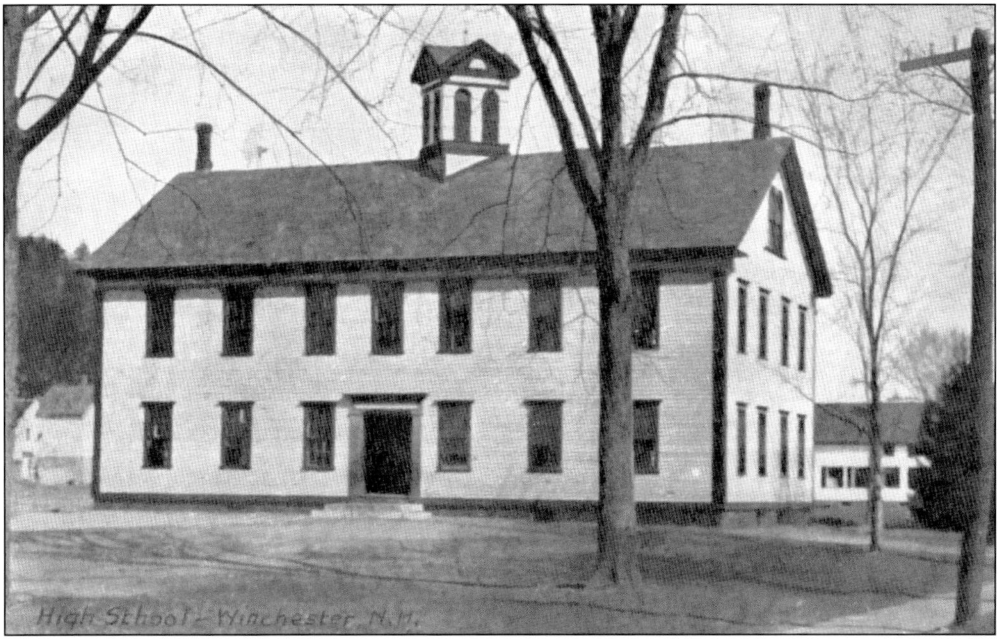

The earliest schools in Winchester assembled in the meetinghouse or in people's homes. A schoolhouse was built on the common where the brick church now stands, followed by the construction of the academy on Michigan Street opposite the bank. Around 1870, this school was built at the corner of Main and Parker Streets for both secondary and elementary school students.

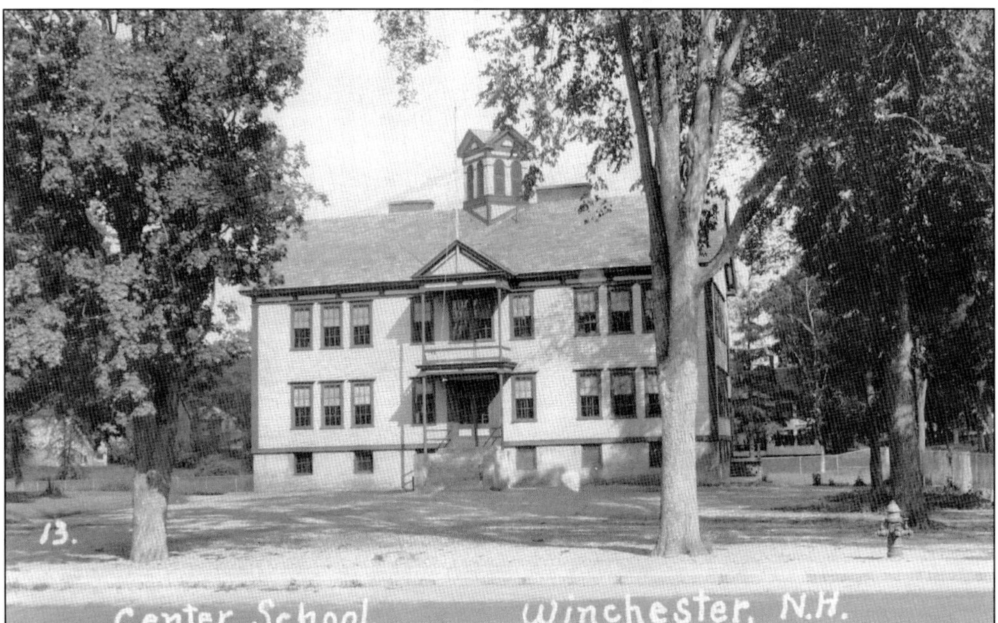

The Center School underwent several renovations. It originally sat low to the ground and later had an entrance porch added, more windows installed, and was raised for construction of a basement level underneath. After Thayer High School was built, the Center School remained as an elementary school until 1971, when Winchester Elementary School opened at the east end of Parker Street. (Courtesy of Dorothy Doolittle Farnan.)

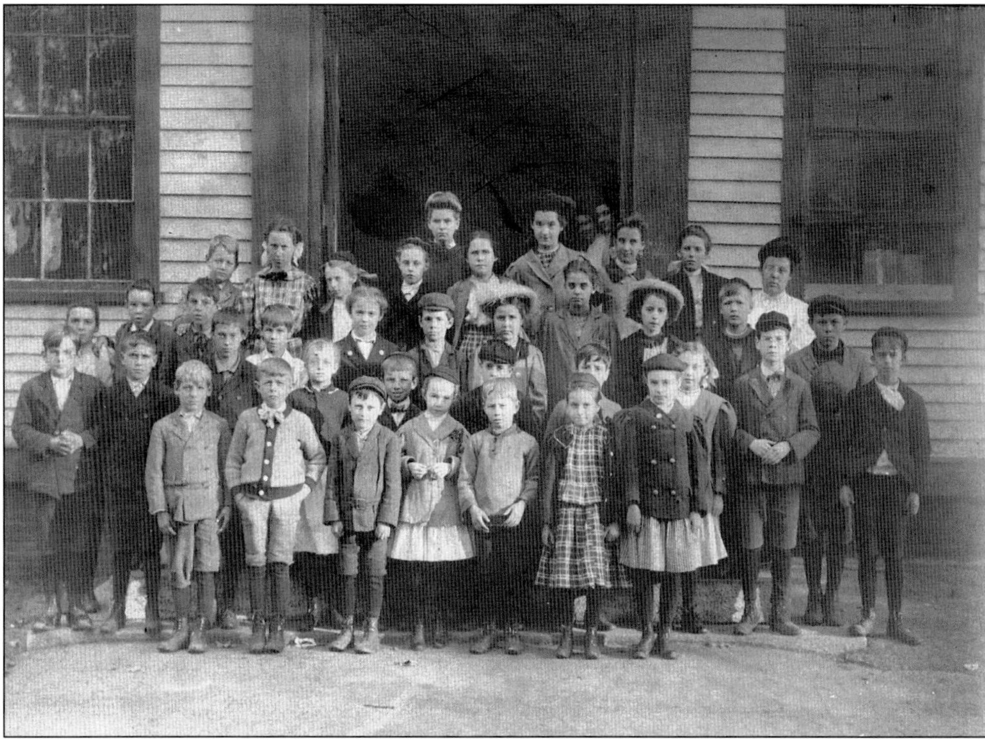

There are many photographs of school classes in which the students are—unfortunately—unidentified. This one was taken at the District School No. 3, later called the Center School, before the entrance porch was added and before the building was raised.

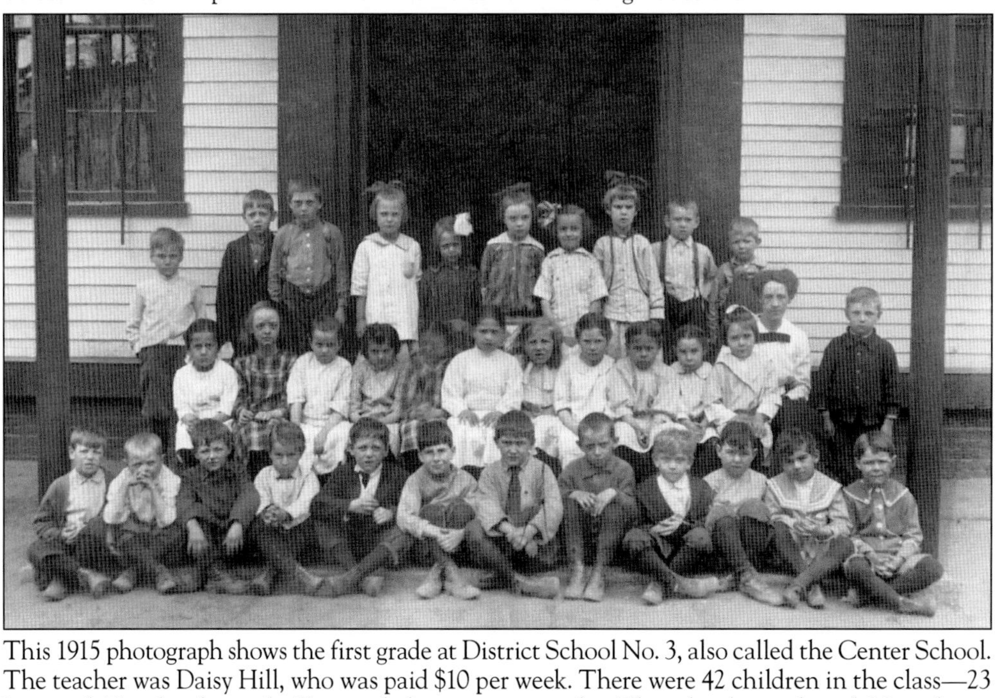

This 1915 photograph shows the first grade at District School No. 3, also called the Center School. The teacher was Daisy Hill, who was paid $10 per week. There were 42 children in the class—23 boys and 19 girls—but only 32 attended on an average day. The school term lasted 36 weeks.

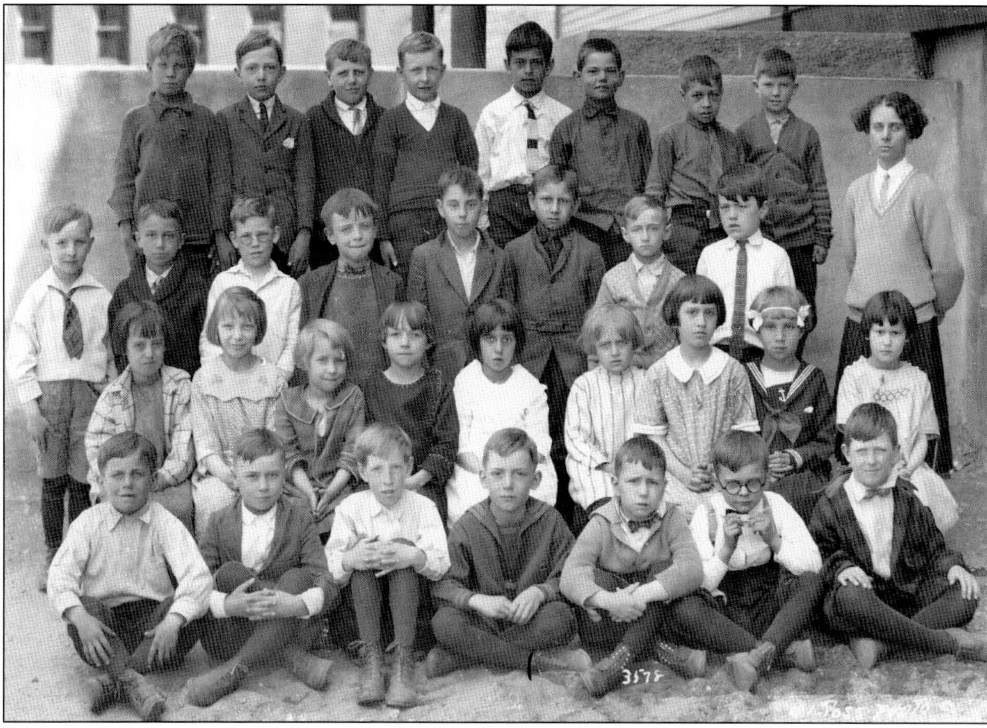

This 1926 photograph is of Dorothy White's Center School class; White is standing at far right. Not all of the students are identified, but some might be familiar to current townspeople. The fifth from the left in the first row is Arnold Conway. Stephen Johnson is third from the left in the third row. If the youngster fourth from the left in the fourth row looks like Butch Plifka, that's because it is his father, "Shady."

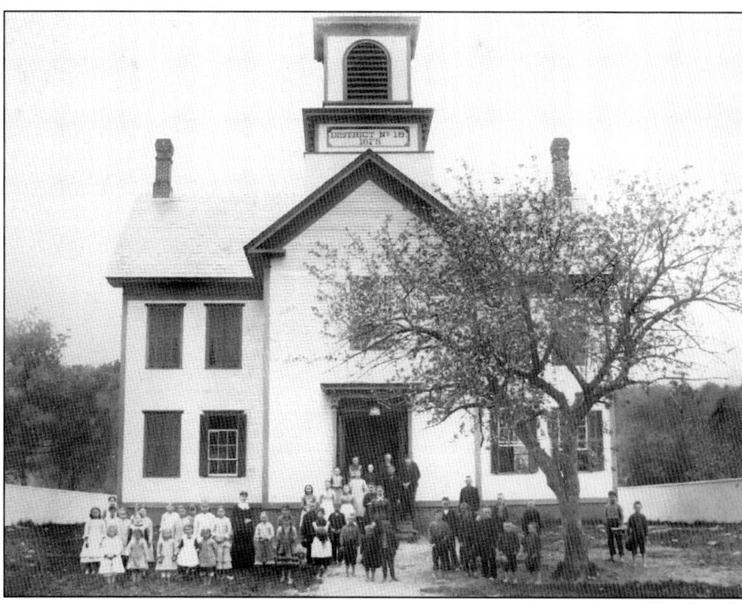

At one time, there were 21 district schools in Winchester. Since most students commuted on foot, schools were located wherever there was a concentration of children. This photograph is of District School No. 18 in the Lower Ashuelot Village. It was located across the street from Broad Brook Road, slightly to the east. The building no longer stands.

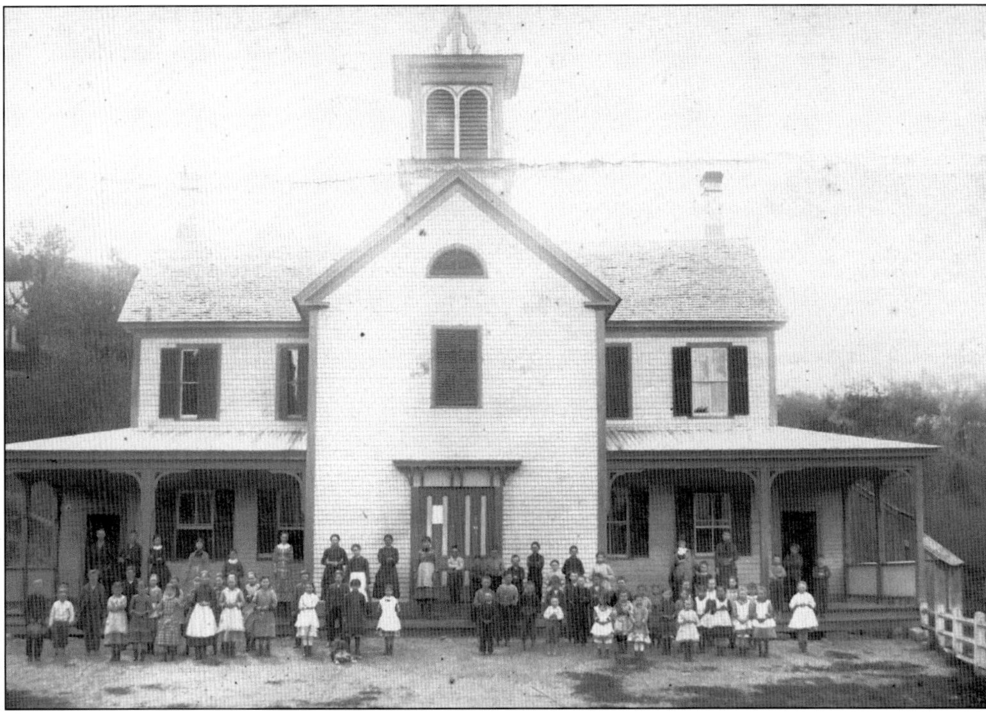

The Upper Ashuelot School, District School No. 2, was located on the south side of the covered bridge, across from the Ashuelot Railroad station. The fence separates it from the railroad tracks. During non-school hours, the building was used for community meetings and religious services. It remained in operation until the newer Ashuelot School was built nearby. A modern, raised ranch house now sits on this site.

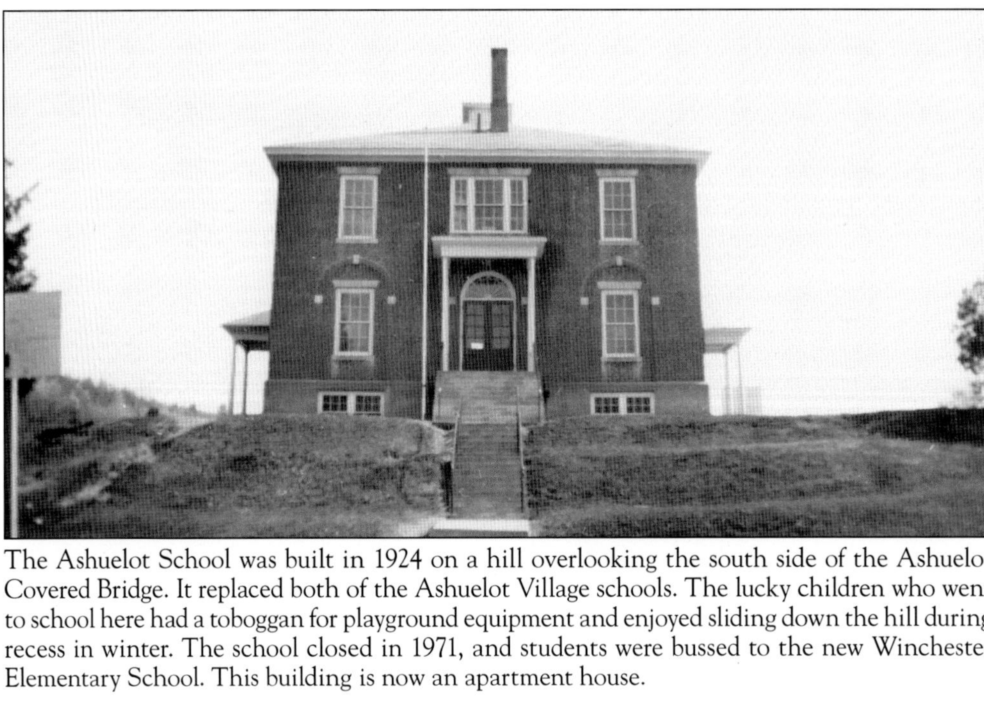

The Ashuelot School was built in 1924 on a hill overlooking the south side of the Ashuelot Covered Bridge. It replaced both of the Ashuelot Village schools. The lucky children who went to school here had a toboggan for playground equipment and enjoyed sliding down the hill during recess in winter. The school closed in 1971, and students were bussed to the new Winchester Elementary School. This building is now an apartment house.

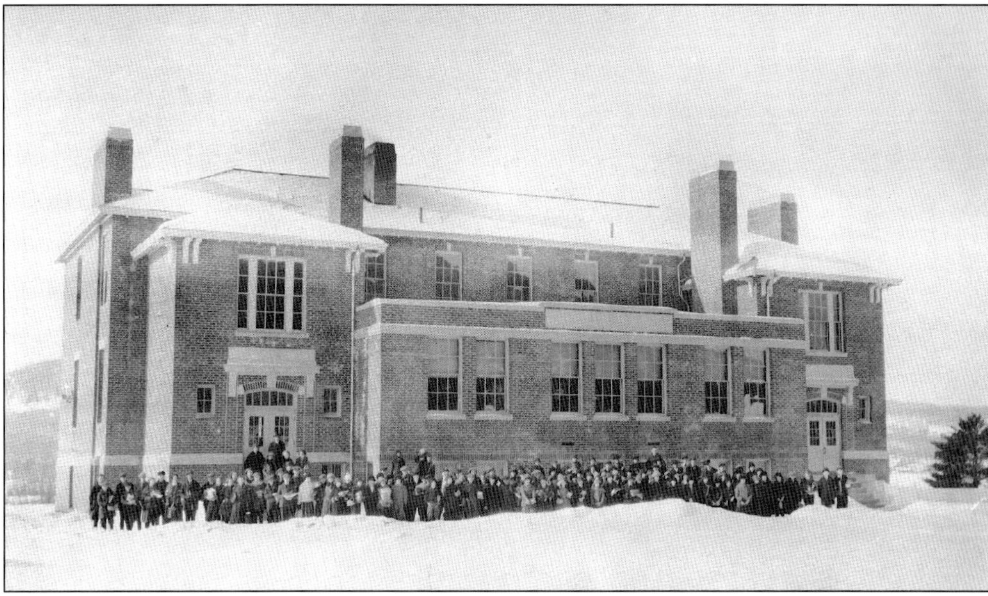

Thayer High School was built with a bequest from Julia Ball Thayer, who was originally from Ashuelot. It opened in February 1923 and boasted 11 classrooms that were "thoroughly modern in design and equipment," according to a newspaper report at the time. It proudly served Winchester's students for many years. In 1963, a new wing was constructed to accommodate junior high students, a cafeteria, and industrial arts classrooms. A gymnasium, an art room, and a band room were also added to the original building. Thayer High graduated its last class in 2005, but remains part of The Winchester School's complex. Winchester high school students now go to school in Keene.

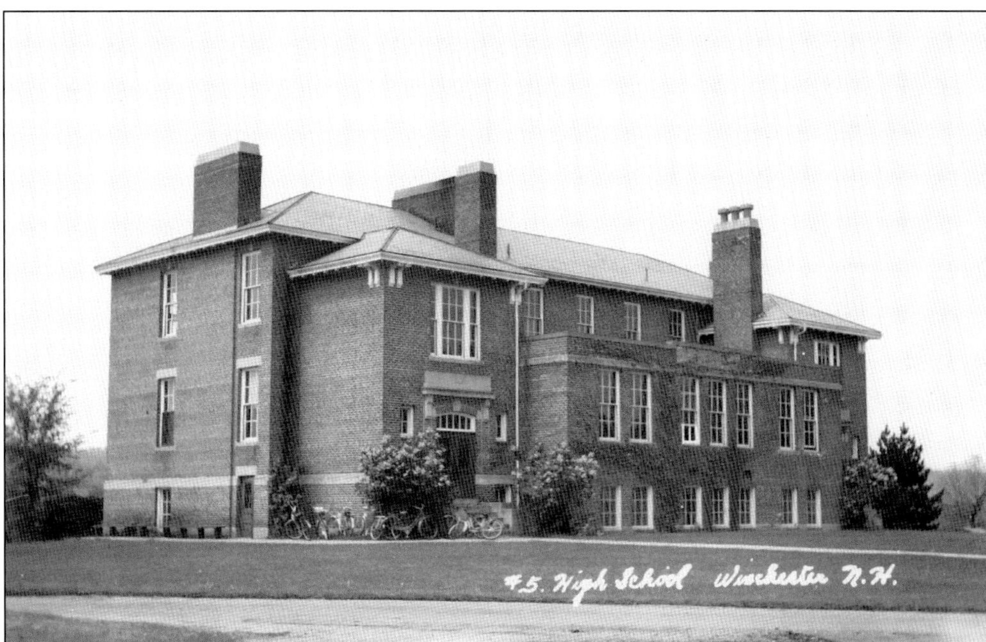

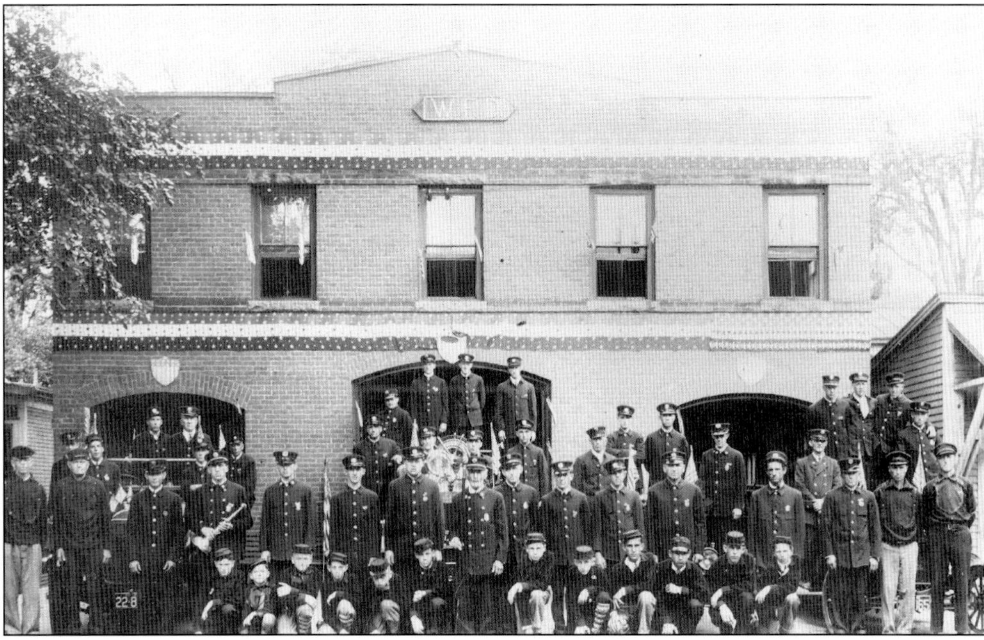

The first Winchester Fire Department was organized in 1843. For many years, their equipment was kept in the old Methodist church building (which later became the Grange Hall). In 1891, a firehouse was built on Ashuelot Street; it burned down two years later. In 1895, it was rebuilt with brick, creating the building these firefighters posed in front of around 1920.

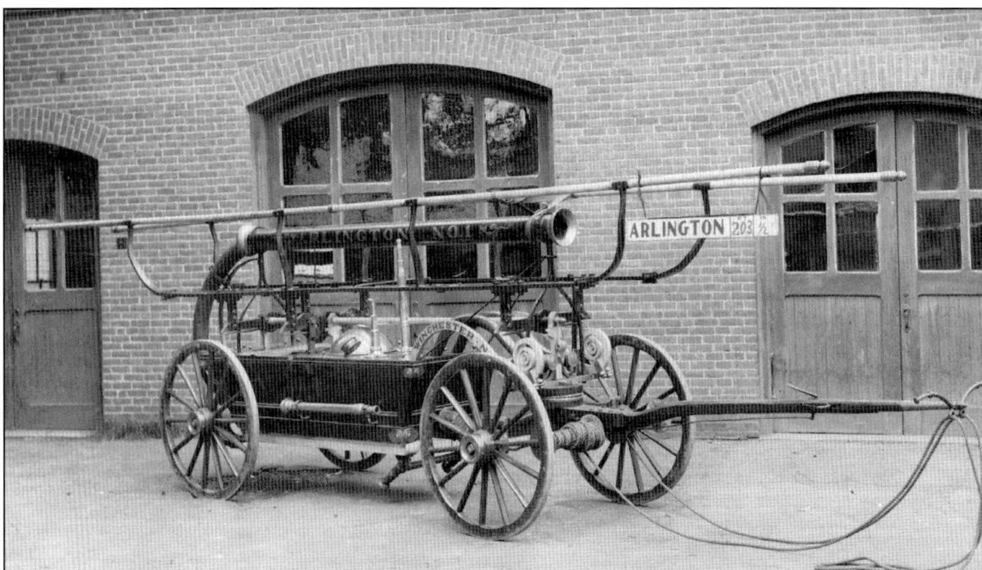

The Winchester Fire Department bought this pumper in 1911 for $200. They named it Arlington No. 1, after the town's early name. In 1925, it won the fireman's muster in Gardner, Massachusetts, by pumping a distance of 202 feet and 1.5 inches. A collection of the fire department's old pumpers can be viewed at the Sheridan House Museum.

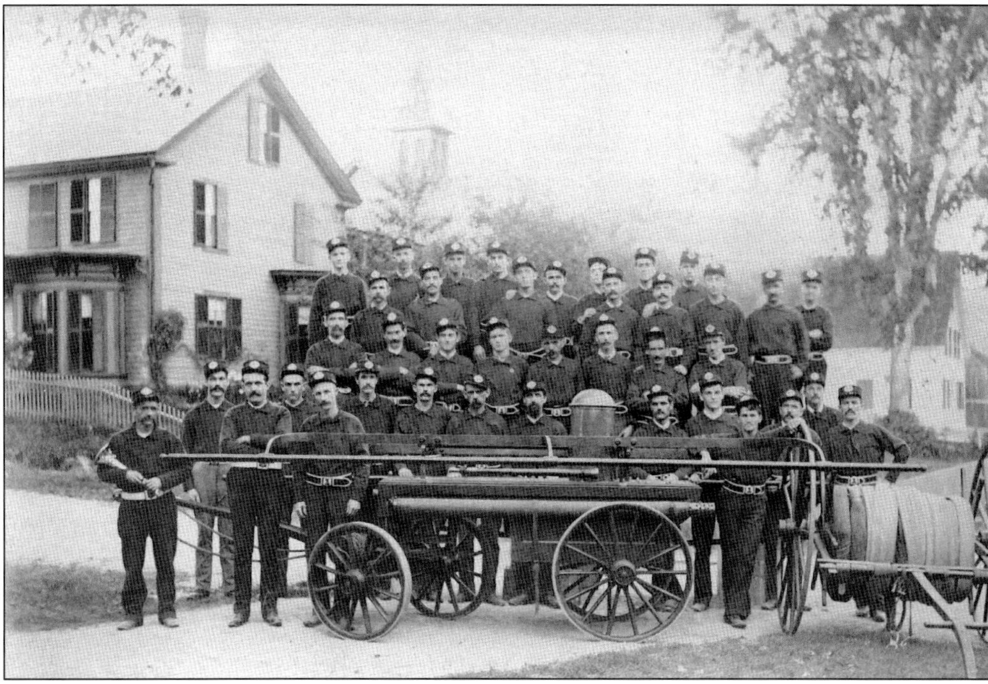

In 1851, the woolen mill in Upper Ashuelot Village burned, and 10 buildings were lost. Perhaps the fire spurred the formation of the Ashuelot Fire Company in 1861. Here, the men pose in front of the pumper house at the north end of the Ashuelot Covered Bridge. The Welch house is visible in the background.

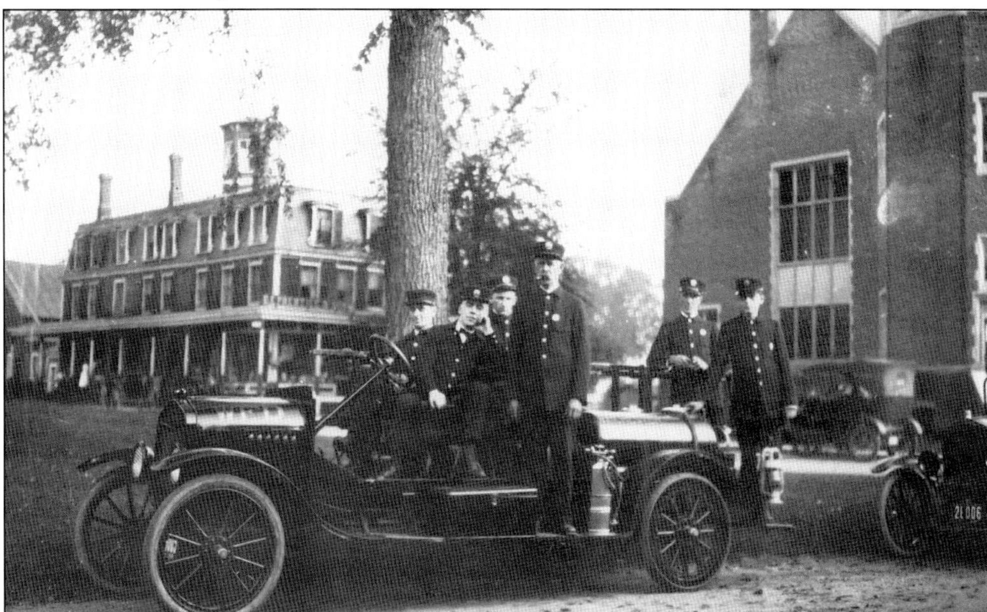

In 1918, the Winchester Fire Department acquired a Model T Ford truck at no cost to the town and refitted it to carry hose. In 1920, they got another free Model T Ford and refitted it to carry supplies; those Model Ts may be the vehicles shown in this c. 1920 photograph. Both of the Ford trucks were sold in 1935.

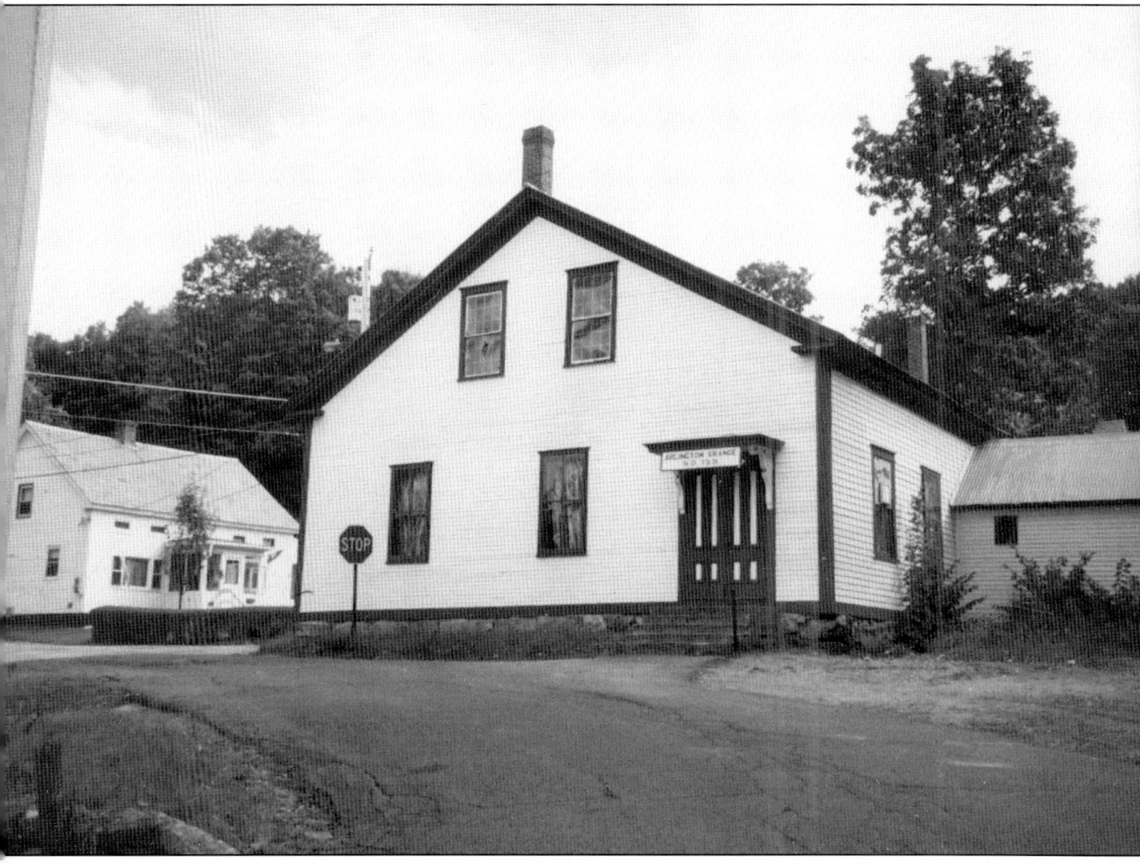

The Arlington Grange No. 139 was founded in 1889. The Grange's first few meetings were held in the Methodist church, and then the group rented the third floor of the Burbank Block (on the northeast corner of Main Street and Richmond Road). In 1891, the Grange rented the GAR Hall, and in 1906, they bought it. The building was the original Methodist chapel that was moved back across Mechanic Street when the new Methodist church was built. When the town meetinghouse burned in 1909, the Grange lent the hall for town business and church services. The Grange is a family fraternal organization that has its roots in the farming community. Its purpose is to help members reach their full potential as citizens and community members. Although the Grange sold this building in 2004, preferring to put its money into the community, the organization is still active in town and has seen its membership grow in recent years. The current Winchester town clerk, James Tetreault, not only heads the local Grange chapter but is also the Worthy Master of the State Grange.

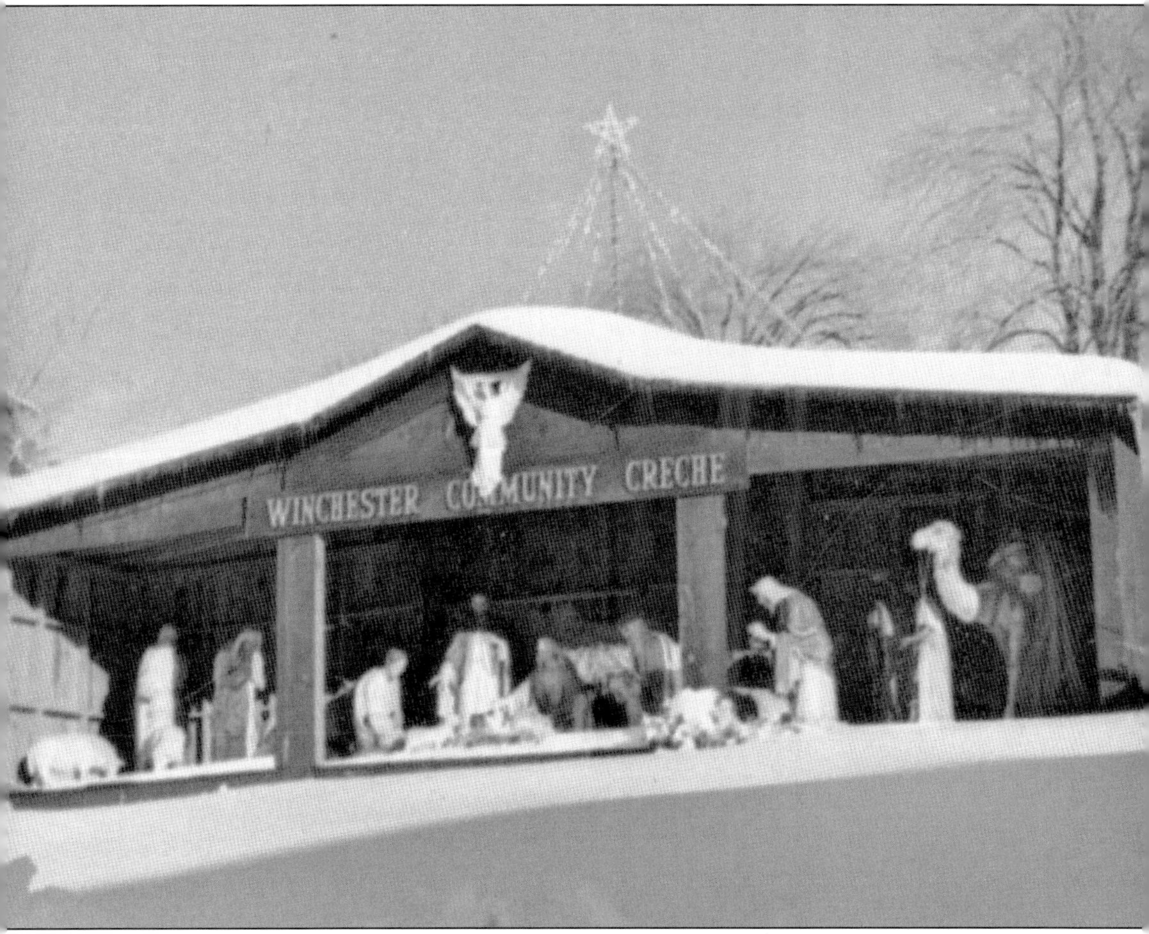

The Winchester Women's Club was formed in 1924 with 125 members. By the end of the second year, there were 153 members paying dues. The Winchester Women's Club was a multipurpose organization that sought to enlighten and entertain its members, improve its community, and contribute to charity. In November 1925, they joined the General Federation of Women's Clubs New Hampshire. Early projects included such things as advocating for hot lunches at school, cleaning up the Ashuelot River, planting a community Christmas tree, and holding a Christmas party for the children of the town. The club's biggest project was this Community Crèche, which was dedicated in December 1958 on the hill next to the Universalist church. Though the club is much smaller now, it still maintains the beautiful crèche, which it supports through an annual dinner held each February.

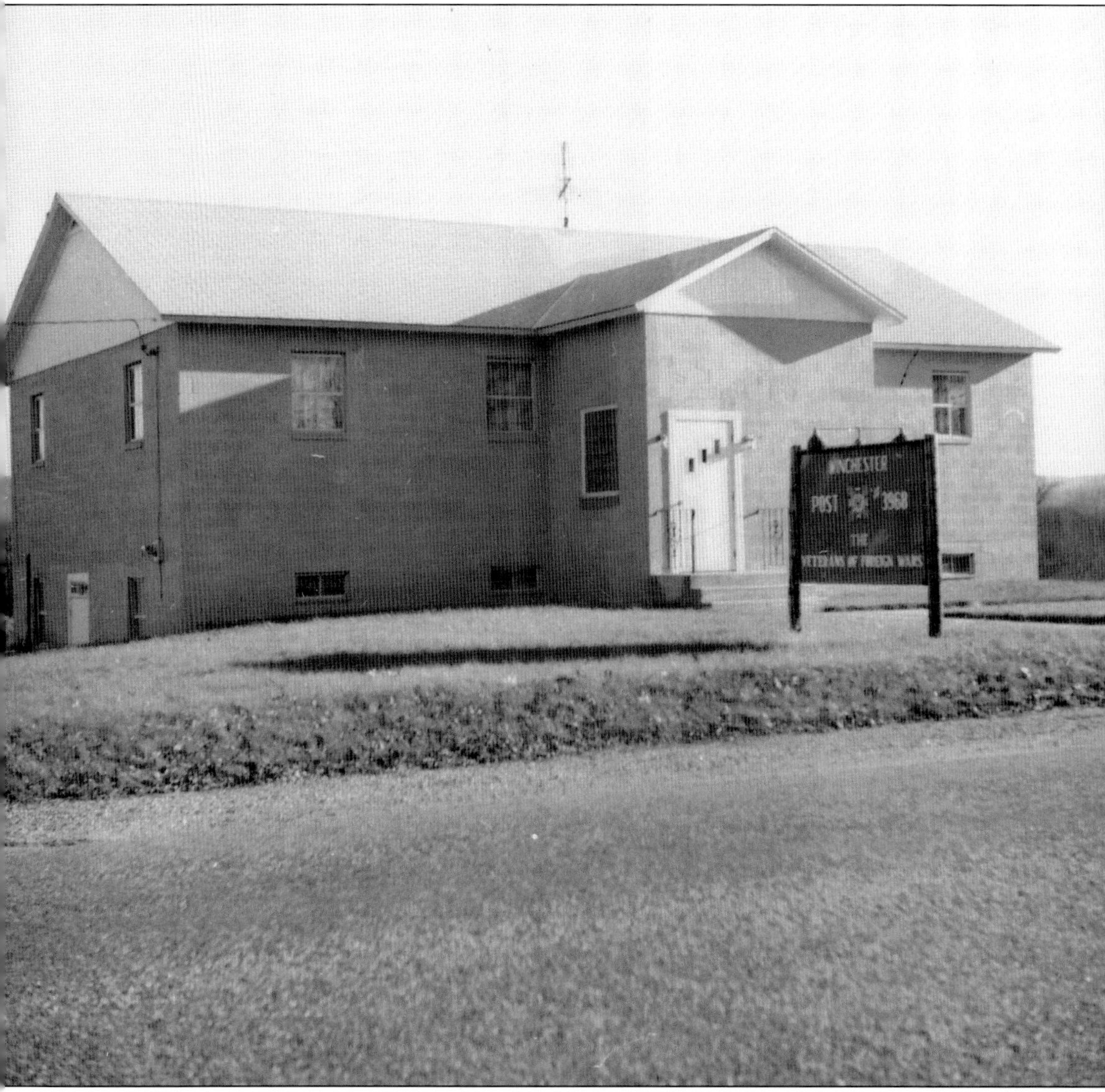

The Winchester Veterans of Foreign Wars Post 3968 was chartered in January 1945. The group first met at the community center before buying the old District School No. 20 building on Scotland Road. In the early 1950s, the VFW bought 16 acres on South Main Street just north of Mirey Brook and began building their new home (pictured) with their own hands. It was completed and dedicated in November 1959. In addition to holding meetings, maintaining a social club, and sponsoring civic events, the VFW organizes the annual Memorial Day parade and observances in Winchester, honors deceased veterans by placing flags on their graves, and places flags along Main Street to mark patriotic holidays from May to November.

Four

FAMOUS SONS AND DAUGHTERS

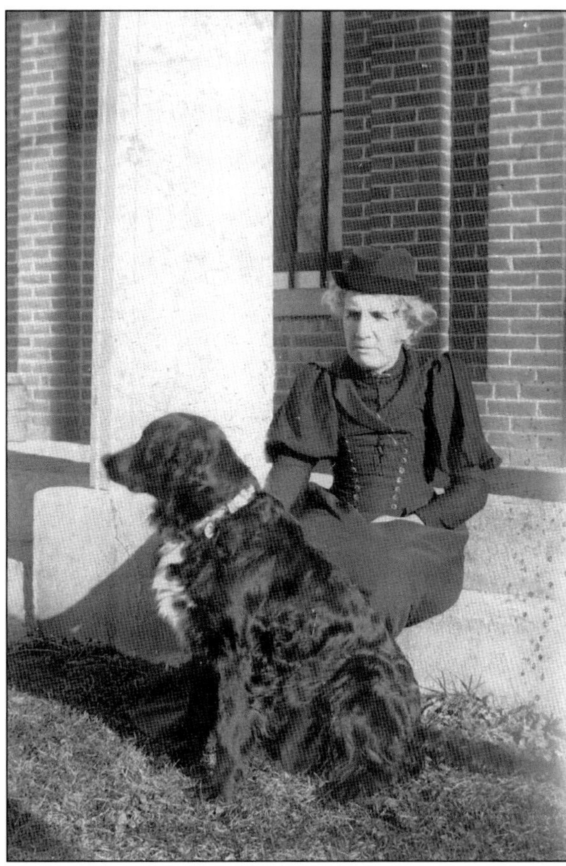

There are a handful of people from Winchester who have earned a place in history with their achievements. Jane Grace Alexander was the first woman to be named treasurer of a bank in New Hampshire. As a young woman, she went to work at the Winchester National Bank. When the Security Savings Bank was formed in 1881, she became its treasurer. She retired after 52 years with the National Bank and died in 1932.

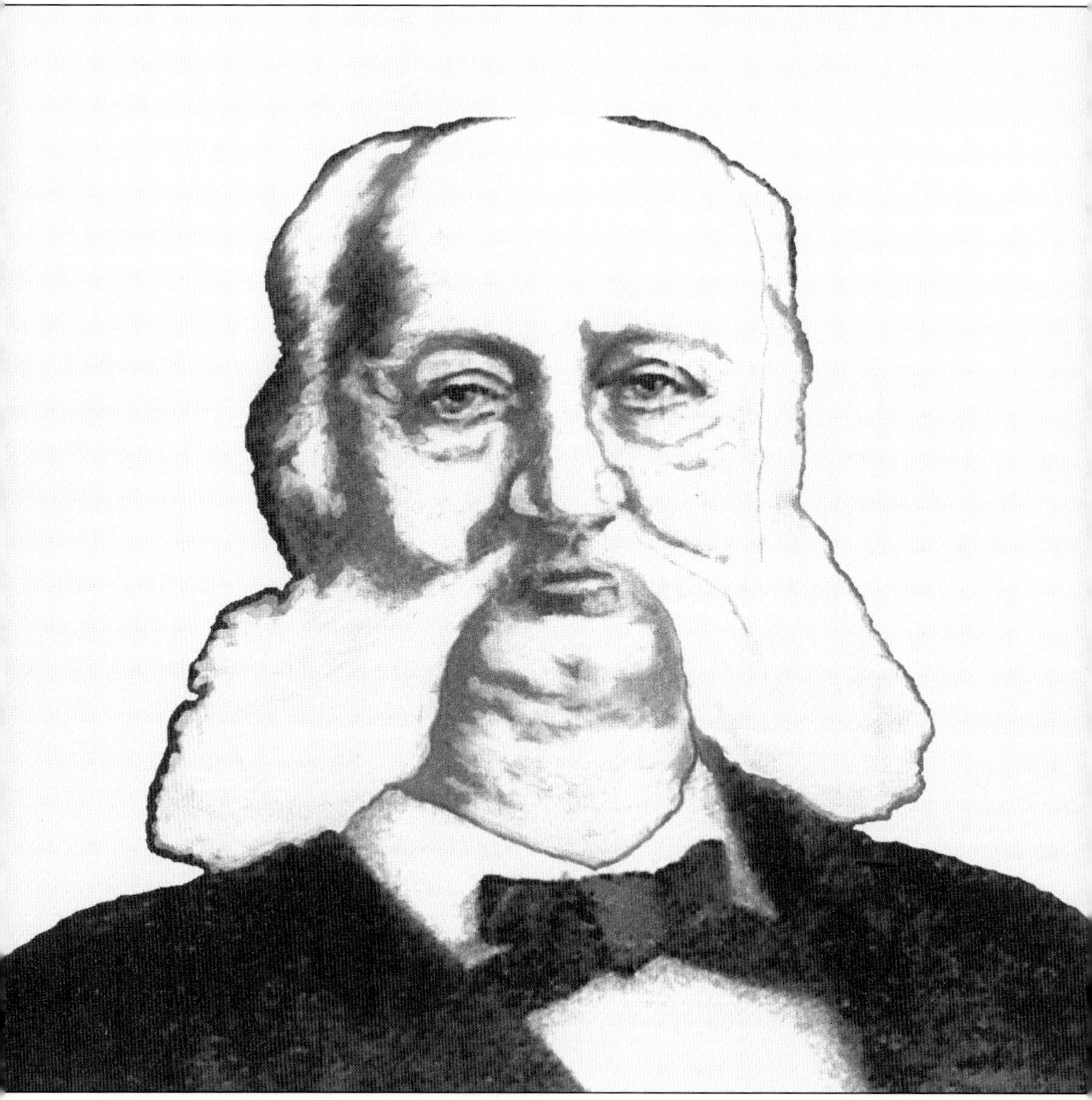

The Jewell brothers can trace their ancestry back to one of Earlington's (Winchester's) original grantees. There were five Jewell brothers in all (and five sisters), great-grandsons of Pliny Jewell, the town's first tannery owner. Two of them became famous. Harvey Jewell was born in 1820 and graduated from Dartmouth College. He then settled in Boston to practice law. He became active in local politics and served on the Common Council. He was later elected to the Massachusetts House of Representatives, where he rose to become speaker of the house, retiring in 1871. His home on Beacon Street was noted for its exceptional library containing many gems of literature. Harvey Jewell was also known for his skill at landing striped bass in the waters off his summer cottage in Swampscott, Massachusetts. He died in Boston in December 1881. Paintings, as well as marble busts, of both Jewell brothers can be viewed at the Conant Library. (Courtesy of Jennifer Bellan.)

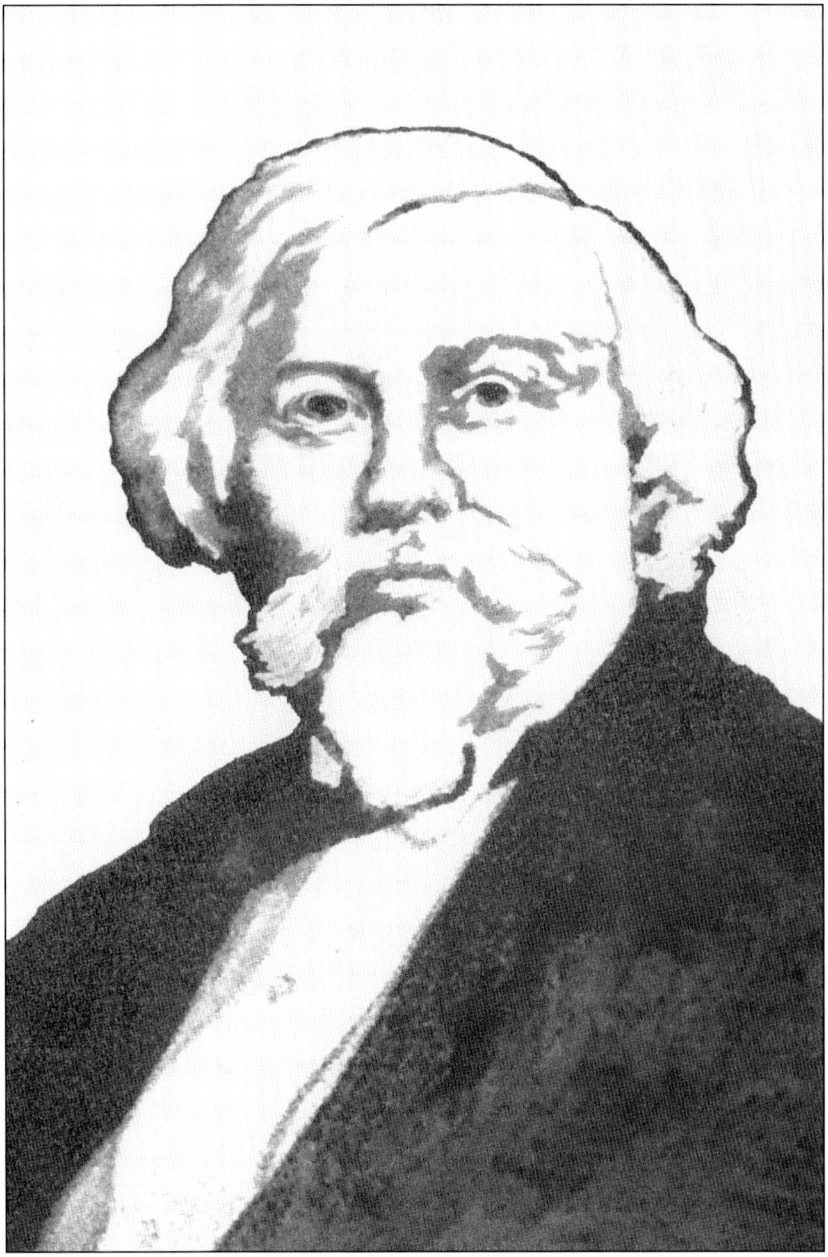

Marshall Jewell, born in 1825, received no more education than Winchester's public schools could provide him but succeeded beyond any of his brothers. His father, Pliny, had moved to Hartford, Connecticut, to start a tannery producing belts, and at the age of 24, Marshall joined him in the company; he became the main force that propelled P. Jewell and Sons to great success. Marshall was called on to serve in several positions in Hartford and state government. In 1869, he was elected governor of Connecticut, where he served two terms. He was then appointed United States minister to Russia by Pres. Ulysses S. Grant, but served only seven months. Grant appointed him postmaster general in 1874. In 1876, Marshall was a candidate for president at the Republican National Convention. He became chairman of the Republican National Committee in 1880 and served until 1883, when he died in Harford, Connecticut. (Courtesy of Jennifer Bellan.)

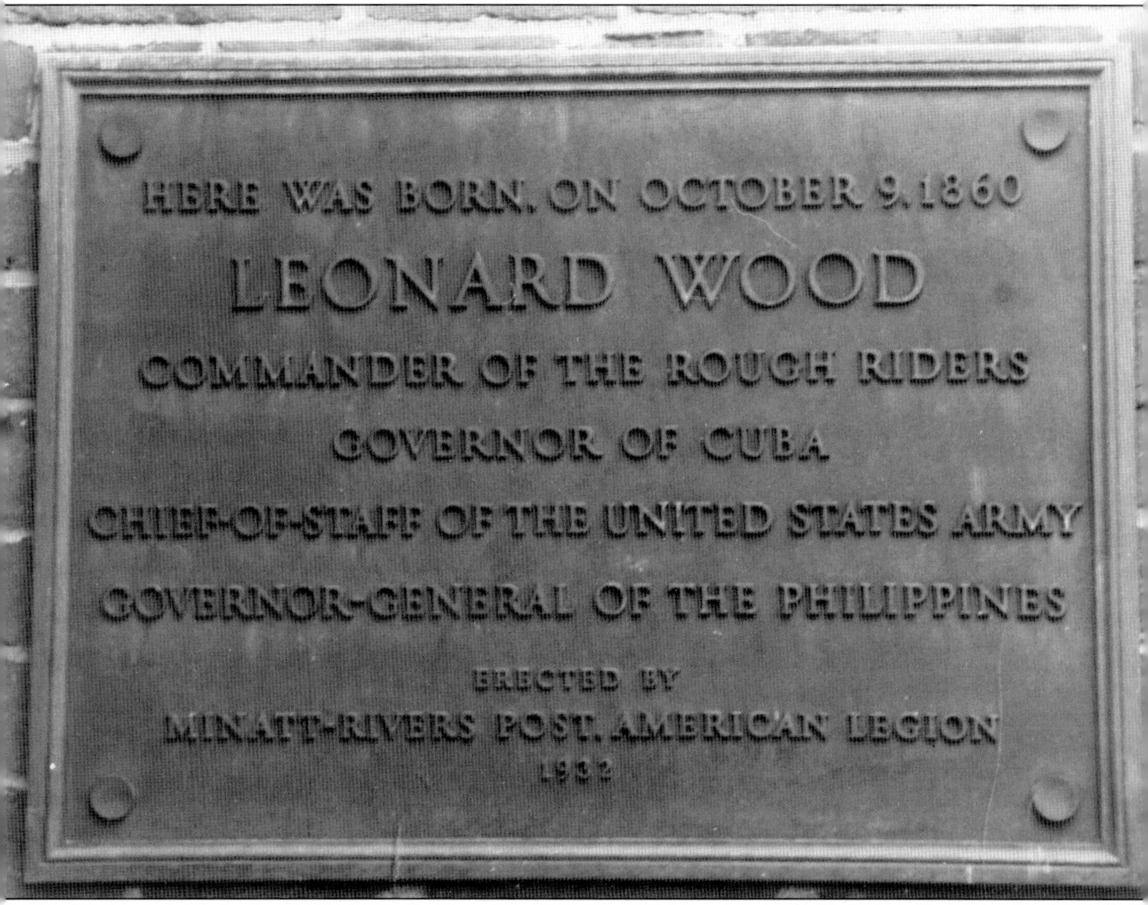

Leonard Wood was probably the most famous son of Winchester. This plaque, located on a brick storefront on Main Street, marks the place where Leonard Wood was born in 1860. The son of a doctor, he went to Harvard and graduated from medical school in 1884. He then became an Army surgeon and went to the southwest United States to fight the Indians. His service was rewarded with the Medal of Honor and a promotion to captain. His next assignment was as a staff surgeon in Los Angeles. In 1895, he was assigned to Washington, DC. He attended Pres. Grover Cleveland and Pres. William McKinley and forged a lifelong friendship with Theodore Roosevelt. In 1898, he was commissioned as a colonel and established a unit of "rough rider" volunteers. Roosevelt was his second in command as Wood led them to fight in Cuba. Their success got Wood promoted to brigadier general and then military governor of Santiago. When Roosevelt became president, he sent Wood to the Philippines to quiet a native rebellion. After Wood returned to the United States, Pres. William Taft made him chief of staff of the US Army, a position he maintained for four years. He died in 1927.

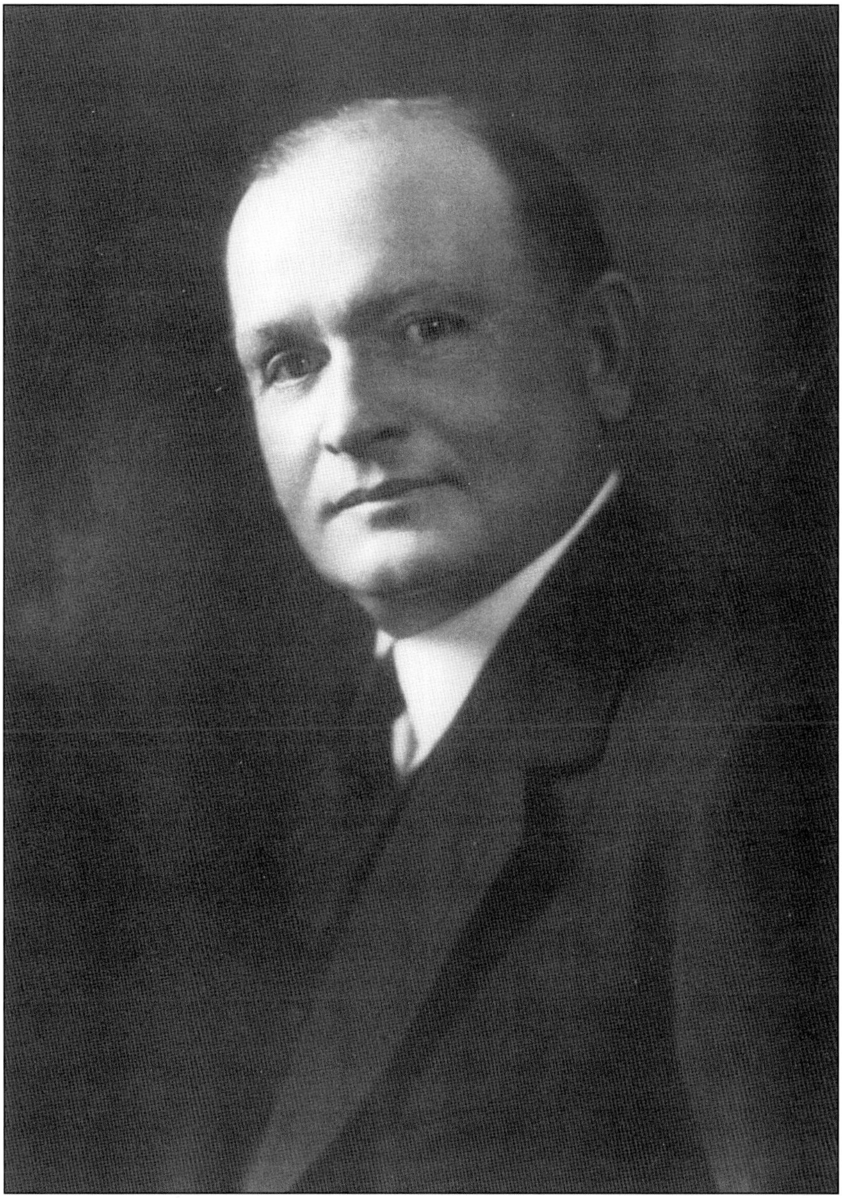

Francis Parnell Murphy was born in 1877 in the Pond Village section of Winchester (the area around the Forest Lake outlet). While still a child, his family moved to Hudson, New Hampshire, where—after he graduated from high school—he got a job nailing packing cases together at a shoe factory. He worked his way up in the company and eventually, with two partners, started the J.F. Elwain Company (shoe manufacturers). Fourteen years later, they had 12 factories and were the largest employers in the State of New Hampshire. Murphy served in many civic positions in Nashua and then in state government. In 1936, he was elected governor of New Hampshire and served two terms. In 1941, after leaving the governor's office, he started radio station WMUR, and with the advent of television, WMUR-TV. Governor Murphy came from humble beginnings as one of eight children of an immigrant tannery worker and did not forget his roots. In 1938, he financed the purchase of the Alexander estate to be turned into the Ellen Lambert Murphy Memorial Community Center in memory of his mother. Governor Murphy died in 1958.

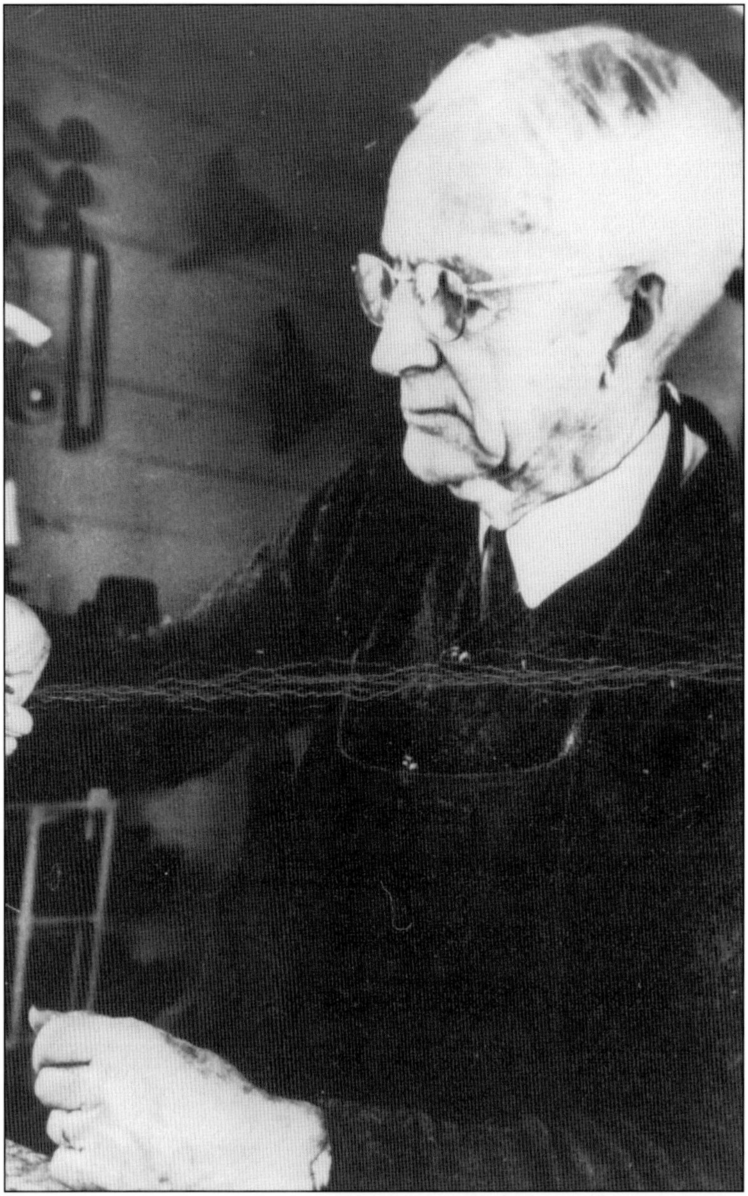

Luman Ranger Nelson was born in 1874 and grew up in Bernardston, Massachusetts. After he married, he and his wife settled in Winchester in the house on the eastern corner of Richmond and Swan Streets. Nelson had a barbershop on Main Street and was a car dealer, selling from his home on Richmond Street and from another lot in Bernardston. He was also a state representative, but his national fame came as a taxidermist. He began preserving birds, and then branched out to other species. A special permit allowed him to kill animals for his collection, and he also traded for specimens from other parts of the country. For many years, he had a museum in the barn behind his house. He gave collections of his work to the State of New Hampshire, the Mount Hermon School (now called Northfield Mount Hermon School), Brewster Academy, the Bernardston Historical Society, and the Conant Library. After his death in 1966, his collection of over 650 specimens found its way to Hogback Mountain in Marlboro, Vermont, where it is displayed at the Southern Vermont Natural History Museum (originally called the Lumen R. Nelson Museum).

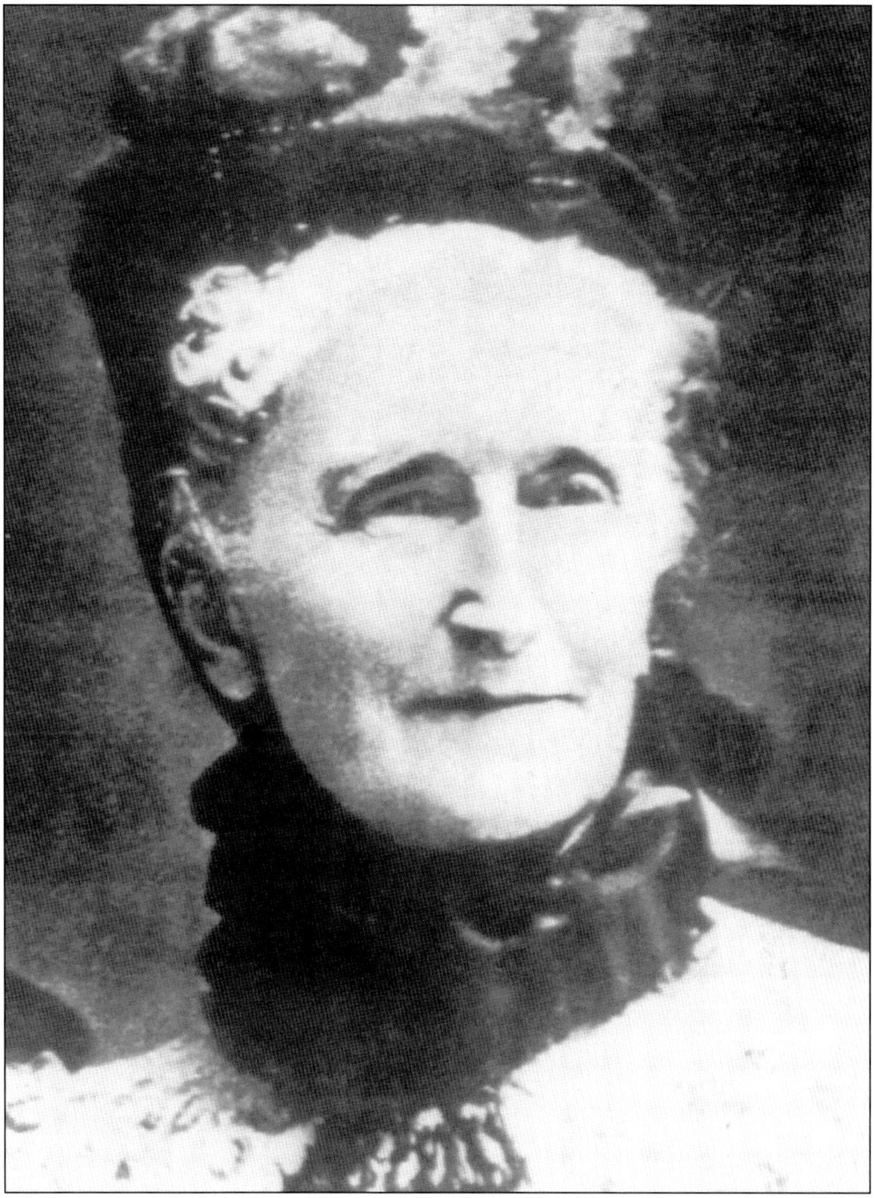

Persis Foster Eames Albee was born in Newry, Maine, in 1836. She married Ellery Albee, and they settled in Winchester to raise a family. Ellery was a lawyer, state senator, and bank treasurer. The Albees also kept a store in their house, which was just across the Ashuelot River from Main Street on the north side of Depot Street (now Elm Street, where the house still stands). David McConnell had dealings with Persis when he was selling books and admired her business sense, so when he founded the California Perfume Company in 1886, he knew she would be the perfect person to market his products. Persis went from door to door selling perfume and recruited other women to do the same, establishing the direct marketing system that is still used today. Persis was very successful, the business thrived, and David McConnell dubbed her "the mother of the California Perfume Company." The company's name was later changed to Avon; thus, Persis Albee was the world's first "Avon Lady." Each year, the top sellers among Avon representatives in 140 countries are given an Albee Award to honor their achievements. Persis Albee died in 1914.

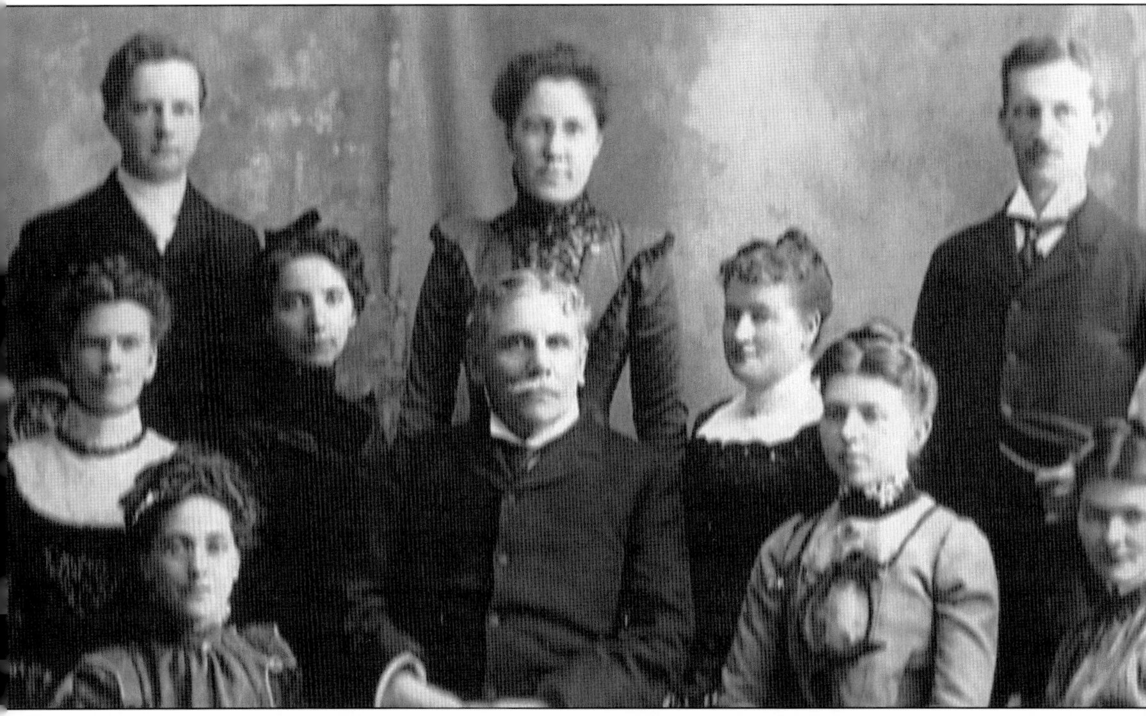

Cyrus Ingerson Scofield is not actually a son of Winchester, but he lived here while doing most of the work he is famous for. Scofield was originally from Michigan, but lived in several states before being called to East Northfield, Massachusetts, to minister at Dwight Moody's Trinitarian Congregational Church in 1895. Scofield, an evangelical Christian who had become friends with Moody, bought land on what is now called Scofield Mountain in Ashuelot and built a home and a chapel. He named the place Crestwood. (The property is currently owned by Gary O'Neal.) People would come from miles around to attend Scofield's weekend retreats or to hear him preach. His contribution to Christian study was to produce the first annotated Bible. The *Scofield Reference Bible*, published in 1909, made Scofield a rich man. This picture shows Scofield surrounded by his children and second wife. Though it had been reported that Scofield died at Crestwood in 1919, he actually died on Long Island in 1921.

Five

INDUSTRY

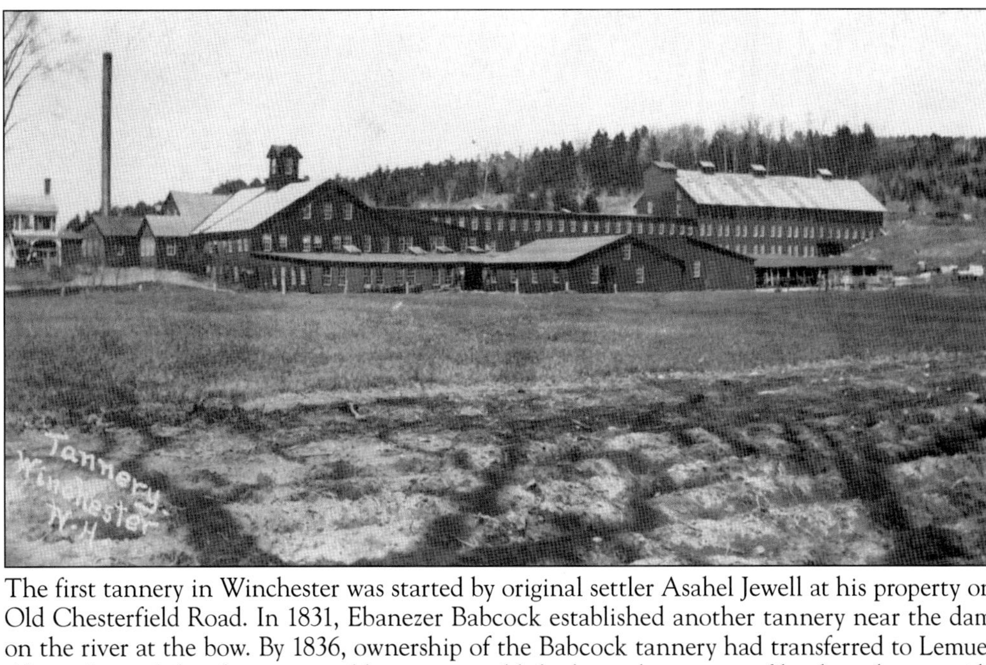

The first tannery in Winchester was started by original settler Asahel Jewell at his property on Old Chesterfield Road. In 1831, Ebanezer Babcock established another tannery near the dam on the river at the bow. By 1836, ownership of the Babcock tannery had transferred to Lemuel Alexander and the plant pictured here was established on a large tract of land on the east side of the Keene Road, south of what is now Lawrence Street.

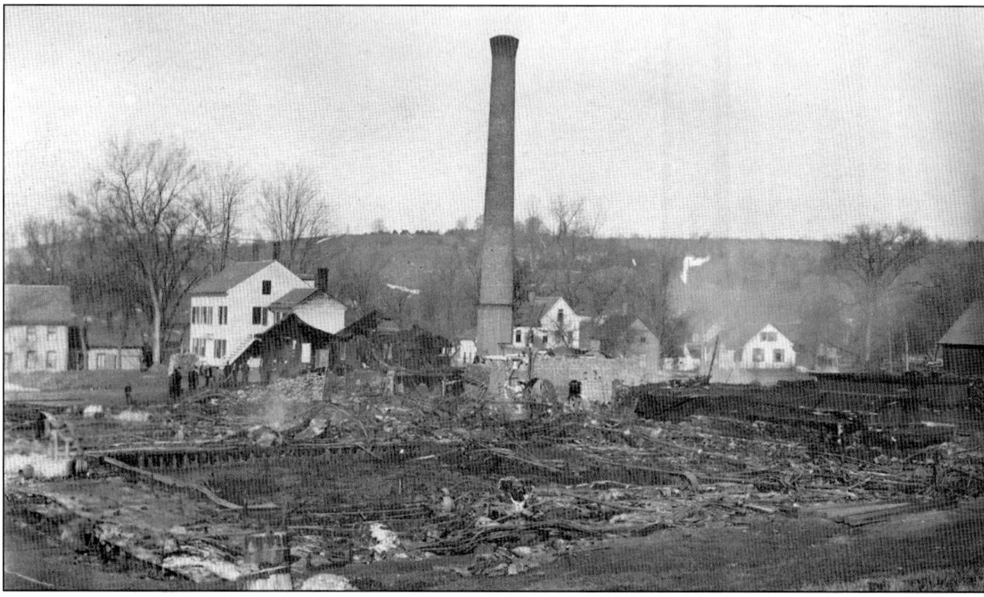

In 1894, A.C. Lawrence took over ownership of the tannery from Nathanial Stevens. In 1909, a fire destroyed the plant and put 115 men out of work. The plant was rebuilt on the other side of the Ashuelot River, giving it direct access to the railway. The tannery continued to be a major employer in town through most of the 20th century.

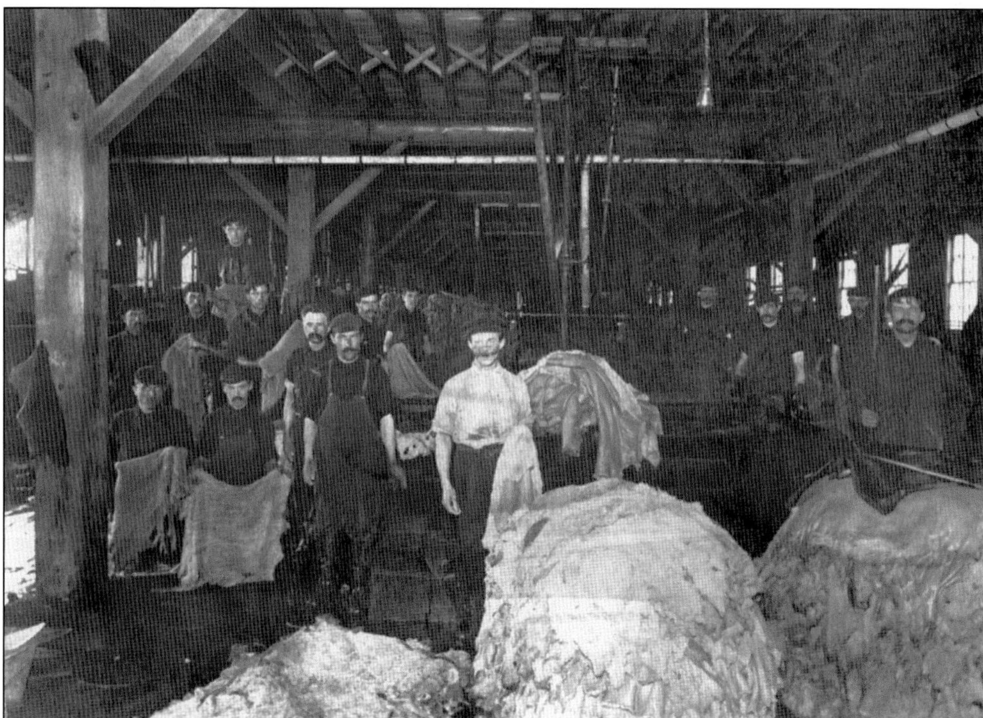

The men in this photograph of the old tannery on Keene Road may have been "fleshing," which was the process of draping the hide over a waist-high beam and scraping bits of flesh off the hide with a blade made specifically for the job.

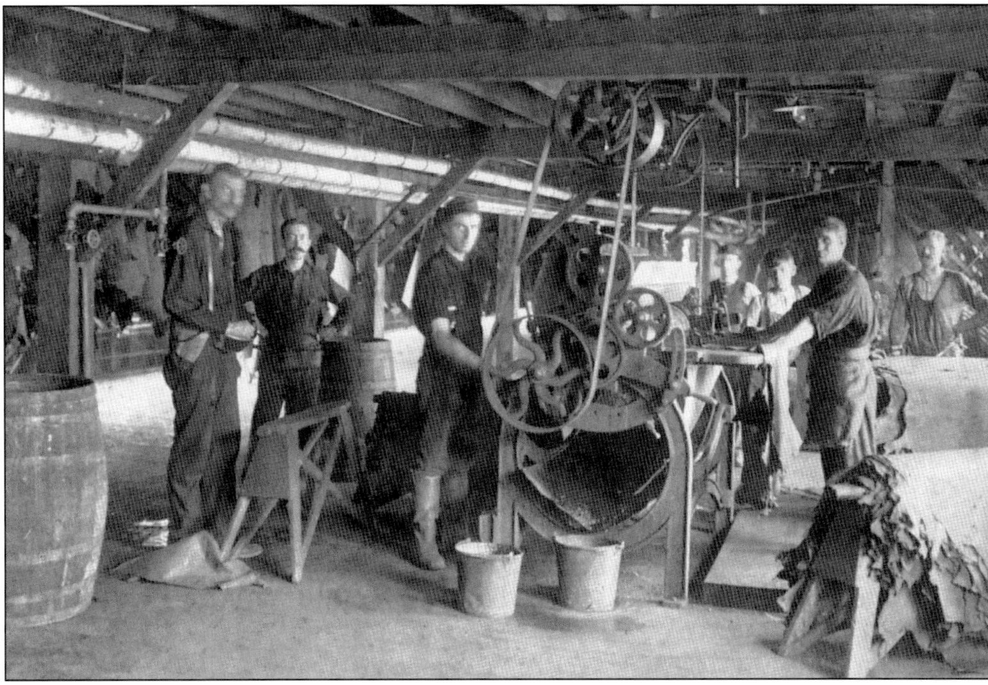

This is the "staking" room in the old tannery, which burned down in 1909. "Staking" is the process of passing the skin between two drums fitted with a tough leather strap to soften it. Note that one of these workers is still a boy.

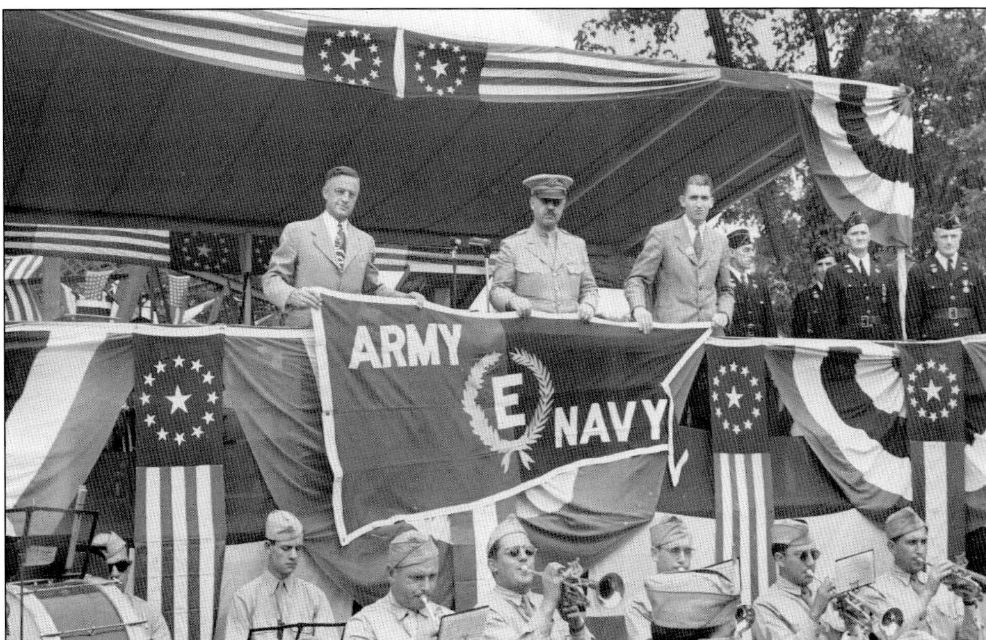

Winchester's A.C. Lawrence Tannery was recognized for its contribution to the World War II effort with a day of celebration. The "E" awards were presented to war suppliers who maintained exceptional excellence. The Winchester plant produced half of all the hides used to make uniforms for airmen in the war.

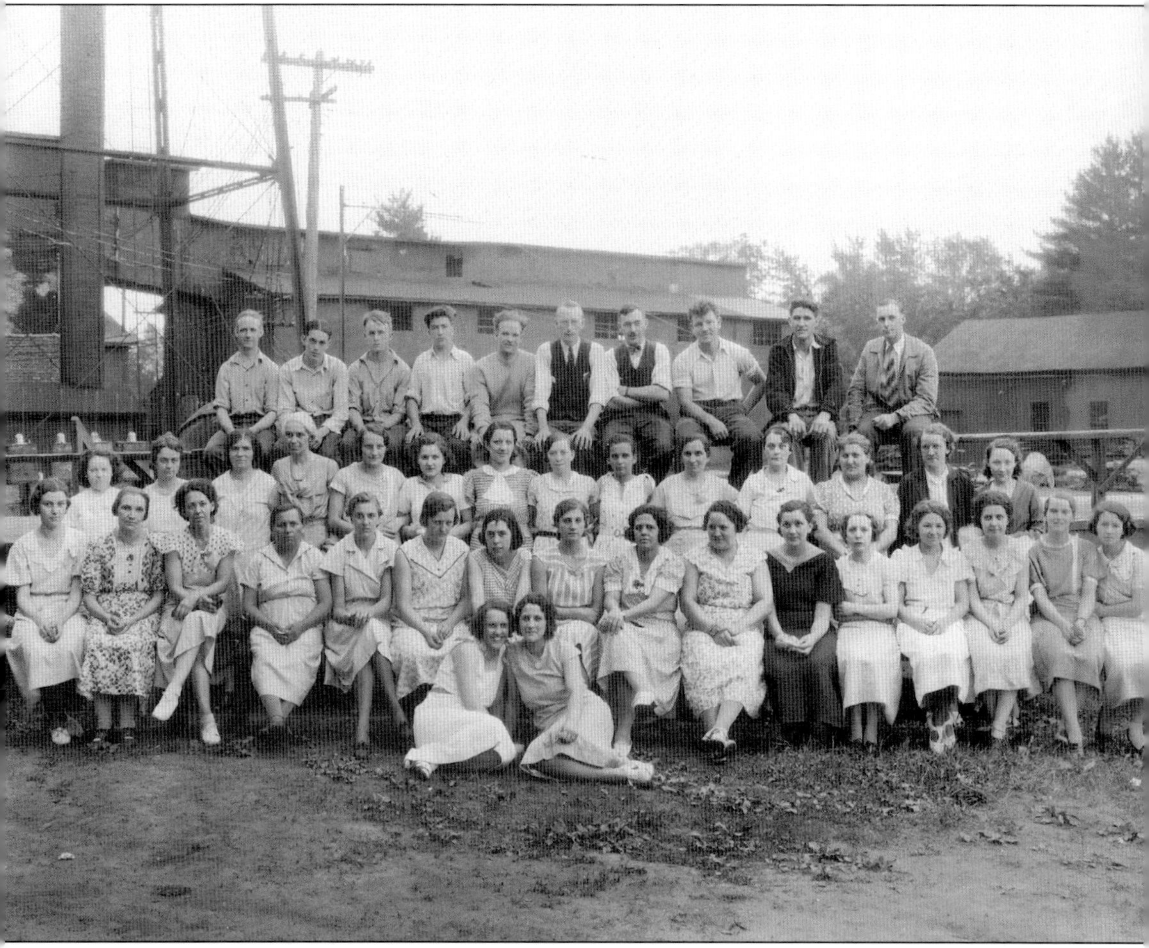

Though the toy division of A.C. Lawrence was eventually sold and became Granite State Toys, it was instrumental in keeping the tannery open during the Great Depression. The shearling toys that were produced enabled the tannery to stay open, though with a much reduced staff. This photograph shows the toy shop employees in June 1934. Seated on the grass are Sophie Zwolinski (left) and Annie Poreda. From left to right are (first row) Frances Manning, Mrs. Seroka, Evelyn Petite, Mrs. Rogalski, Helen Kilanski, Mildred Dick, Hilda Scott, Varja Poreda, Elizabeth Warren, May Kelly, Sophie Zabielski, Feley Smofski, Mildred Manning, Muriel Packard, Goldy Robb, and Nellie Zabielski; (second row) Doris Barber, Nina Baker, Marie O'Connor, Louise Johnson, Evelyn Jackson, Pauline Krenski, Agelina Wasileski, Doris Curtis, Mary Adams, Mrs. Kilanski, Margaret Orde, Jennette Stancliff, Sophie Napierkoski, and Bogda Zwolinski; (third row) Percy Hill, Eldon Thompson, Harlan Hildreth, Donald Guyette, Clayton Bean, Elmer Kibbe, Howard Little, George Moore, Bill Miner, and Jack Brown.

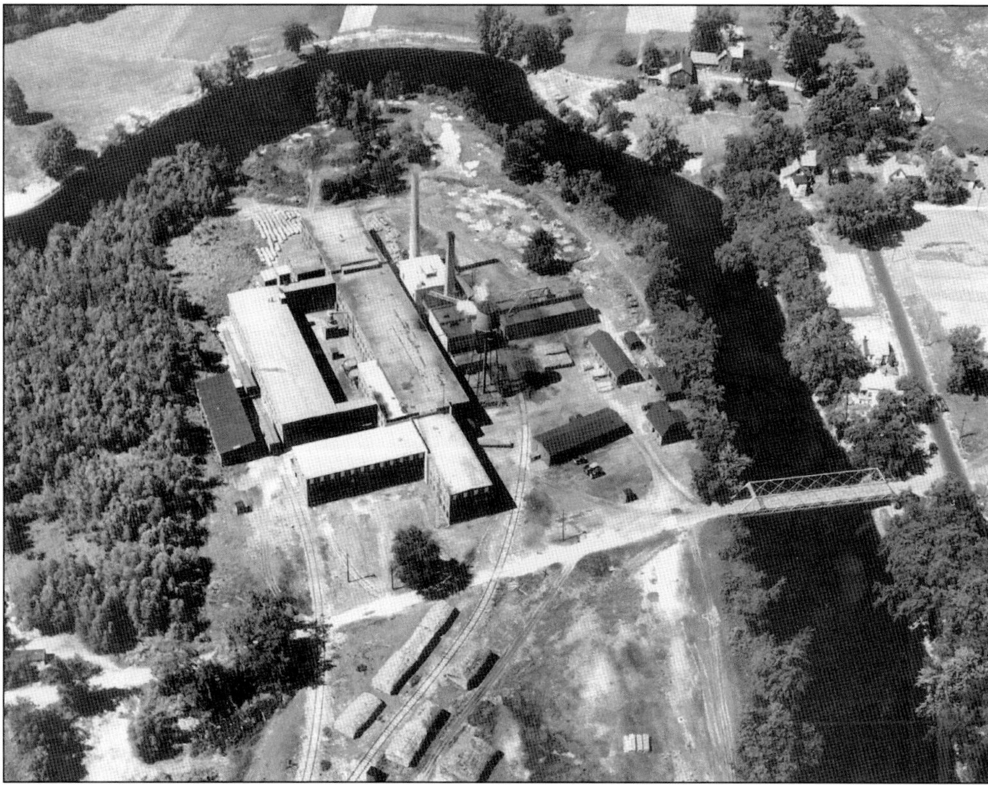

The A.C. Lawrence Tannery, located on the west side of the Ashuelot River, was quite extensive. The plant specialized in shearling production. By adapting to the changing market, it was able to stay in business until 1987. The tannery buildings are now vacant.

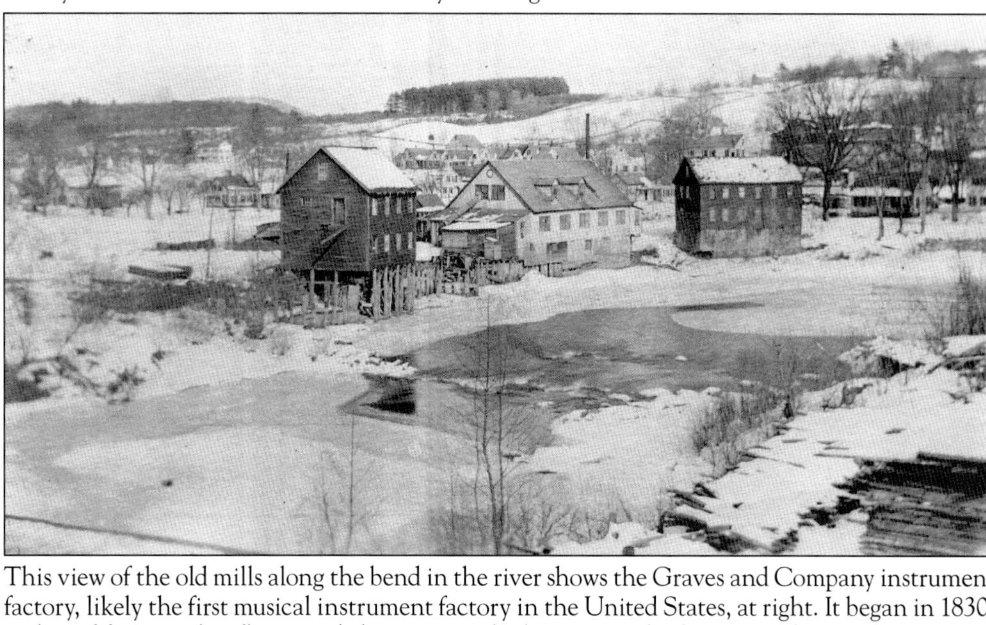

This view of the old mills along the bend in the river shows the Graves and Company instrument factory, likely the first musical instrument factory in the United States, at right. It began in 1830, making fifes, piccolos, flutes, and clarinets. By the late 1840s, the factory made brass instruments exclusively. The business moved to Boston in 1850.

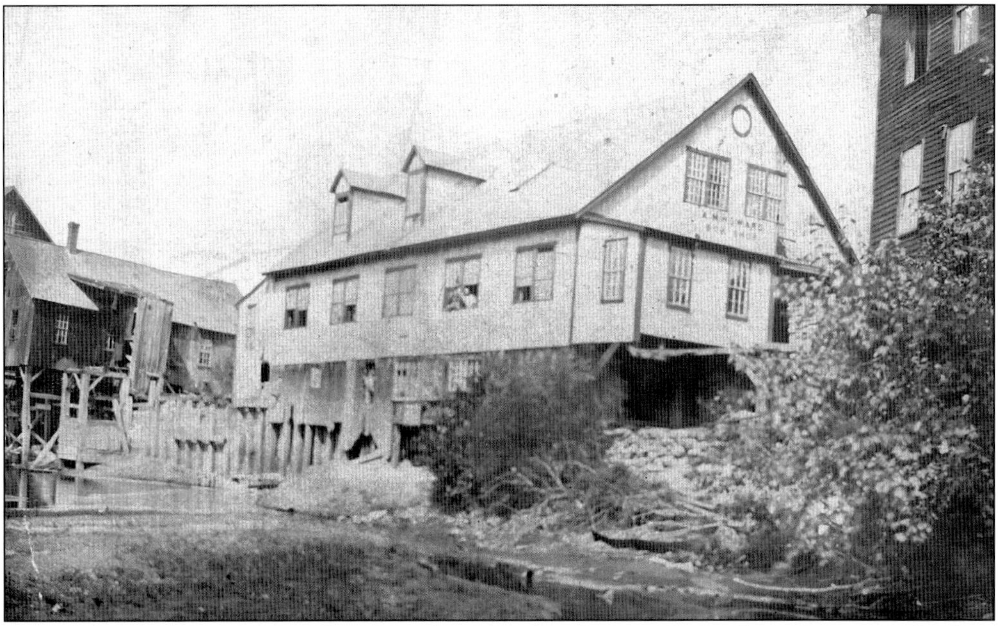

A.M. Howard and a Mr. Chandler opened the first box factory in Winchester in 1863. The shop was destroyed by fire in 1870, and when it was rebuilt, it was renamed the A.M. Howard Box Shop. It was located on the bank of the Ashuelot River on what was called Mill Street, behind the present-day location of Kevin's Automotive Service on Keene Road.

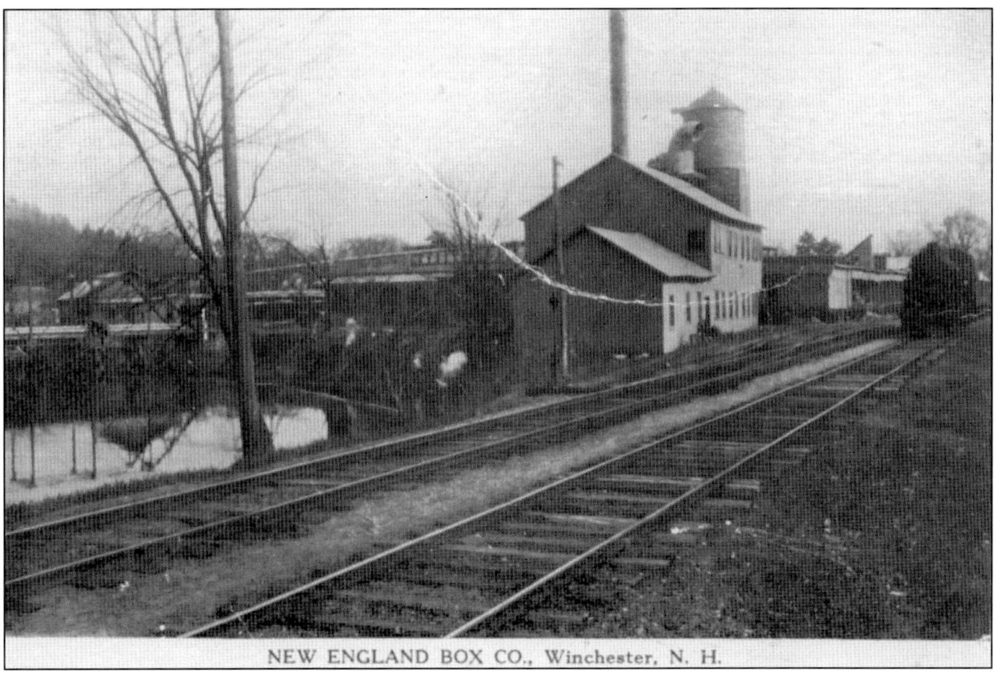

This building was originally the Munsell Box Shop. It was acquired by Ansel Dickinson and became part of the New England Box Company. It was located on Mill Lane, a road that ran along the east side of the Ashuelot Railroad tracks from Elm Street to the bend in the Ashuelot River.

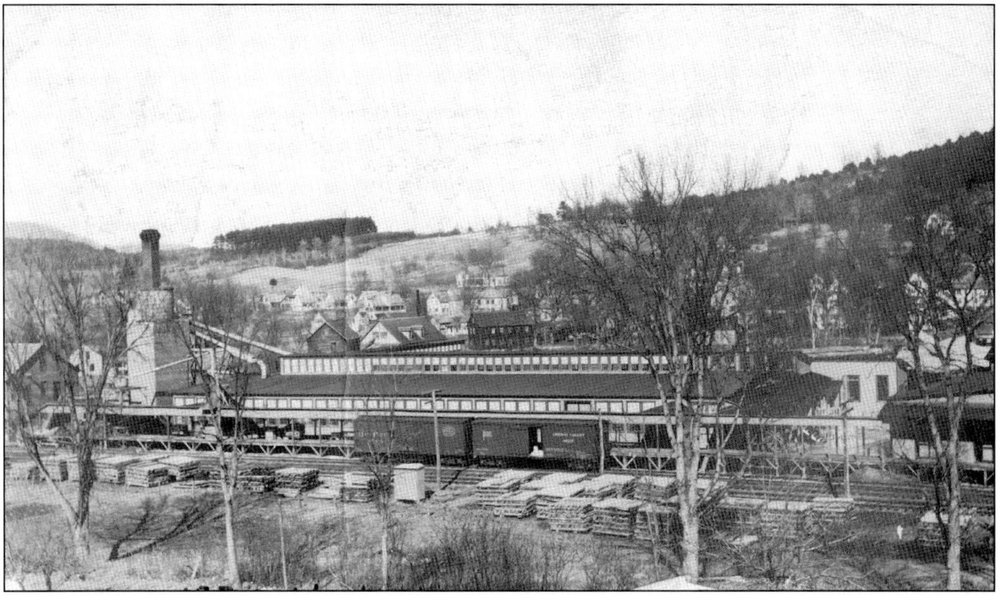

This photograph shows the extent of the New England Box Company's Winchester plant along Howard Street. It was originally one of Ansel Dickinson's shops. In 1899, the New England Box Company was formed by merging Dickinson's two shops with shops in Orange and Baldwinville, Massachusetts.

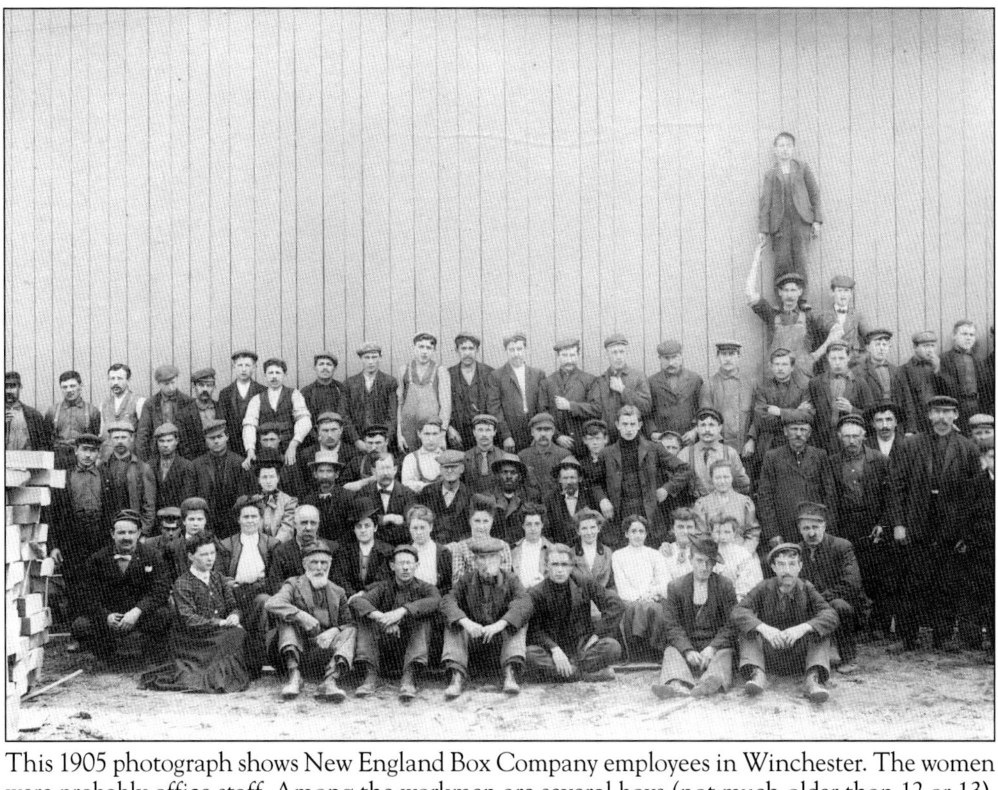

This 1905 photograph shows New England Box Company employees in Winchester. The women were probably office staff. Among the workmen are several boys (not much older than 12 or 13). Working-class families relied on income from every family member who could contribute.

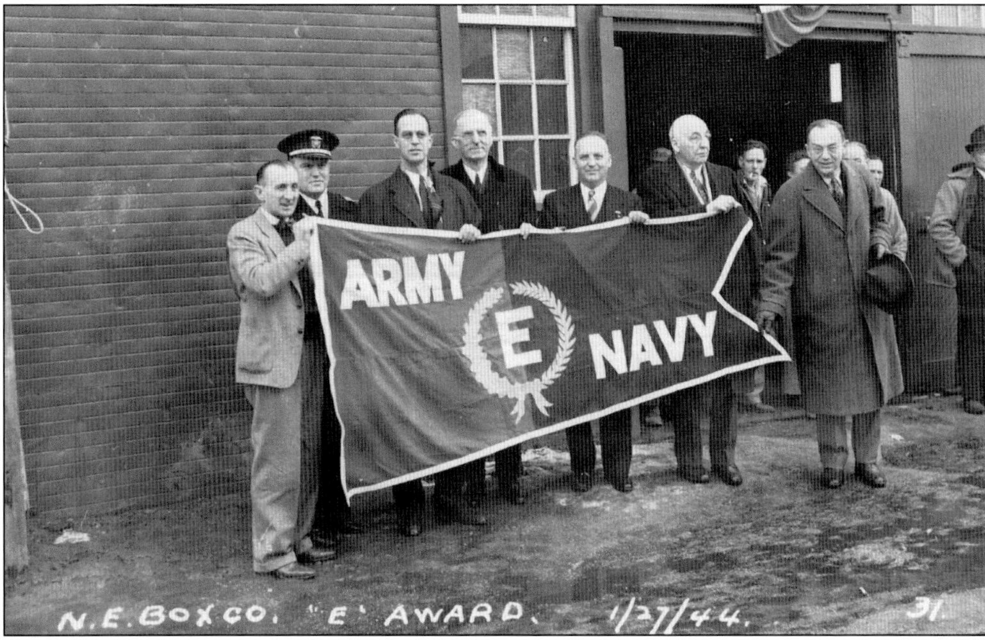

The Winchester plant of the New England Box Company was recognized for its service in World War II with an "E" award (the "E" is for excellence). Only four percent of companies engaged in war work received the award. Among other products, the plant produced sturdy lock-corner boxes for ammunition. The factory received a flag and each employee was awarded a pin.

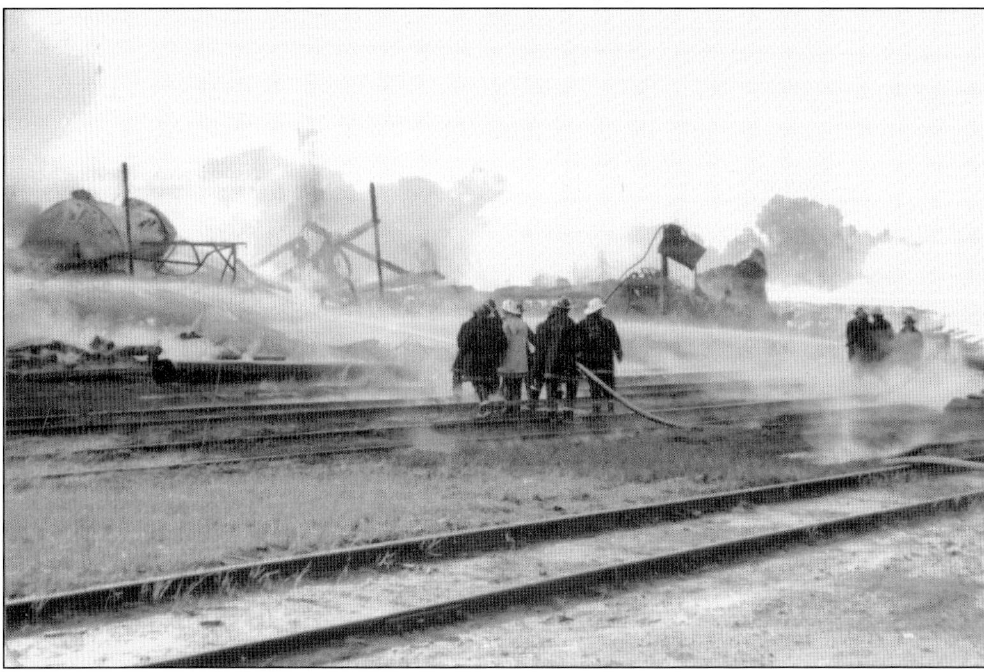

The New England Box Company was the site of many fires over the years. It was leveled four times, with the final incineration (pictured) occurring in 1977. Since the company had ceased operations in 1976, it was not rebuilt. The foundations of the buildings are still clearly visible between the old Ashuelot Railroad bed and Howard Street.

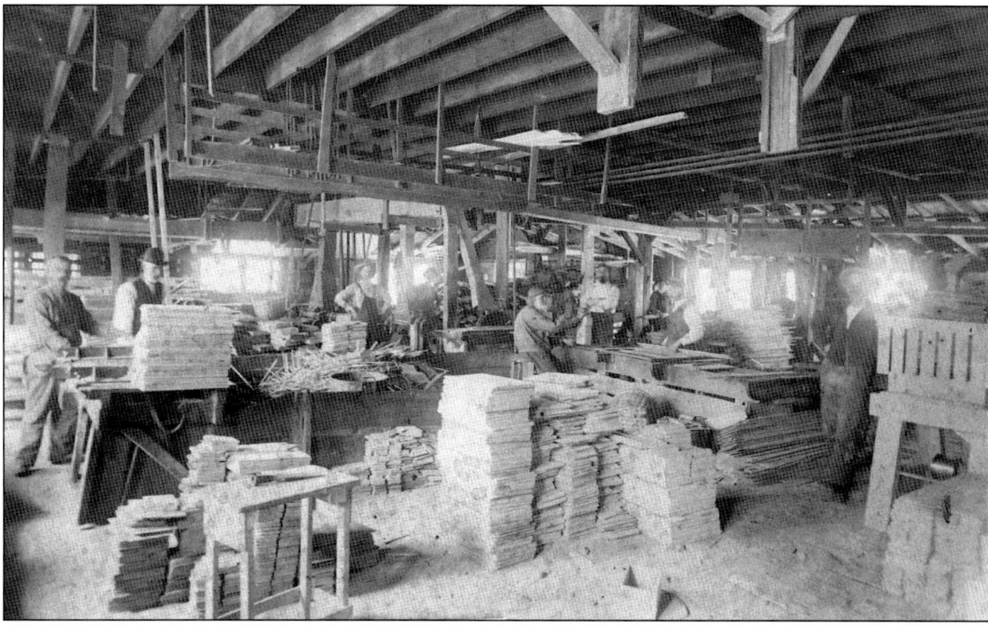

The box shop shown here is not identified, but it is most likely a New England Box Company shop. The lock-corner box was invented in the Winchester plant. In 1900, the owners of the Winchester plant added a machine that would cut and assemble the boxes when a correctly sized piece of lumber was fed into it.

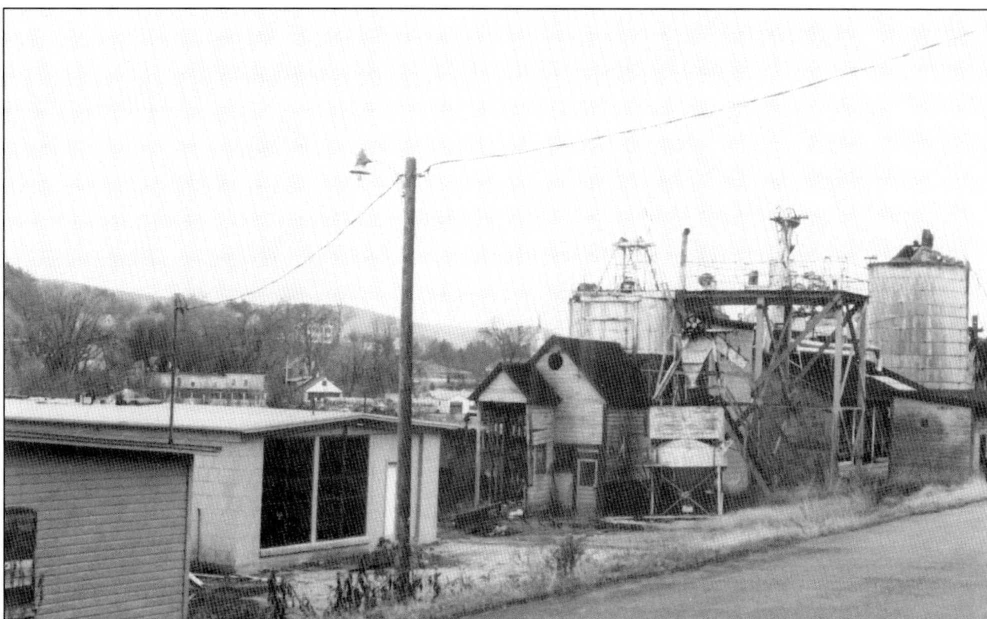

This photograph of the Wood Flour Plant on Howard Street is about the only documentation available. The plant was active for many years in the 20th century, producing pulverized wood—known as wood flour—that was used in the production of items such as linoleum and plastic. The vacant plant was lost to arson in 1982.

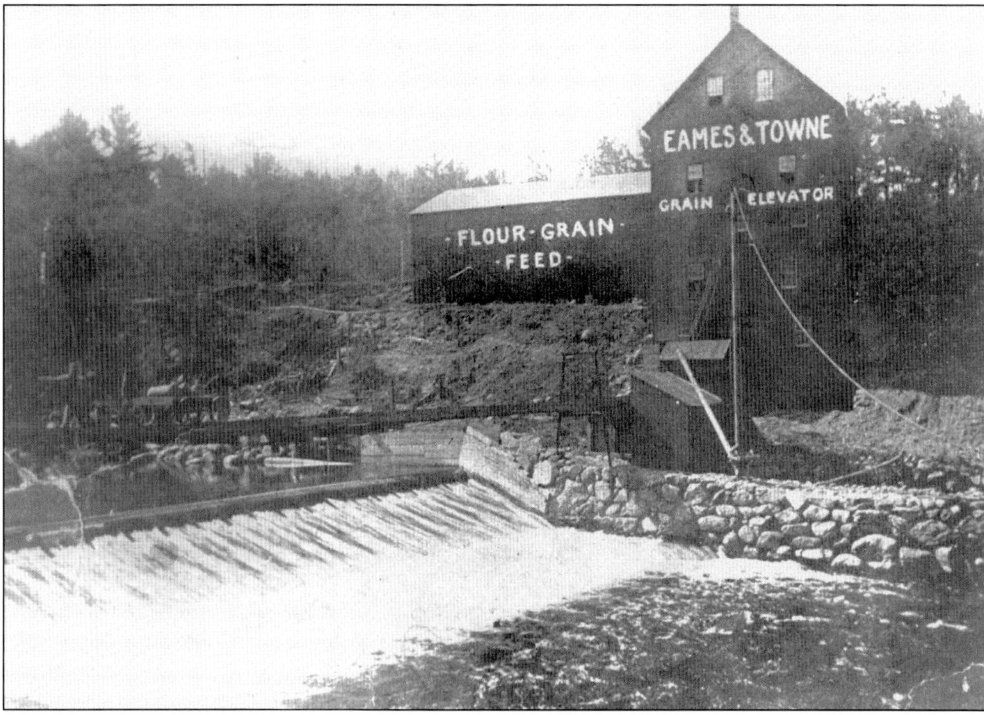

The Eames and Towne gristmill was located beyond the Lower Village of Ashuelot on the south side of the Ashuelot River. Ashuelot Paper was eventually built on the site. This image shows a dray being pulled across the river on the pedestrian bridge. In 1902, the town raised $600 to replace the nearby bridge over Pisgah Brook.

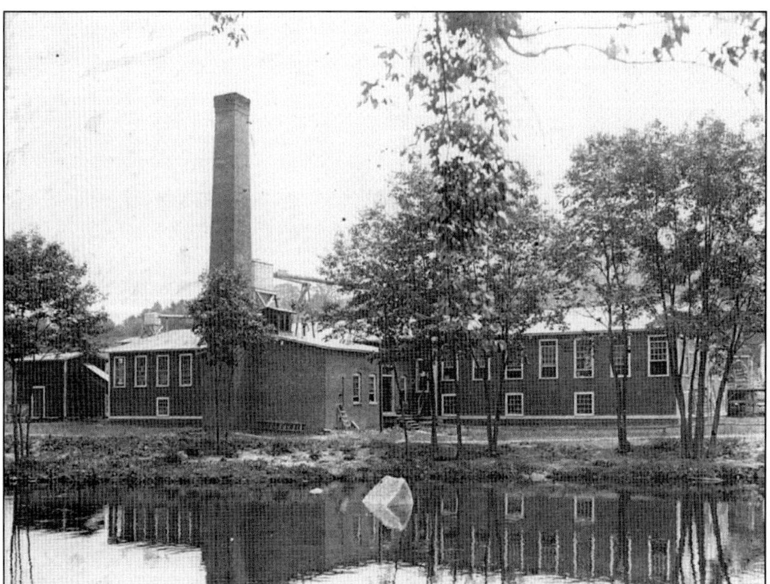

The Hampshire Box Factory was one of several "box shops" in Winchester. It was built in 1906 by the Welch brothers and later became part of the New England Box Company. It was located between the Ashuelot River and the Ashuelot Railroad tracks, about 100 yards east of the depot. Parts of its foundation remain on the site.

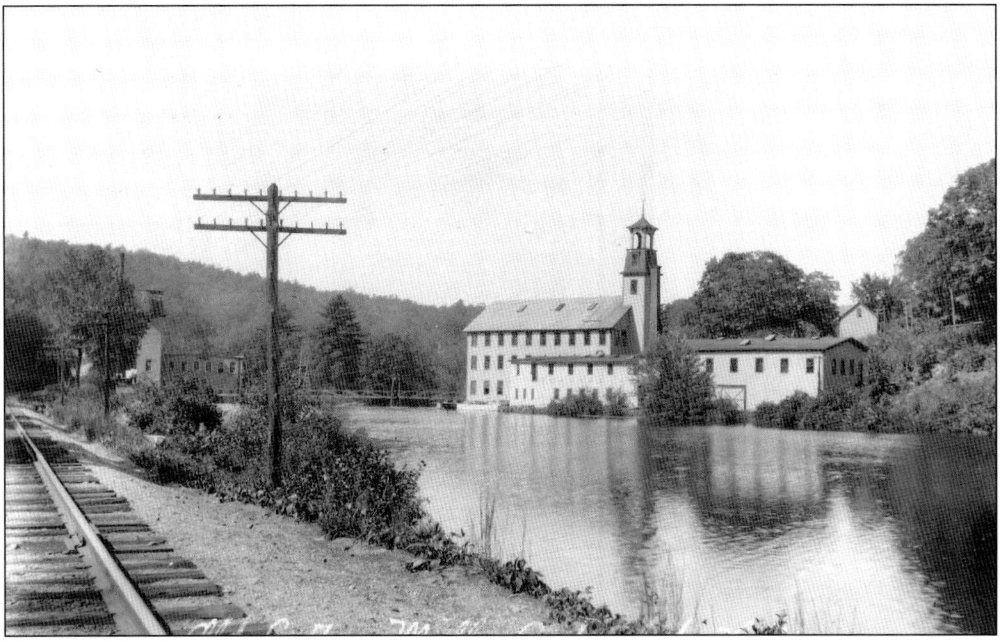

The Ashuelot Warp Mill and the Ashuelot Union Mill sat on the banks of the Ashuelot River near the foot of Fiddle Hill in Lower Ashuelot Village. The buildings later housed a paper mill. The fabric mills in Ashuelot were largely responsible for the influx of Polish immigrants in the late 1800s, as they were actively recruited to come to Winchester to work for the mills.

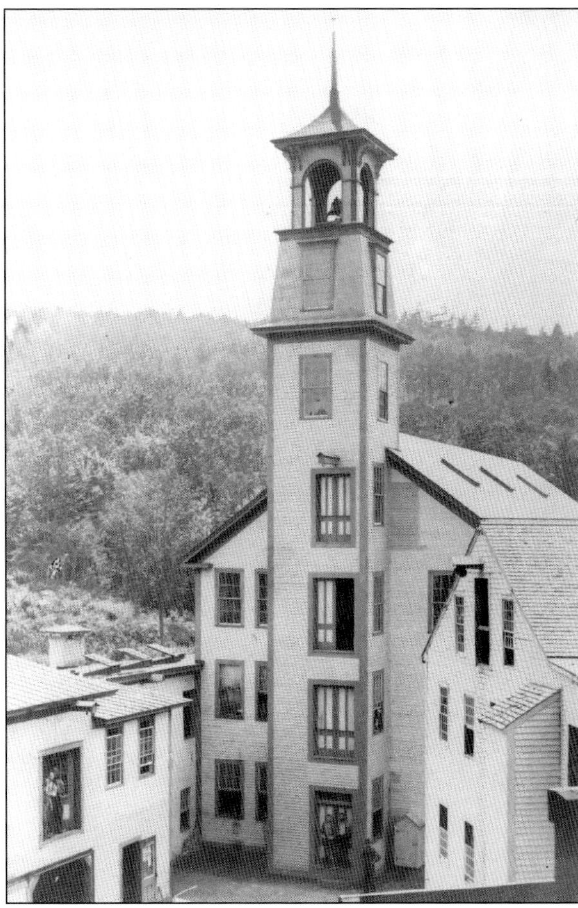

The building with the beautiful bell tower is the Ashuelot Warp Mill in its second incarnation. The original building burned down. It is sometimes called the cotton mill because it manufactured cotton warp. It was well known for the high quality of its thread, which was used extensively in woolen mills throughout the Northeast.

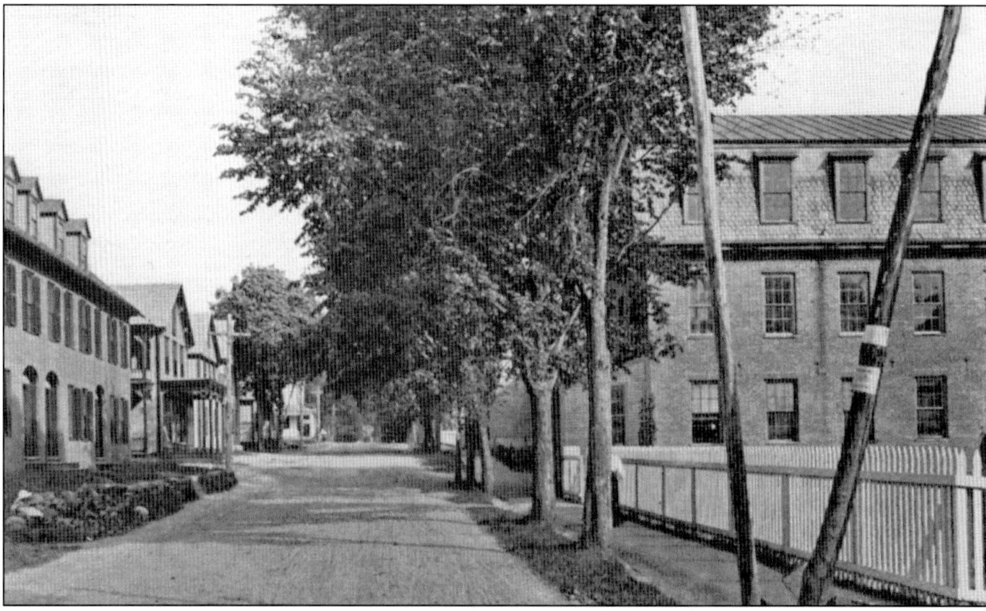

A woolen mill was in operation in the Upper Village of Ashuelot as early as 1850. It changed ownership several times and was leveled by fire and rebuilt before it was purchased by Hugh Sheridan in 1901. He sold it in 1916, but it continued to be called the "Sheridan Mill" locally.

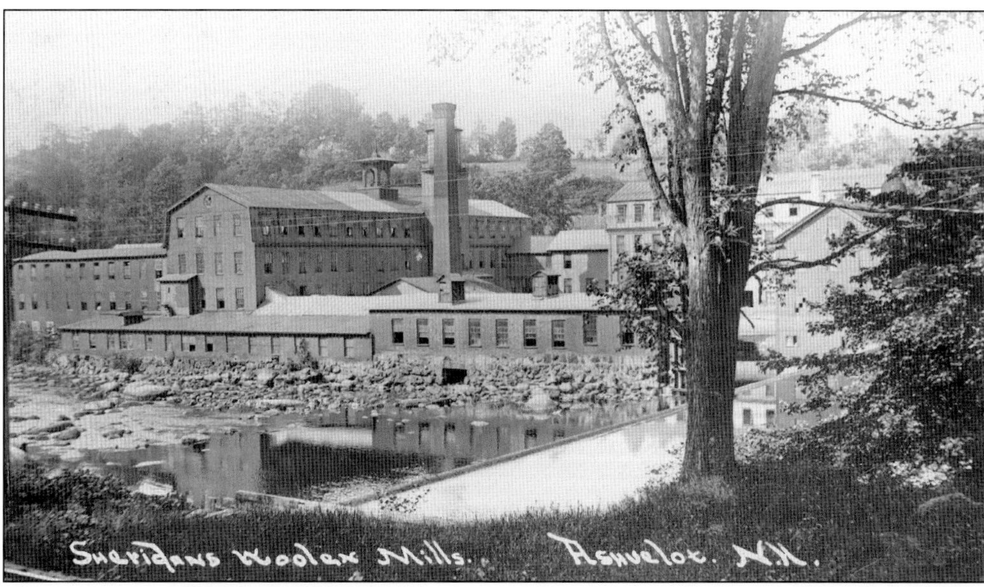

This view of the Sheridan Woolen Mill from across the Ashuelot River shows the extent of the complex. The manufacturing plant contained 16 buildings. The mill closed for good in the 1920s. Two brick buildings that belonged to the mill but were not part of the factory still stand along Main Street. The factory buildings have been demolished.

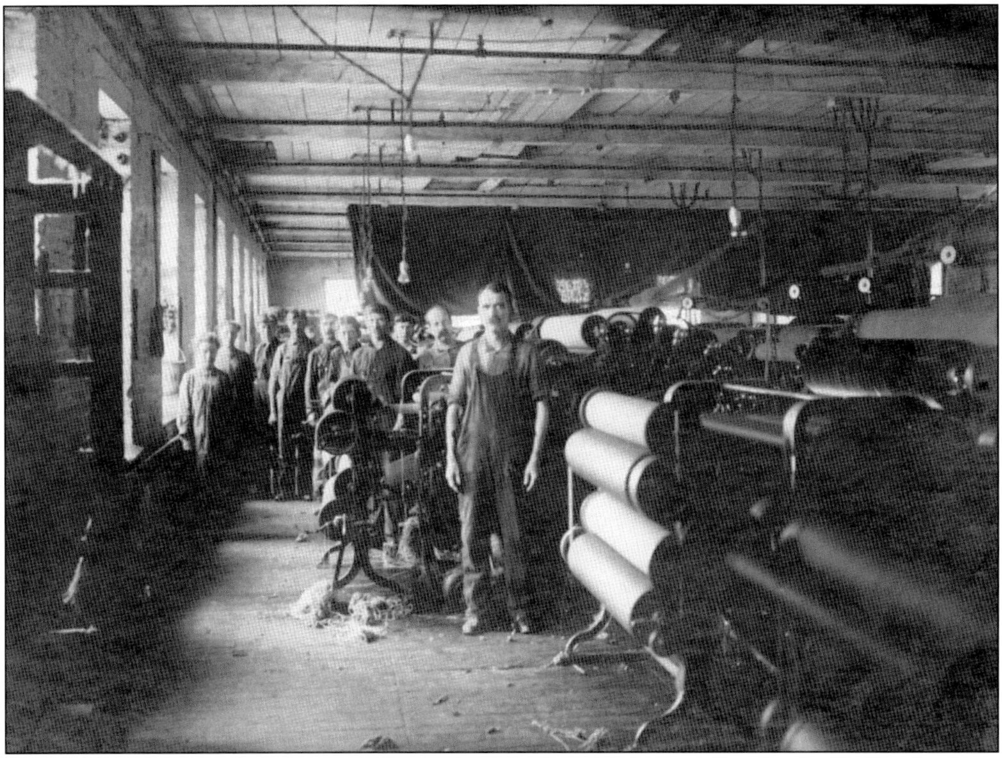

This interior photograph of a mill is—unfortunately—unidentified. However, it is evidently a textile mill, and since it is a brick building, it is possible that it belonged to the Sheridan Mill. Note the girl to the left near the windows. Mills employed girls as young as 10 years old as "bobbin girls."

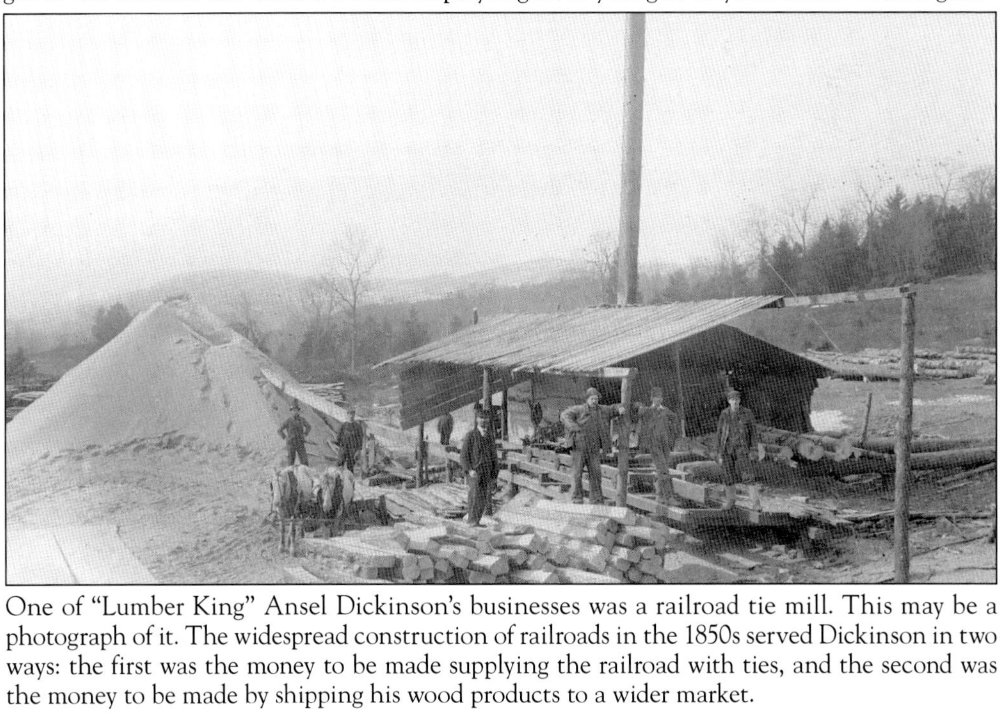

One of "Lumber King" Ansel Dickinson's businesses was a railroad tie mill. This may be a photograph of it. The widespread construction of railroads in the 1850s served Dickinson in two ways: the first was the money to be made supplying the railroad with ties, and the second was the money to be made by shipping his wood products to a wider market.

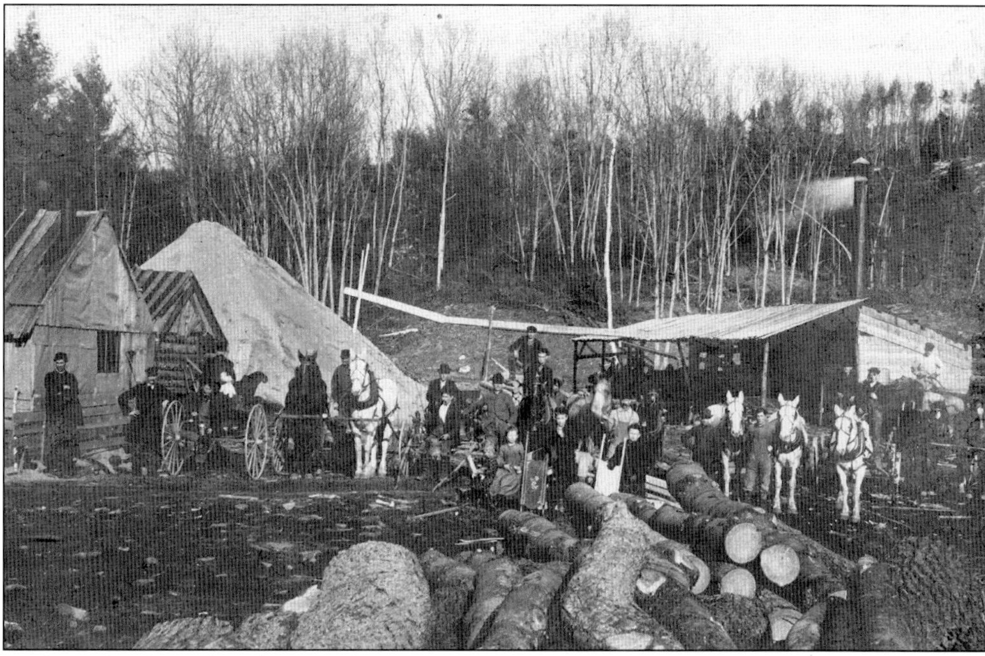

Looking closely at this photograph of one of Pisgah's sawmills, children can be seen, and some seem to be showing off their sleds. Families usually lived in housing owned by the mill. They were located close enough to the mills so that fathers could walk to work. Often, children would carry a hot lunch to their fathers at noon.

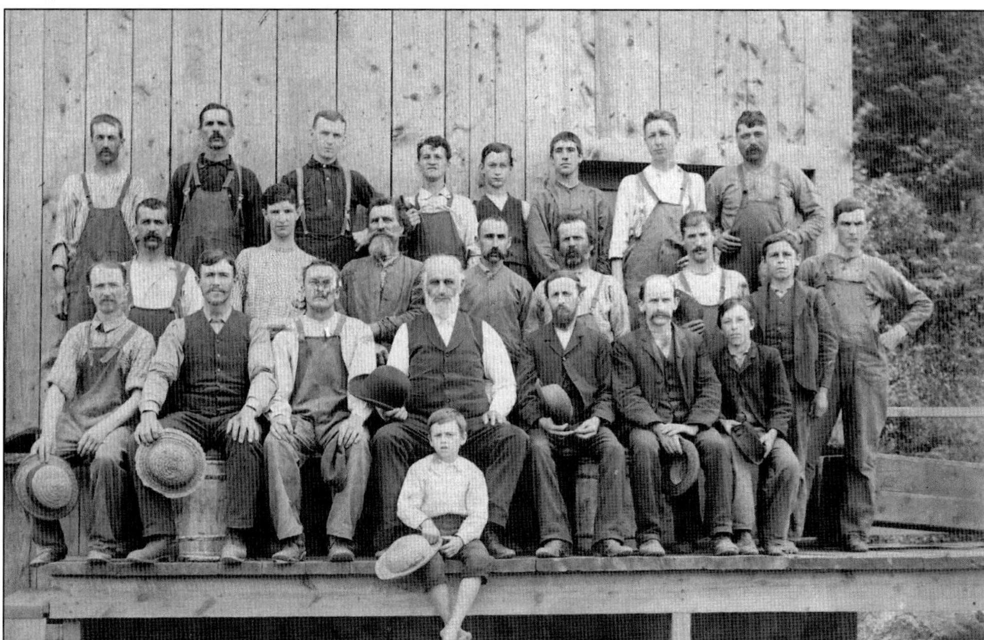

This photograph is identified as the crew at the "old box shop in Ashuelot." It is one of Ansel Dickinson's mills, but "old" would suggest it is the Welch shop in the Upper Village. Ansel is the big gentleman in the center of the first row, his son LaFel is just over his left shoulder, and his son John is the last man on the right in the back row.

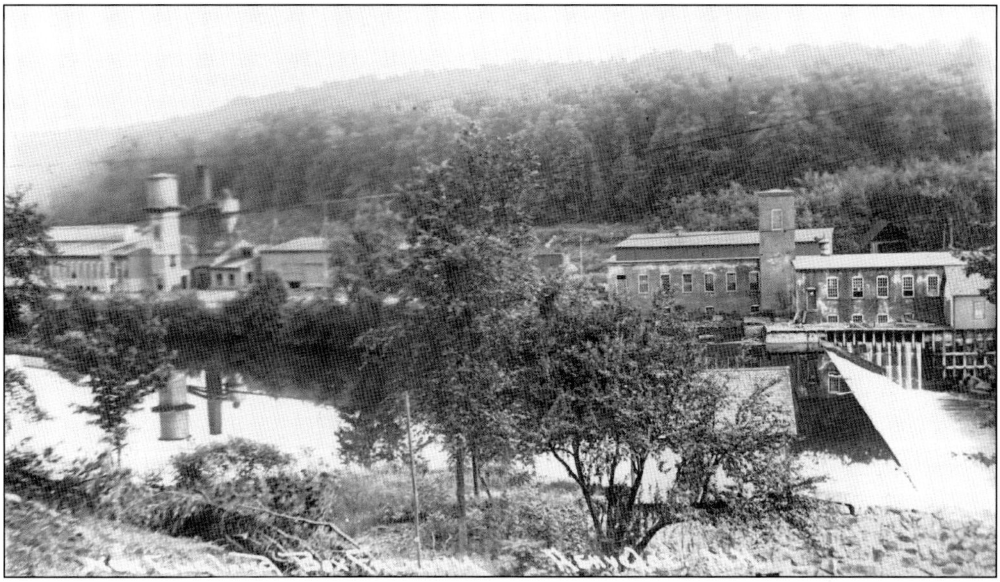

This view from the Main Street side of the Ashuelot River shows some of the mills near the dam in Lower Ashuelot. Although this image is undated, it included a notation labeling the mill at right as the Robertson Mill. The building at far left was the Ashuelot Box Company.

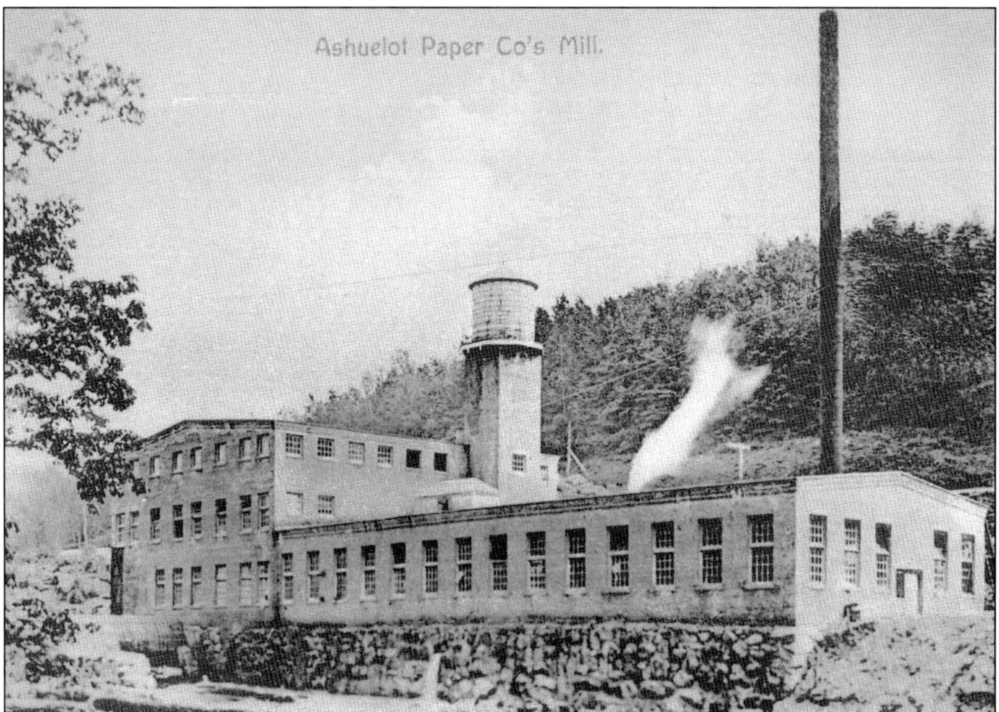

The Ashuelot Paper Company was built in 1904 on the former site of the Eames and Towne gristmill. It was located on the south side of the Ashuelot River across from the old road to Hinsdale. It originally produced industrial paper that was used in the production of other goods. The mill changed ownership several times and managed to stay open into the 1990s. The buildings now sit idle.

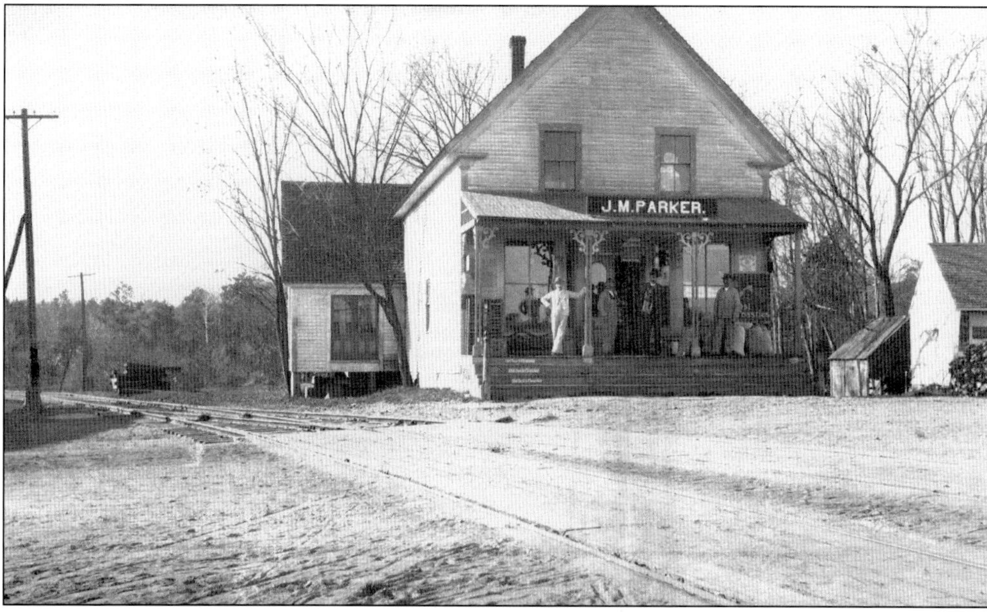

The building in the photograph, Parker's store, was opposite the depot on Elm Street. Parker's was the home of Cheshire Chemical Company from 1920 until World War II. Cheshire Chemical was a distributor of cleaning supplies, but was best known for Dust Void, a cleaning compound developed by owner James Bliss. The green substance was sprinkled on old wooden floors. When it was swept up, it brought the dust with it, leaving an oil treatment on the wood.

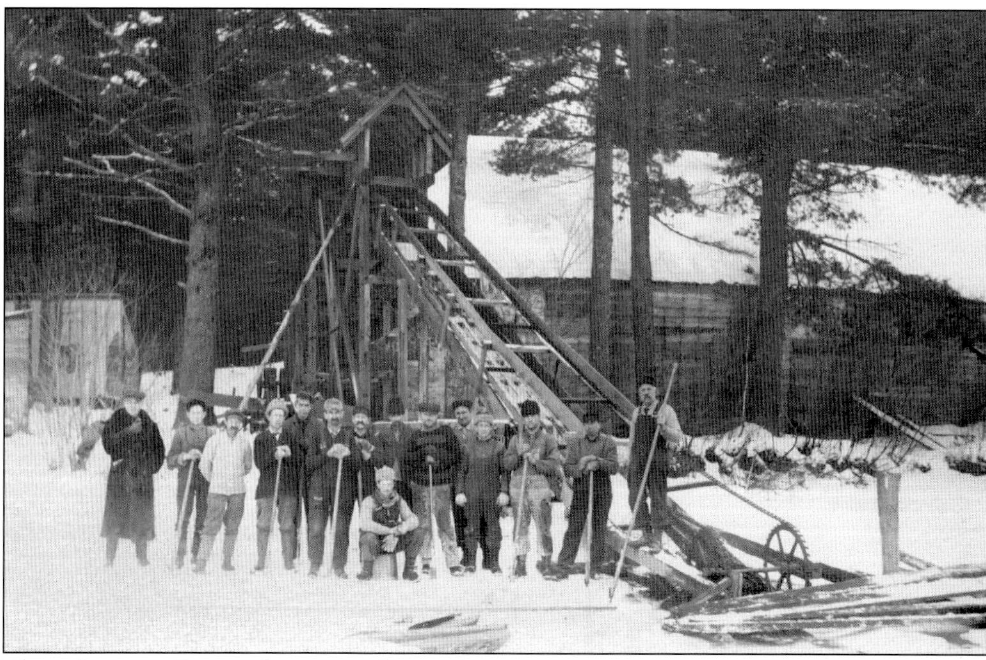

The icehouse on Forest Lake remained active for many years. In winter, blocks of ice were harvested from the lake and stored in the icehouse with sawdust (for insulation). Before refrigerators, the iceman would deliver ice to homes during warmer months. The icehouse was located near the brook in what is now Forest Lake Campground.

Six

FARMING

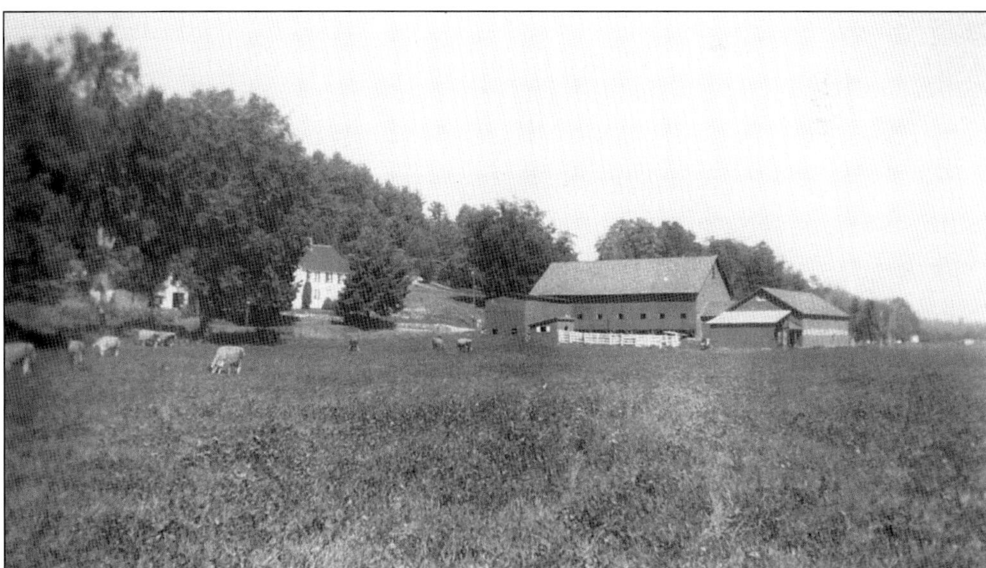

Winchester's farming history goes back to the earliest settlers, who farmed to feed themselves. Farming was also an important industry in Winchester—especially dairy farming. More than a half-dozen farms produced milk commercially. In this c. 1900 image, some contented cows graze at an unidentified farm. (Courtesy of Dorothy Doolittle Farnan.)

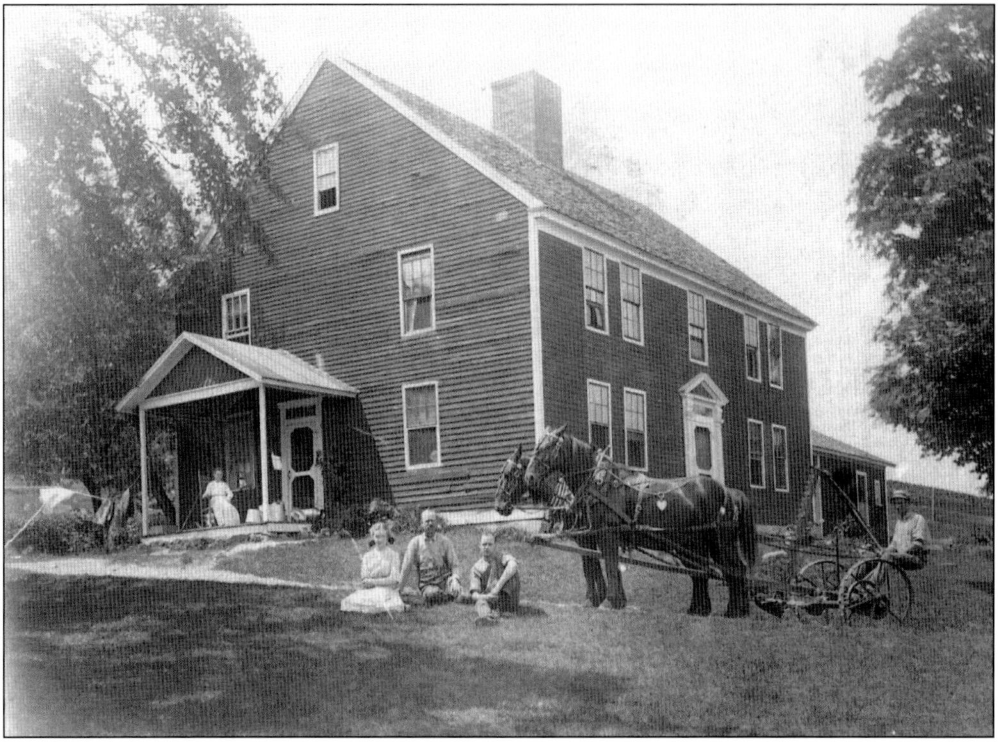

This c. 1920 photograph shows Maplewood Farm. The house still stands and is easily recognizable today. Nellie Johnson is sitting on the porch. Seated on the lawn are, from left to right, Ethel, William Sr., and S. Guy Johnson. Ralph Johnson is riding on the mowing machine. (Courtesy of Stephen Johnson.)

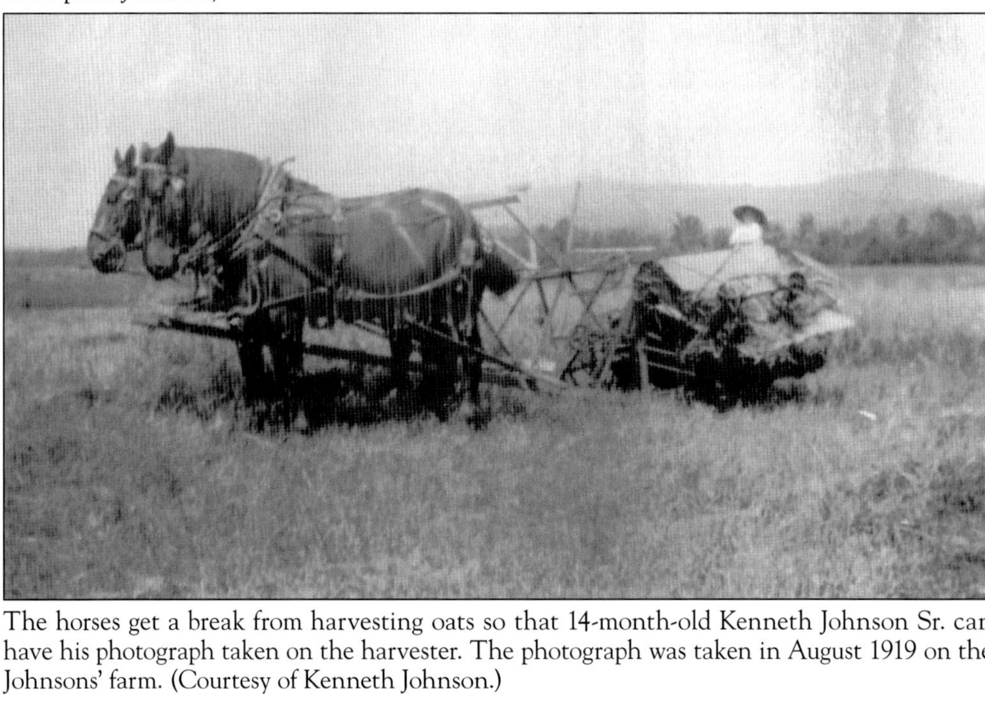

The horses get a break from harvesting oats so that 14-month-old Kenneth Johnson Sr. can have his photograph taken on the harvester. The photograph was taken in August 1919 on the Johnsons' farm. (Courtesy of Kenneth Johnson.)

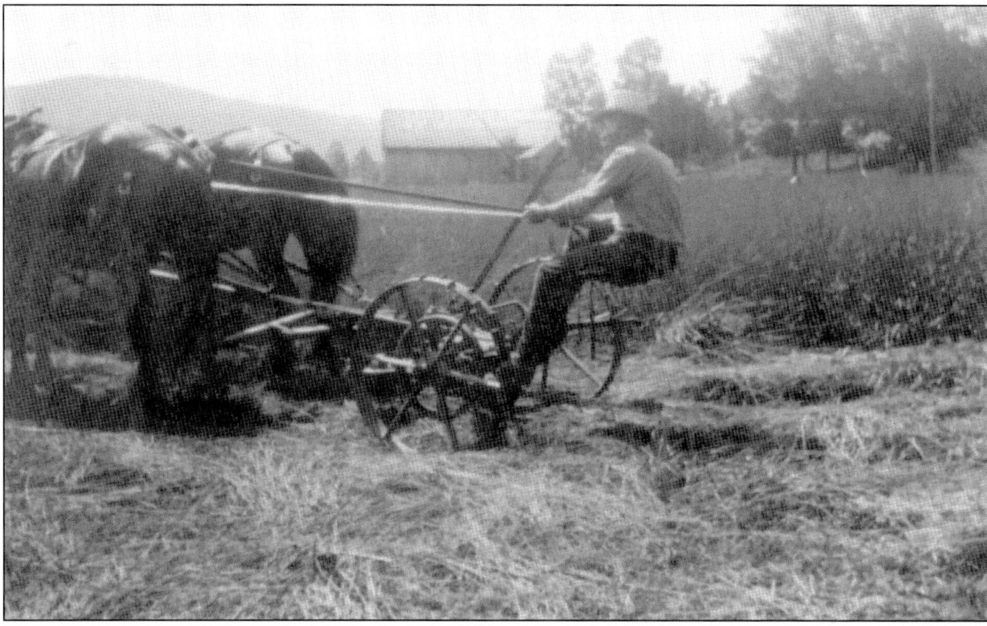

The driver of this hay-cutting team is not identified, but is most likely Ralph Johnson. If not for the antiquated equipment, the picture might have been taken this year. The view down Sunny Valley along Warwick Road remains the same. At one time, Sunny Valley contained seven family farms. (Courtesy of Stephen Johnson.)

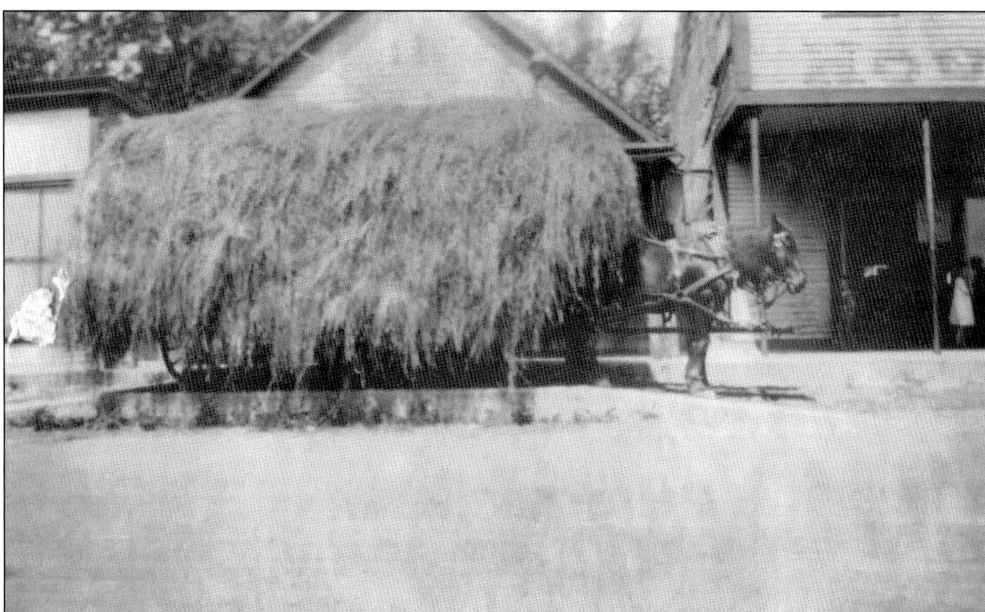

This is the largest load of hay ever placed on the scales on Main Street in Winchester. It weighed 4,650 pounds and came from the Johnson farm. The scale is across the street from the library. The building at right was destroyed in the 1971 fire. (Courtesy of Kenneth Johnson.)

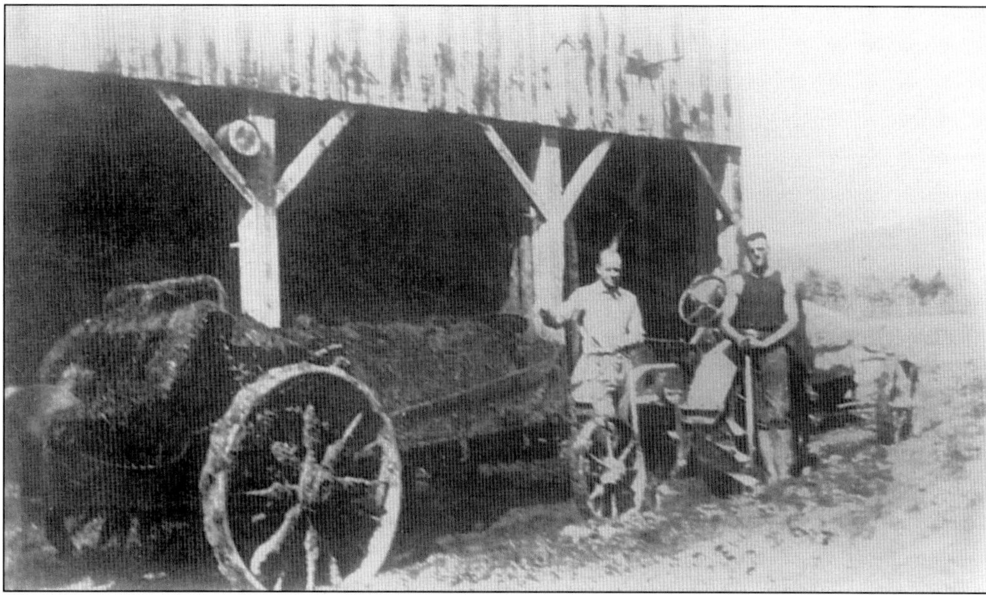

Farming is not all riding on wagons and bucolic scenery. This is a manure spreader that was obviously well used. The significance is that it is being pulled by the first tractor on Maplewood Farm, a c. 1916 Farmall made by International Harvester. (Courtesy of Stephen Johnson.)

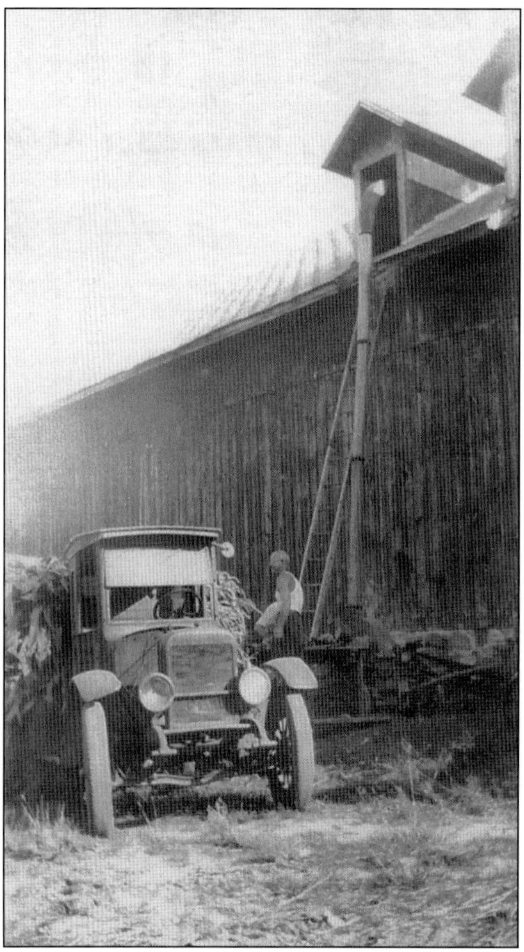

This photograph is of Maplewood Farm's first truck, a 1922 International Harvester that was nicknamed "Big Red." A man could actually stand up in the cab. Here, corn is being fed into the chopper and then blown into the silo, where it is stored for feeding the cows throughout the winter. (Courtesy of Stephen Johnson.)

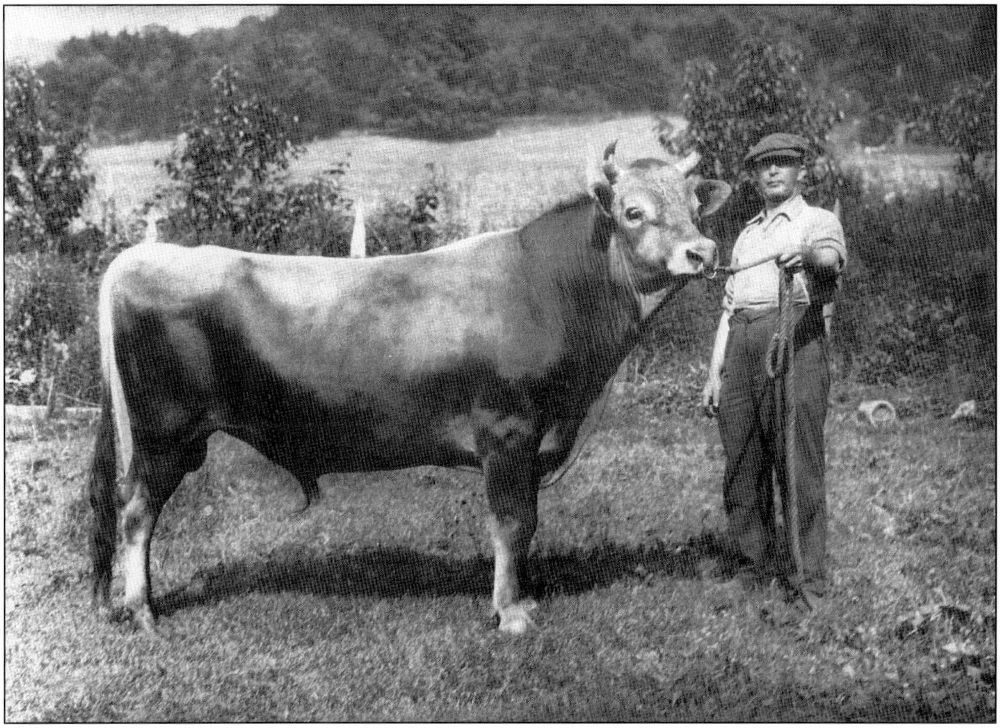

This photograph is of Judge A.F. Pierce showing off his prized Jersey bull, Raleigh's Lodestar No. 124668. Judge Pierce owned Shoemet farm on the east side of Pleasant Valley. Miscreants who came before the judge were often sentenced to spend time working on the farm. (Courtesy of Kenneth Johnson.)

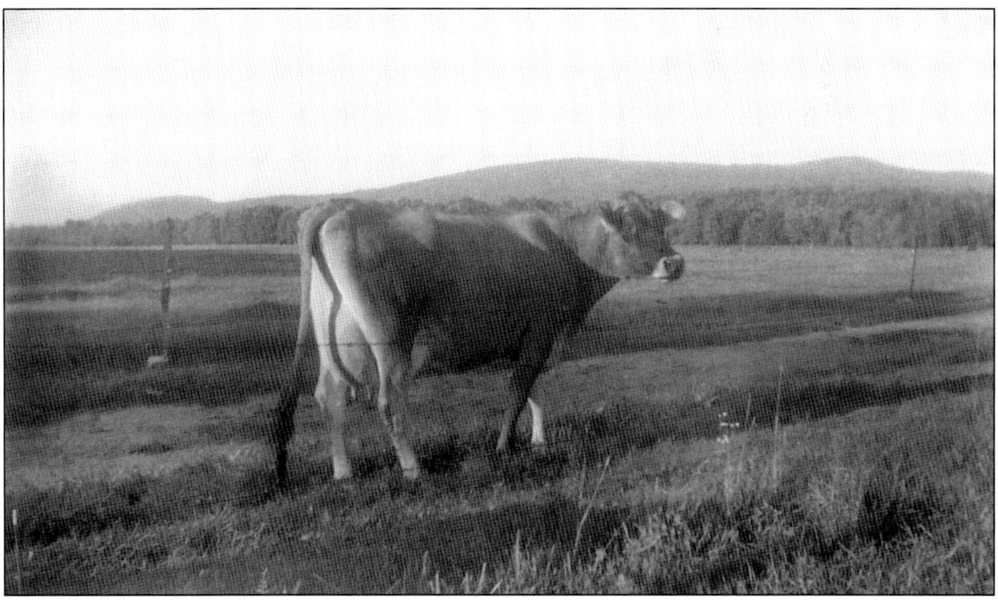

Maplewood Basilica was a prized, registered Jersey cow on the Johnson farm in the 1950s. She produced up to 60 pounds of milk per day. The average cow's production was around 25 pounds. Jerseys were prized for the high butterfat content of their milk. (Courtesy of Stephen Johnson.)

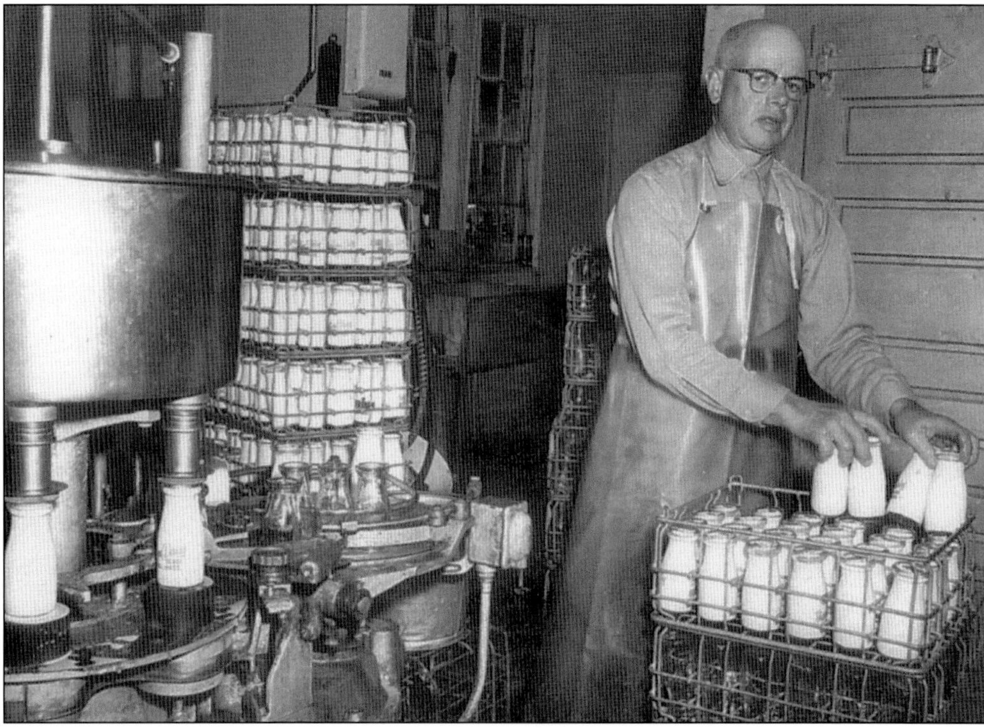

Maplewood Farm was unusual in that they bottled their own milk. Here, S. Guy Johnson bottles milk, possibly for school lunches. Maplewood Farm provided the school milk in Winchester in the 1950s. Other farms usually sent their milk to market in bulk cans via train. (Courtesy of Stephen Johnson.)

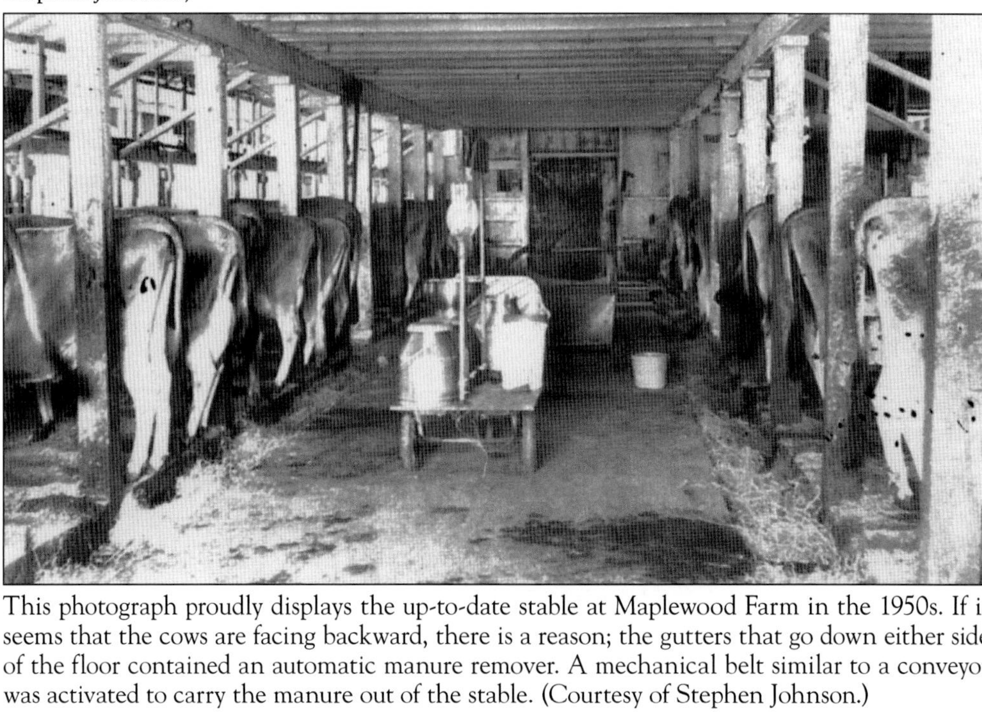

This photograph proudly displays the up-to-date stable at Maplewood Farm in the 1950s. If it seems that the cows are facing backward, there is a reason; the gutters that go down either side of the floor contained an automatic manure remover. A mechanical belt similar to a conveyor was activated to carry the manure out of the stable. (Courtesy of Stephen Johnson.)

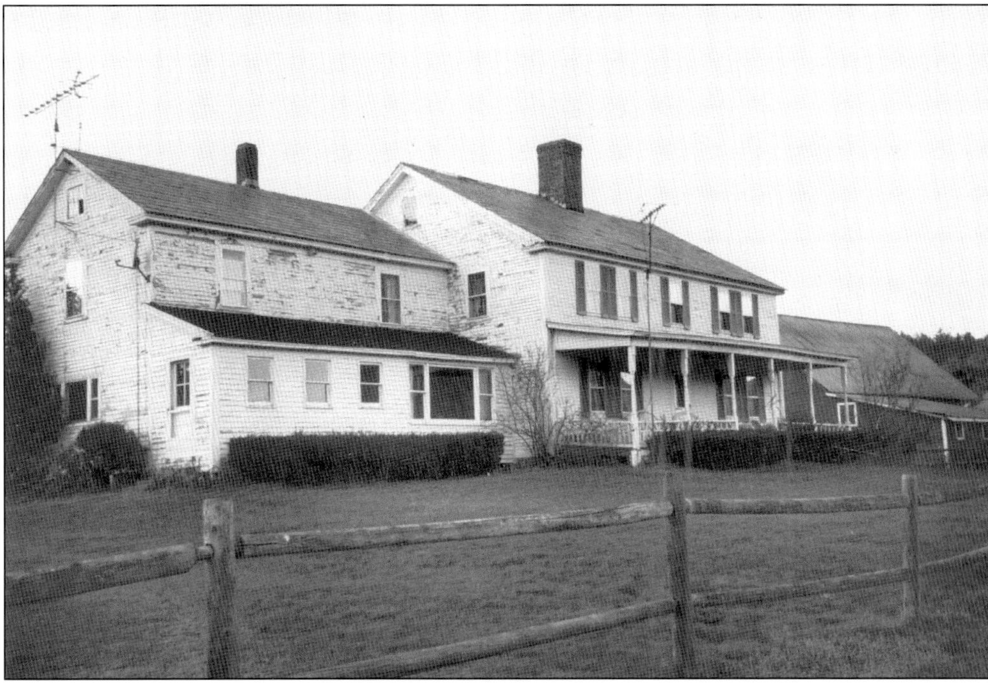

The Kelly View Farm (formerly the Thompson farm) on Old Westport Road is the only dairy farm left in Winchester. At one time, there were more than six dairy farms in town, but small farms can no longer compete with large agribusiness operations.

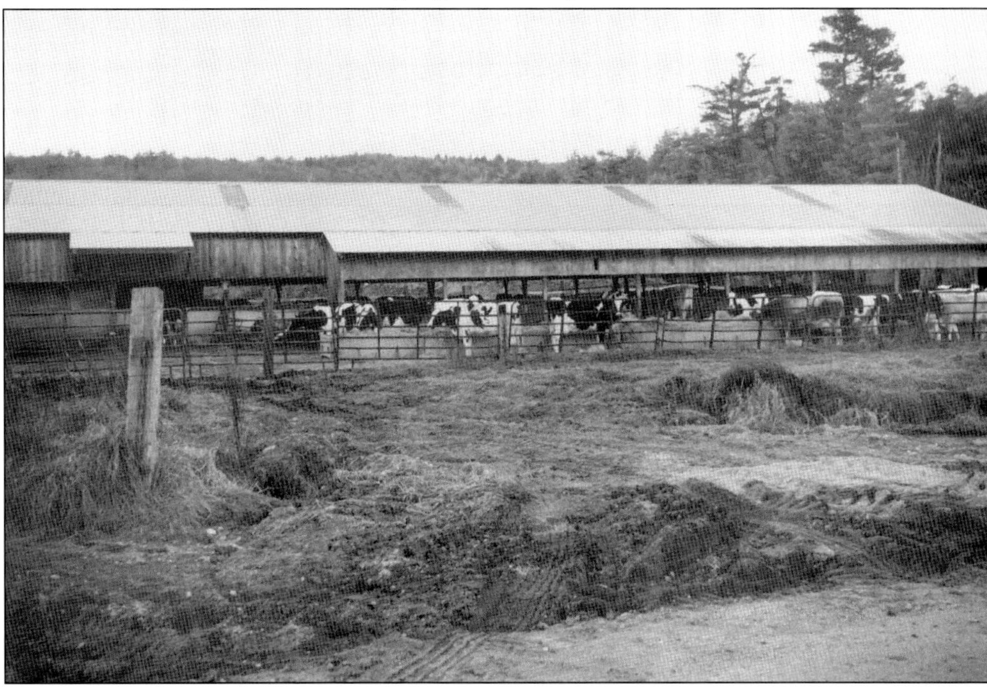

The Kelly farm milks Holsteins, though they have also had Brown Swiss. At one time, there were two Kelly farms on Old Westport Road. William Kelly Sr. ran one farm, which was farther north, and his two sons, William Jr. and Thomas, ran Kelly View Farm (pictured).

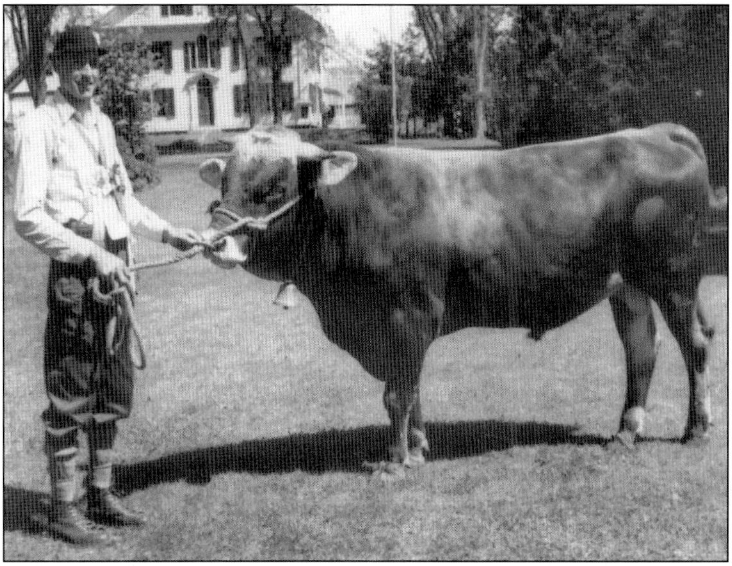

Elmer Johnson preferred Brown Swiss cows. He joined five farms along Warwick Road into one, which he dubbed Pleasant Valley. At one point, he also had another farm in Hinsdale. In this 1940s photograph, Johnson is dressed as a Swiss to show off his state champion bull in front of the Ellen Lambert Murphy Memorial Community Center. (Courtesy of Kenneth Johnson.)

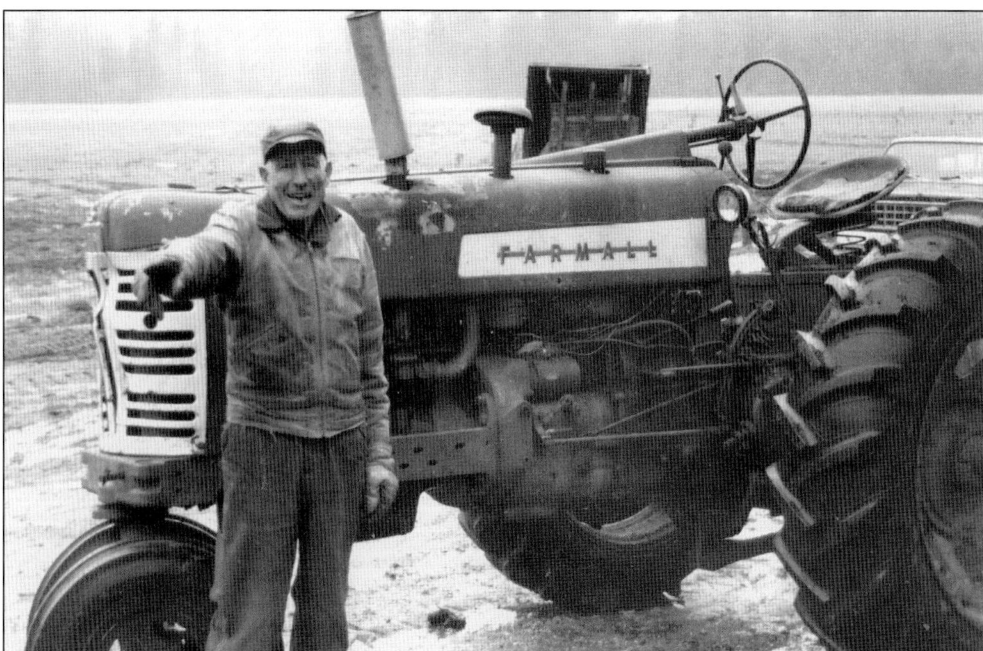

This photograph shows Elmer Johnson on his farm in the 1980s. Johnson served in many positions in local government. He was town moderator for 40 years, on the budget committee for 40 years, and was a state representative for 20 years.

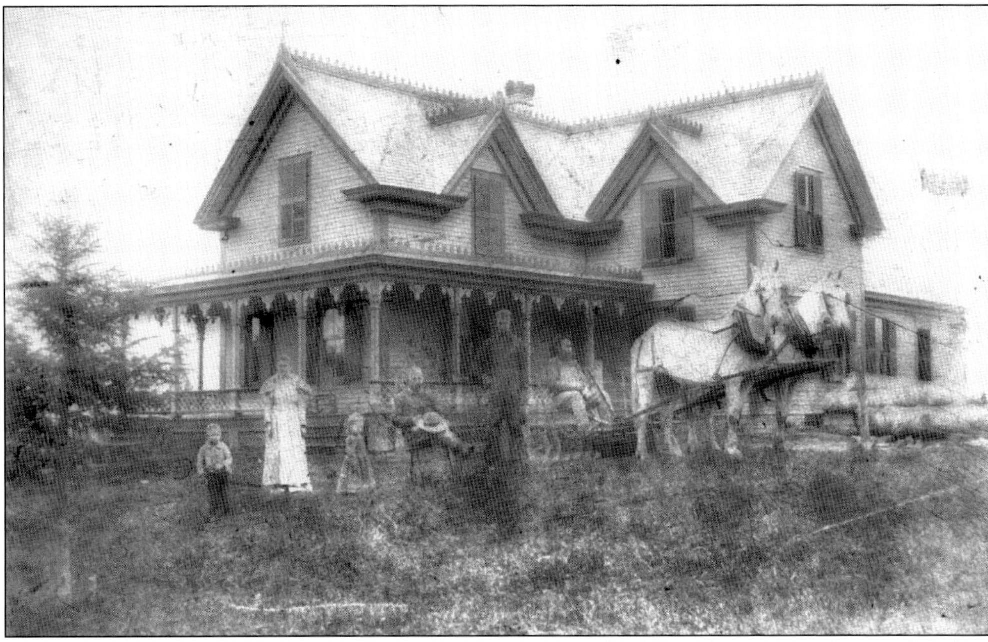

This photograph shows the Fisher family at their farm, which was located on the north side of Old Chesterfield Road just before the present-day location of the entrance to Pisgah State Park. The impressive house is testimony to their success at farming. Unfortunately, the beautiful house fell on hard times, and then was destroyed by fire in 1989.

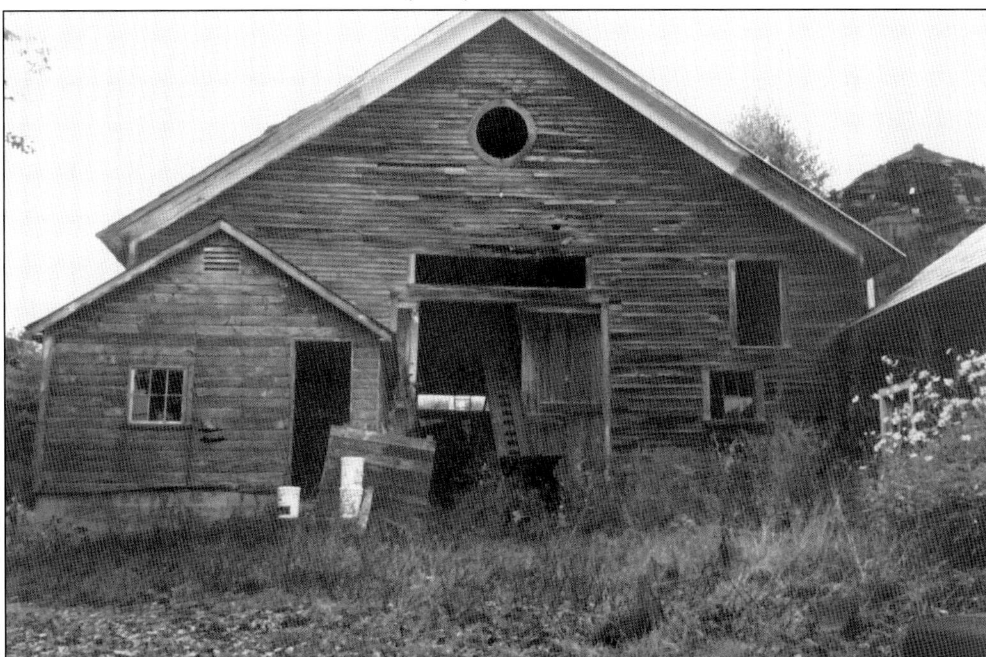

This barn, which is slowly returning to the earth, was part of the once-successful Solasz dairy farm on Burt Hill. In the early 1990s, Elmer Johnson compiled a list of 151 barns that had disappeared in Winchester since 1900. Some had burned down, some had been torn down, and some fell on their own.

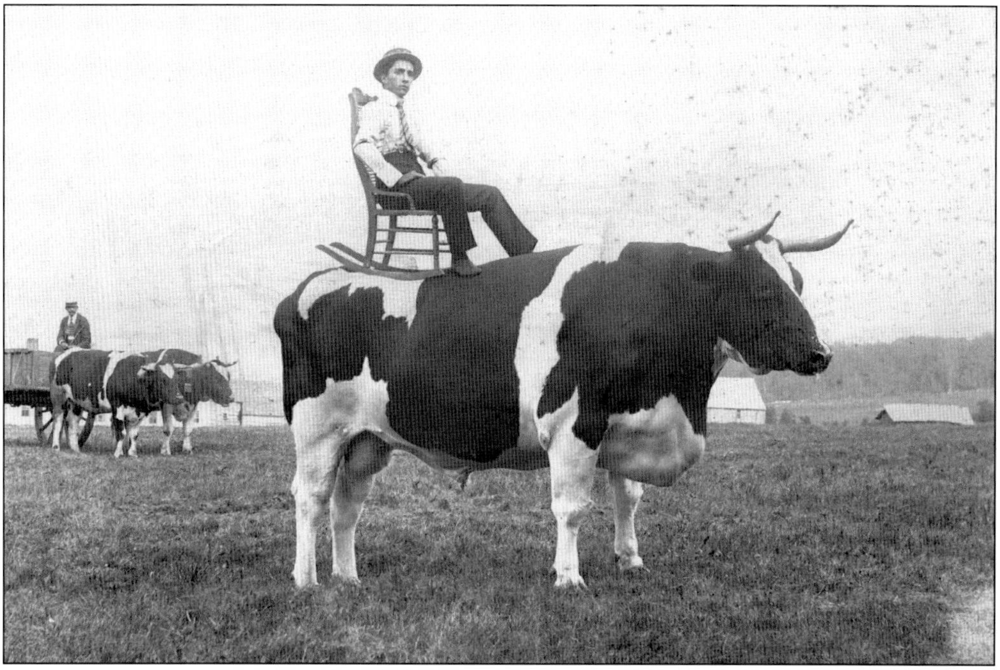

Oxen do not really fall under "farming." They were industrial animals—beasts of burden—that brought heavy loads out of places without roads and delivered goods to market. Obviously, men took great pride in their beasts, as the photographs above and below attest.

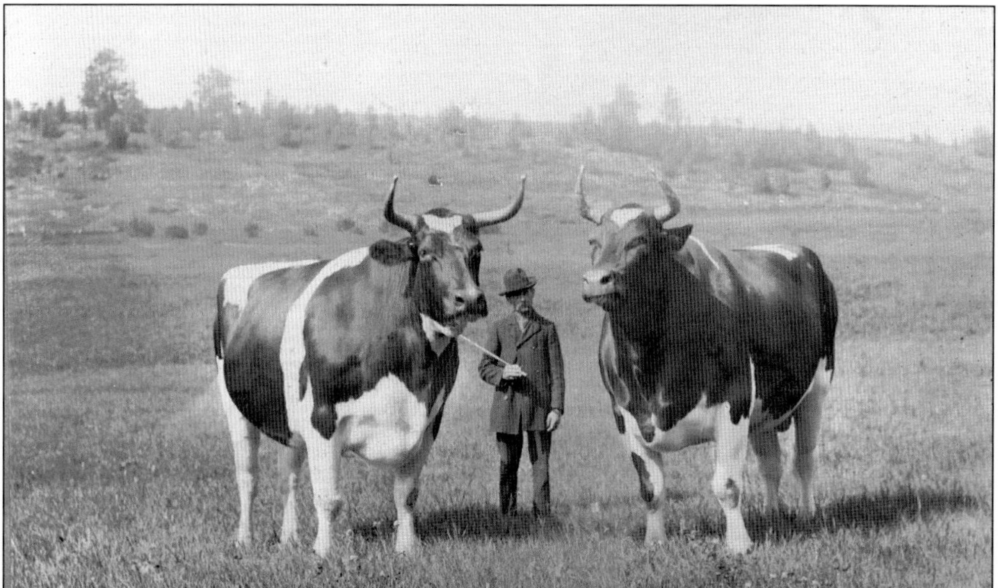

We cannot identify the man in this photograph, though it has been suggested that it is Ansel Dickinson. Dickinson was described as a big man, but this does not look like a big man. However, it may be just the size of the animals that makes him look small. The ox at left in this photograph may be the same one that has a man in a rocking chair sitting atop him in the photograph above this image.

Seven

Recreation

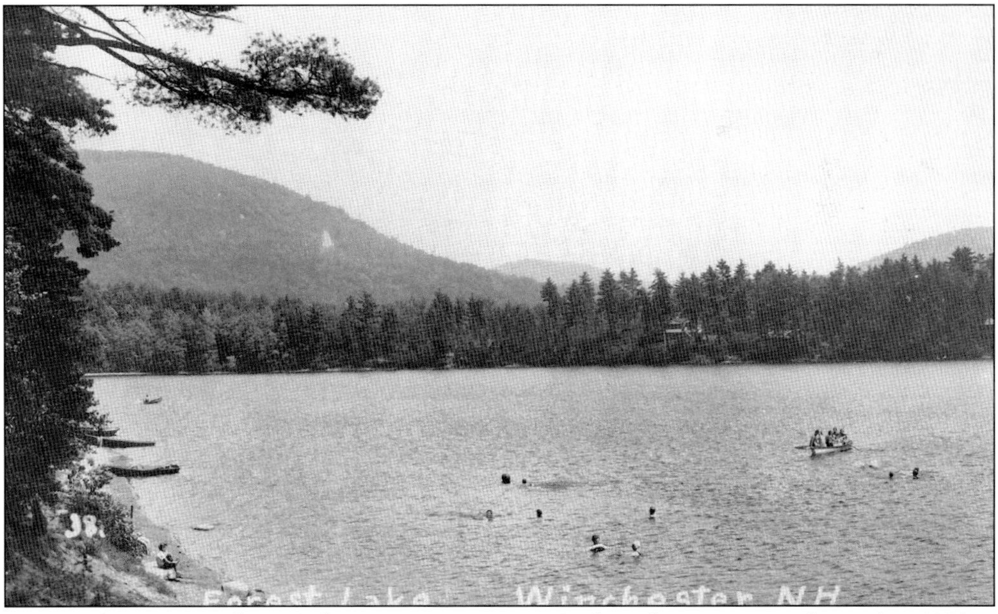

Forest Lake was Winchester's first tourist attraction. In fact, the name was changed in 1883—from Humphrey's Pond to Forest Lake—to make it more attractive to visitors. Today, it is still a summer home for many and a day trip for boaters, bathers, and fishermen. It now competes with the Pisgah Wilderness Area, which attracts fishermen, hikers, and ATV riders in the summer and snowshoers and snowmobilers in the winter. And the Ashuelot River beckons for canoeing, kayaking, and tubing.

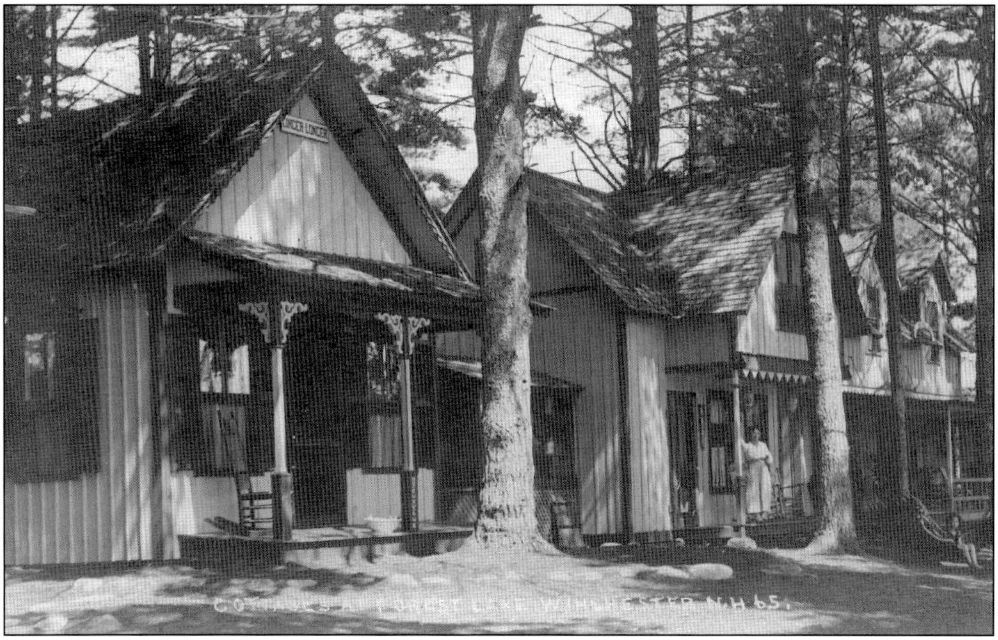

The pine grove on the western shore of Forest Lake was an early attraction for people looking for a cool spot to have a picnic on a hot summer day. In the 1880s, several local residents—and some from as far away as Keene—built cottages there. In 1918, lightning struck the area, knocking over an oil lamp and starting a fire. Ten of the cottages were lost, along with the store and pavilion.

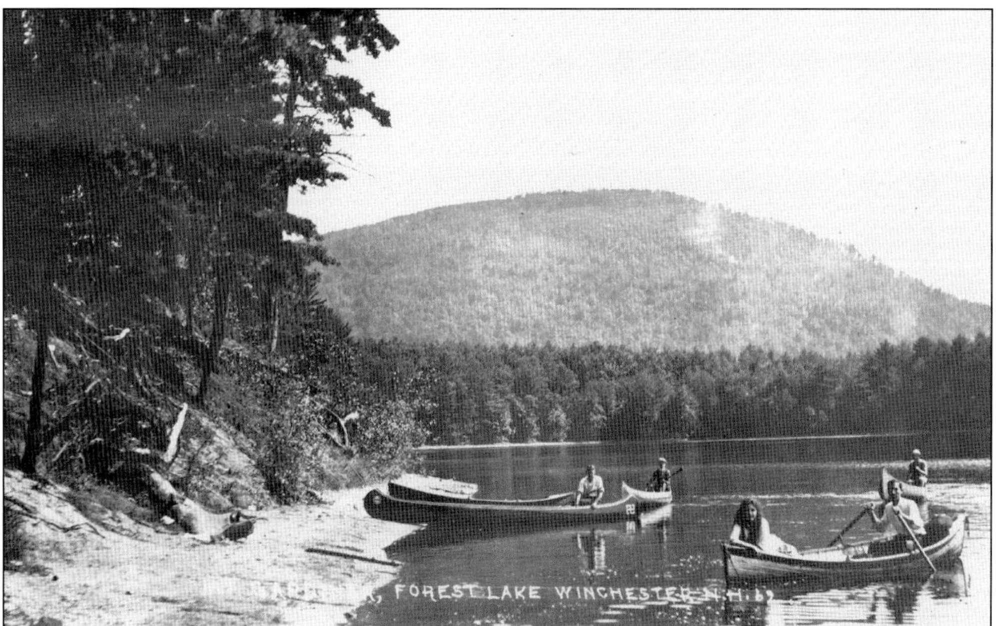

The Connecticut Railroad advanced the idea of having fun at Forest Lake to encourage weekend riders. They sponsored special events, and people could buy a ticket that included the train ride on the Ashuelot Branch. It was a short wagon ride or walk from the flag station across the Melvin Bridge to the grove.

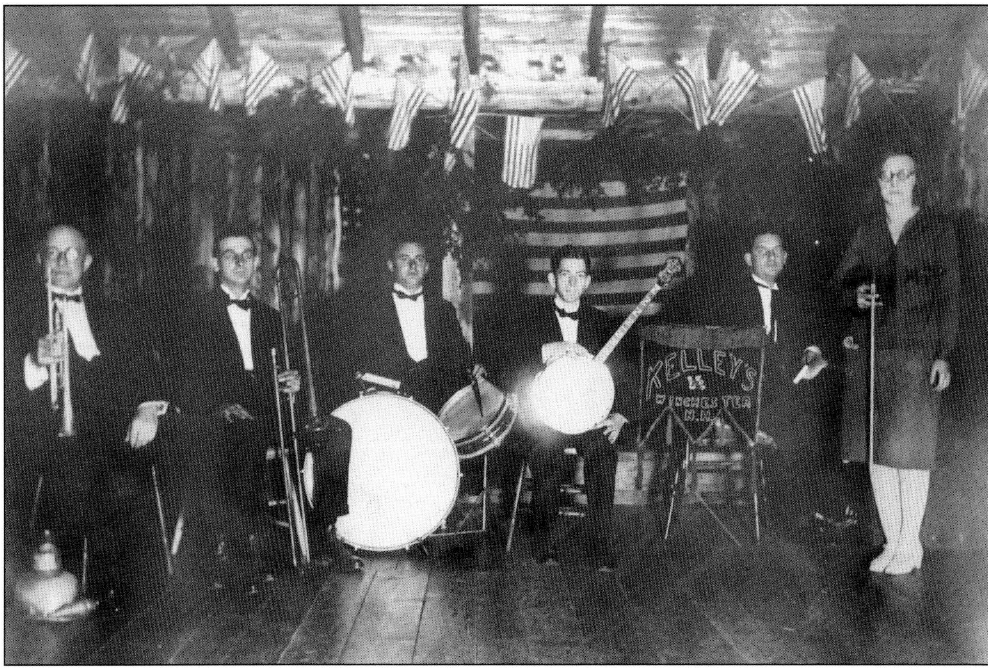

A dance hall eventually grew from an early open-air pavilion at the grove. Local and some very well-known bands played at the weekly dances that attracted young people from all around the area. This band, as evidenced by the banner, is Kelley's. A Kelley family member is on drums, and Celia Payeski is holding her violin.

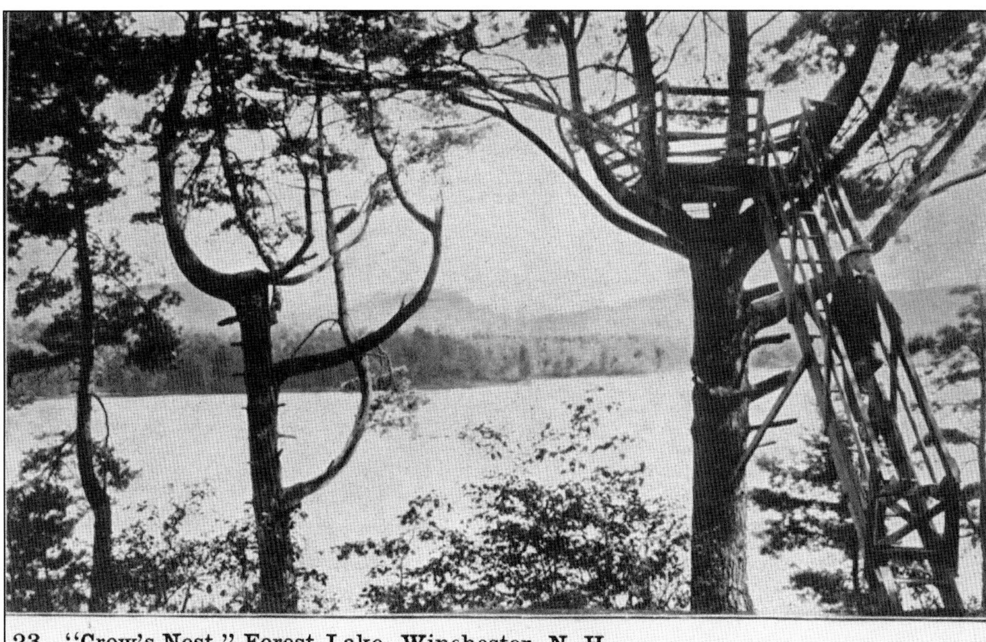

The Crow's Nest offered a panoramic view of Forest Lake. Besides the Crow's Nest, the pavilion, and a cozy seating area called Robin's Nest, there were also excursion boat rides around the lake.

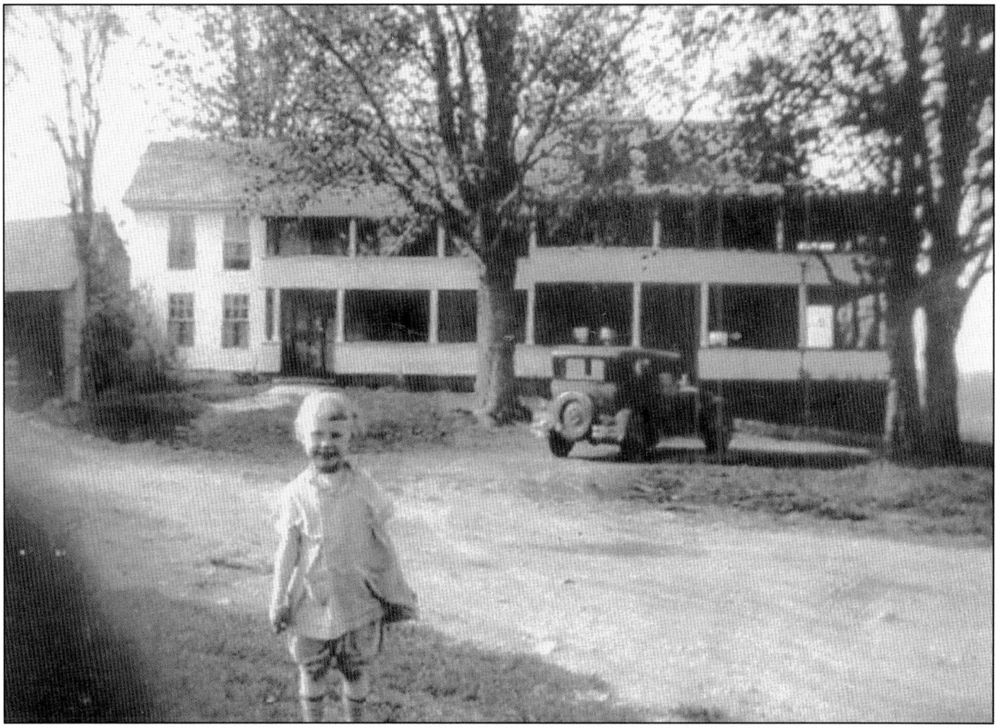

The original Humphrey home was located just north of the inlet on the west side of Keene Road. It was enlarged and then enlarged again, becoming the Humphrey Hotel and later renamed the Forest Lake Inn. Here, Evelyn Thompson Conway poses in front of the inn, which was destroyed by fire in 1945 or 1946.

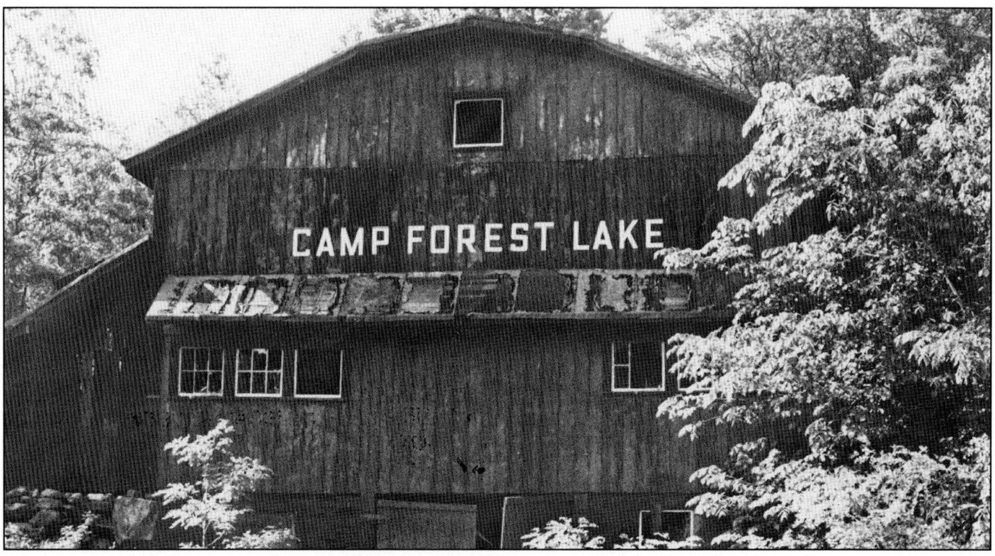

The east side of Forest Lake remained undeveloped until the fire of 1918, when some cottage owners chose to rebuild there instead of in the grove. In 1935, the Northampton WMCA bought part of the headlands and built a camp. Later, the camp was sold to Morningside Community Center in New York City, who operated a camp there in the 1970s that was locally known as "the Negro camp."

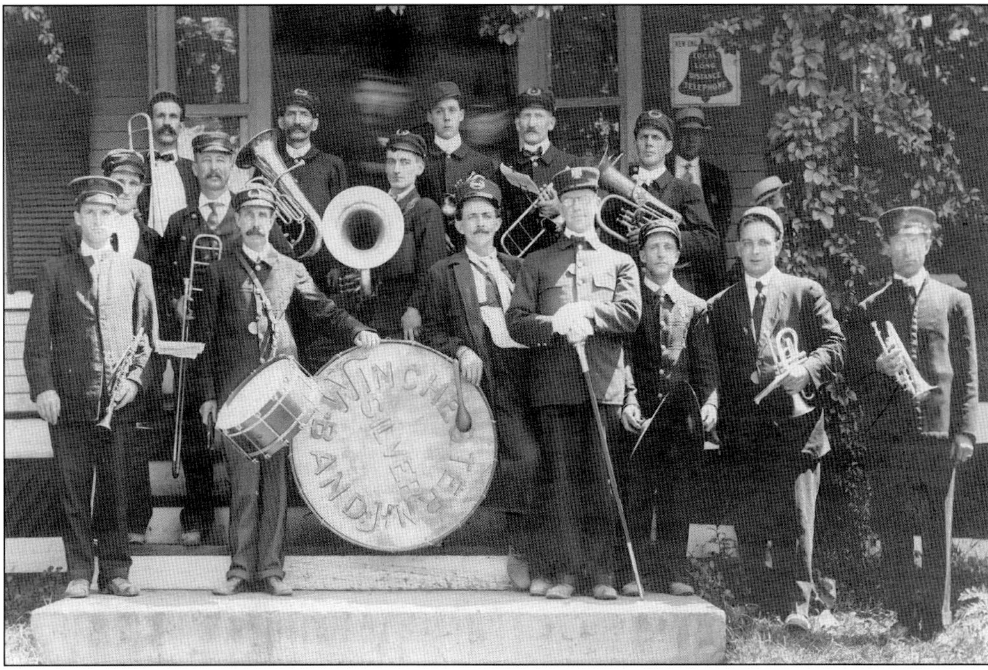

Town bands were often the pride of a community. The Winchester, New Hampshire, band traveled to exchange concerts with the Winchester, Virginia, band. Bands were a source of entertainment for the community and camaraderie for the members. At a time that predated radio—let alone iTunes—people created their own music.

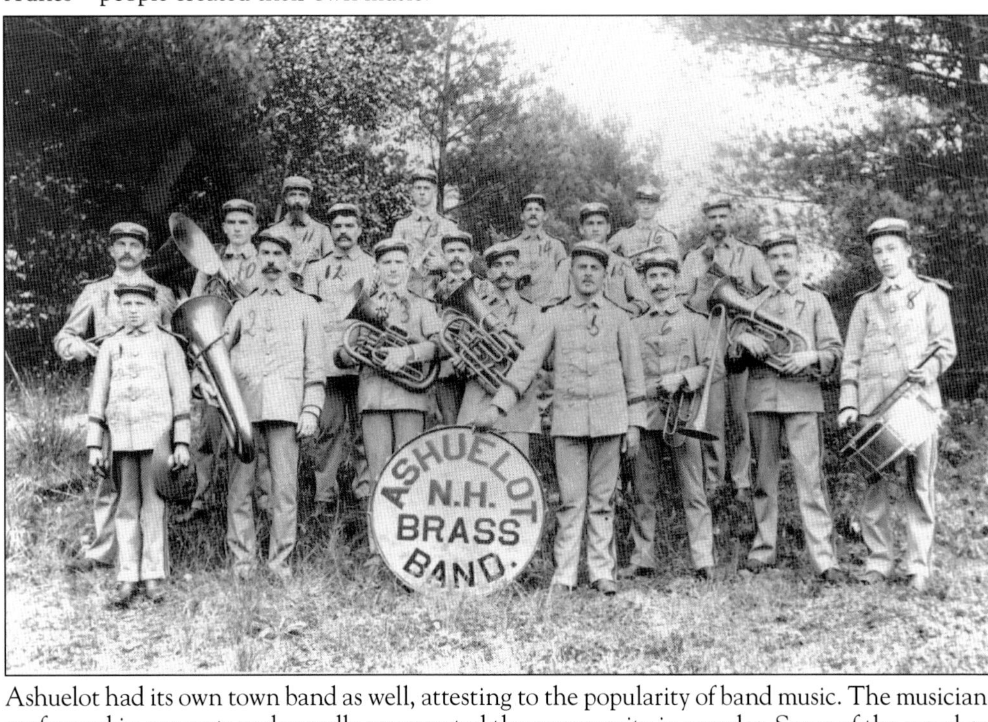

Ashuelot had its own town band as well, attesting to the popularity of band music. The musicians performed in concerts and proudly represented the community in parades. Some of the members here are quite young, but notice that none of them are female.

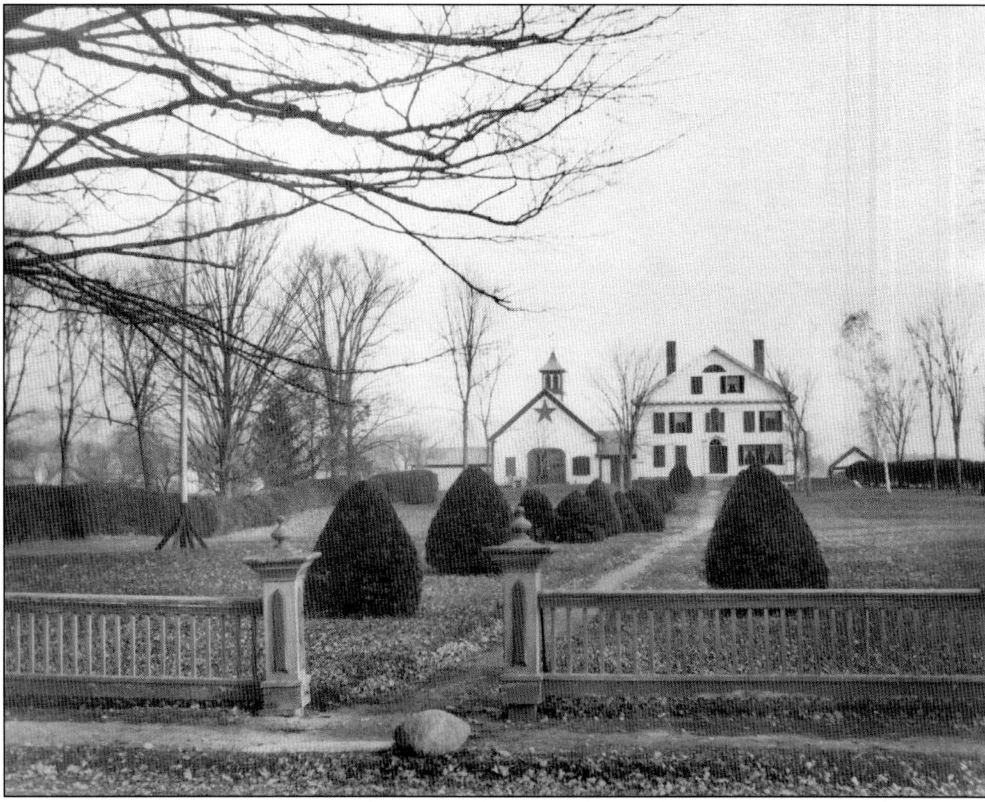

The Ellen Lambert Murphy Memorial Community Center came into being in 1938 primarily due to the efforts of Francis P. Murphy, governor of the State of New Hampshire, and Rev. George Truman Carl, minister of the Federated Church at the time. Reverend Carl thought the vacant Alexander estate would make a perfect recreation center for the people of Winchester, and Governor Murphy thought a community center would be a great way to honor his mother.

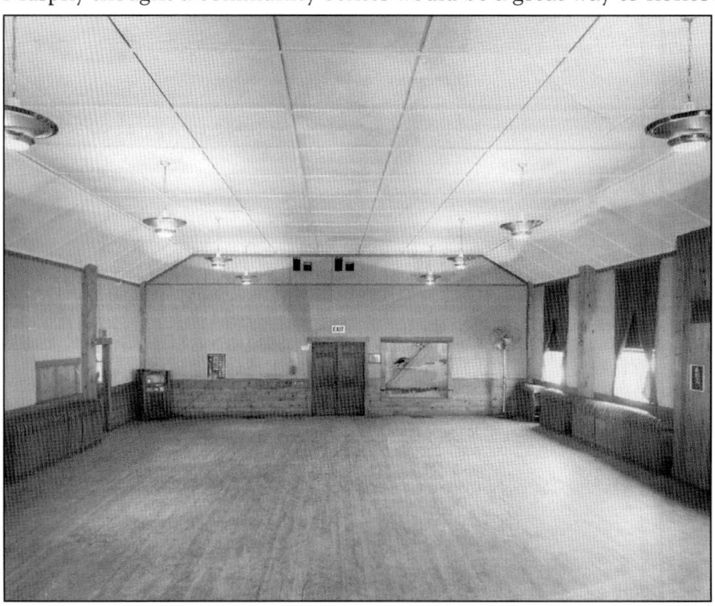

For over 70 years, the ELMMCC has served as a meeting place for Winchester groups, as well as a recreational center. At one time, weekly movies were shown in the auditorium (pictured here), and a kiln in the basement of the house accommodated ceramic classes. Summer camp, Scouts, ball teams, a skating rink, and playground equipment kept youngsters busy.

The ELMMCC originally had two bowling alleys, and two more were added. In 1959, automatic pinsetters enhanced the alleys. Bowling leagues regularly meet to enjoy New England's own candlepin bowling. Until recently, there was a rifle range under the alleys that hosted many sharpshooting teams over the years.

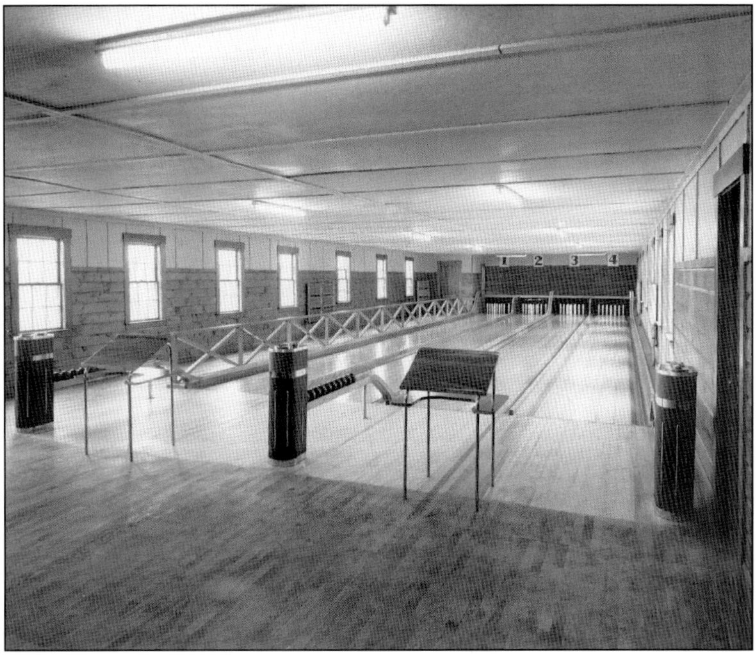

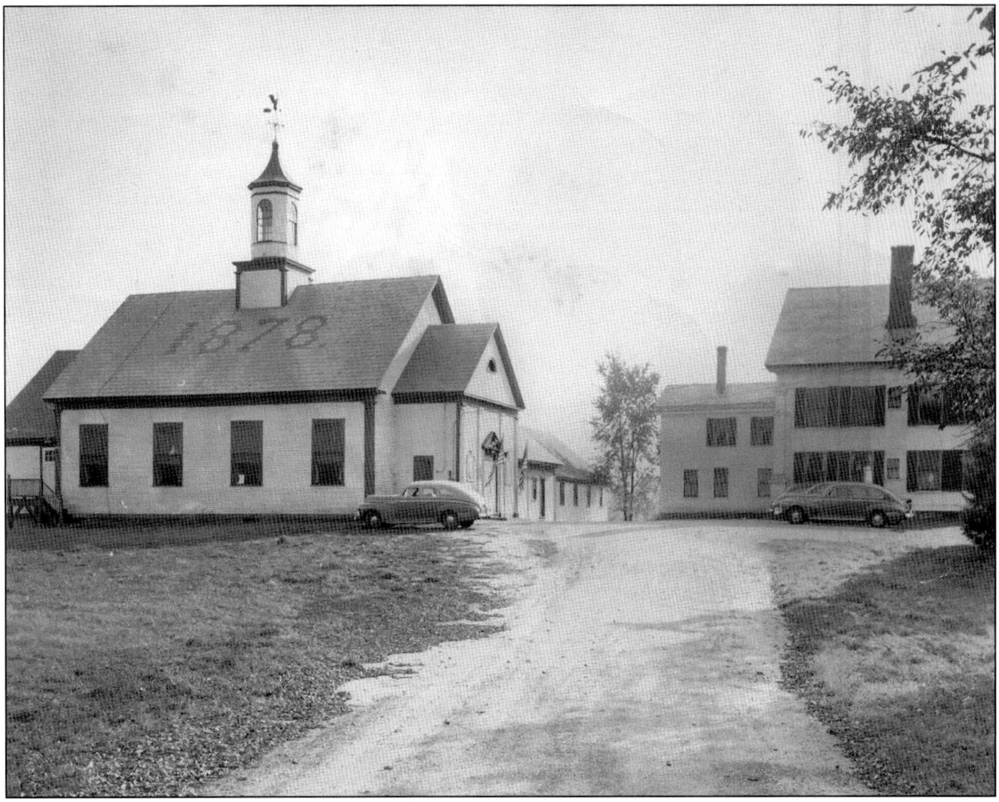

The cars in this photograph help date it, but the buildings still look just the same. This area now contains a large parking lot, tennis courts, and a basketball court. The center also had a shallow pool at one time. Thanks to Gil Conant, two baseball fields are equipped with dugouts.

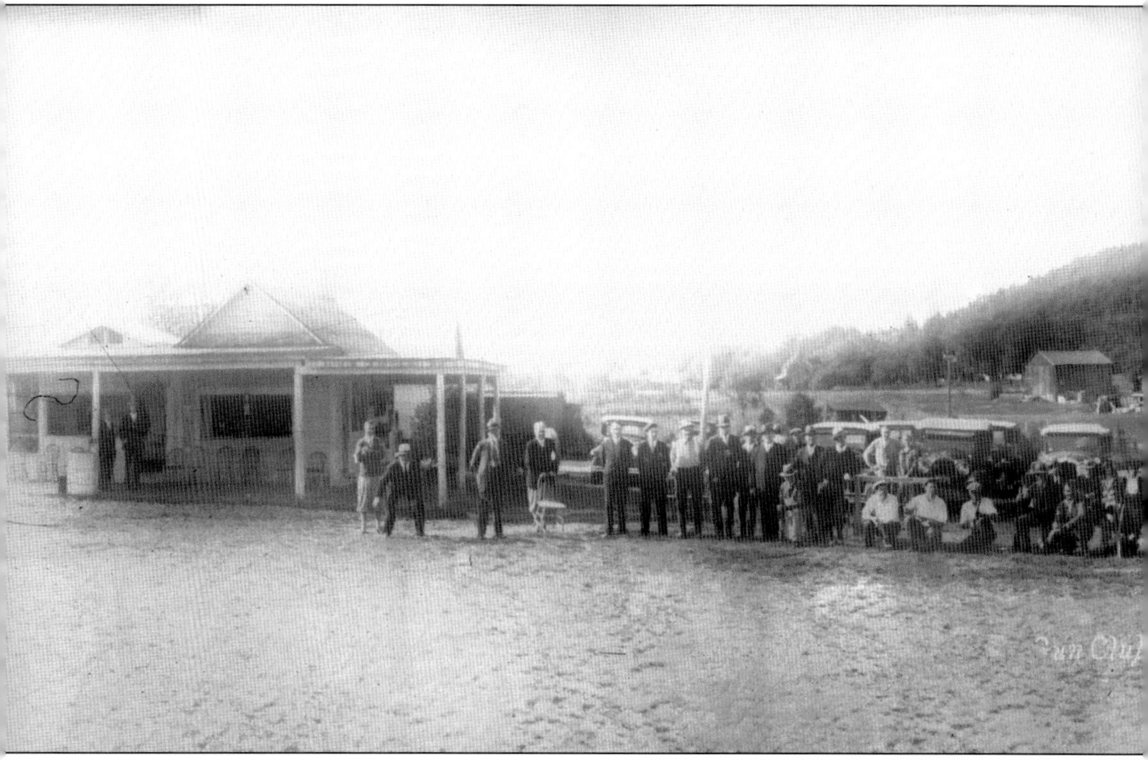

This wonderful panorama shows the Winchester Gun Club meeting for trap shooting in 1931. The location is behind the Winchester School, where the Bi-Lo housing development now stands. The club was very active before World War II, shooting skeet on Saturdays and Sundays when the weather permitted. Sometimes picnics were held at the time of the shoot. The sportsmen hosted

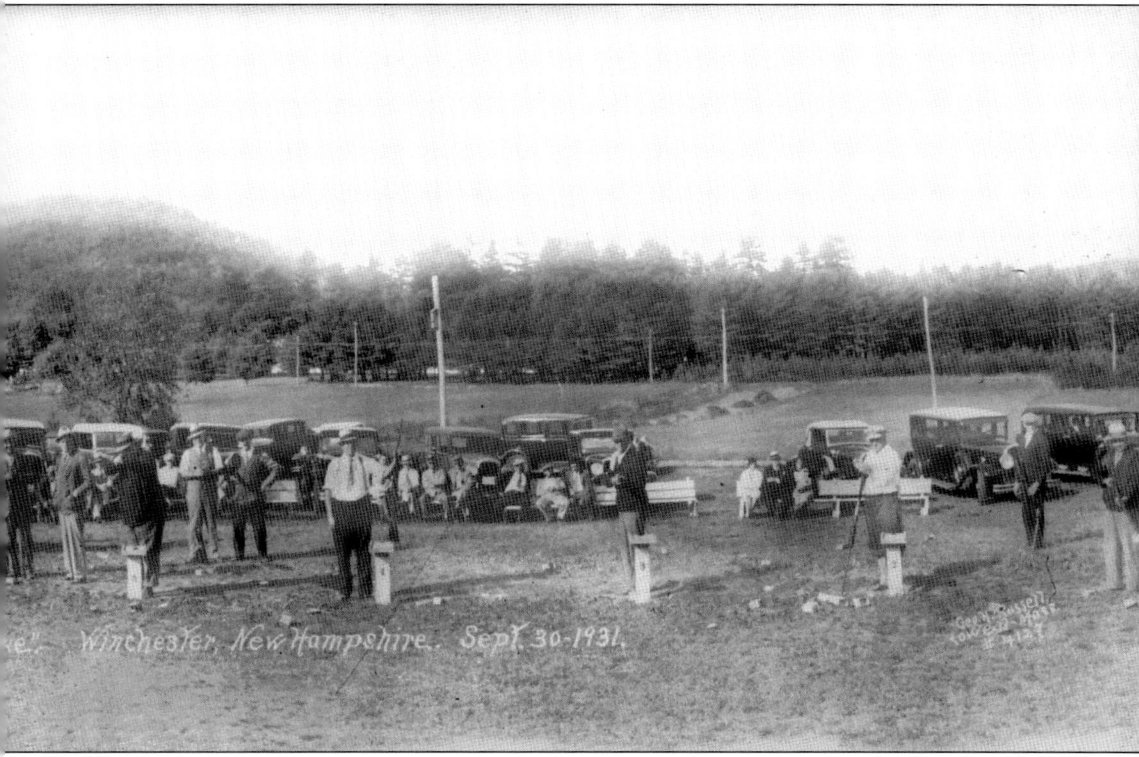

an annual clambake that the whole town looked forward to. Getting a job firing the skeet was a plum for a Winchester teen—it was not only fun, but also paid more than most jobs available to youngsters; in the 1920s, a skeet-firer could earn 35¢ per hour.

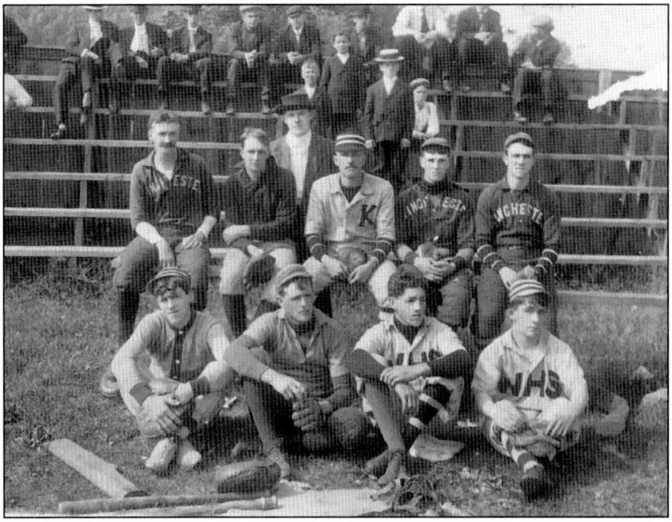

Winchester caught the baseball bug early. As early as the 1890s, the *Winchester Star* was reporting box scores. The town fielded a team that played other teams from surrounding towns, as well as semi-pro traveling teams. The 1905 team is pictured at left. There were five fields in Winchester, plus one just over the state line in Warwick, Massachusetts, for Sunday games; Winchester's selectmen did not allow games on Sundays.

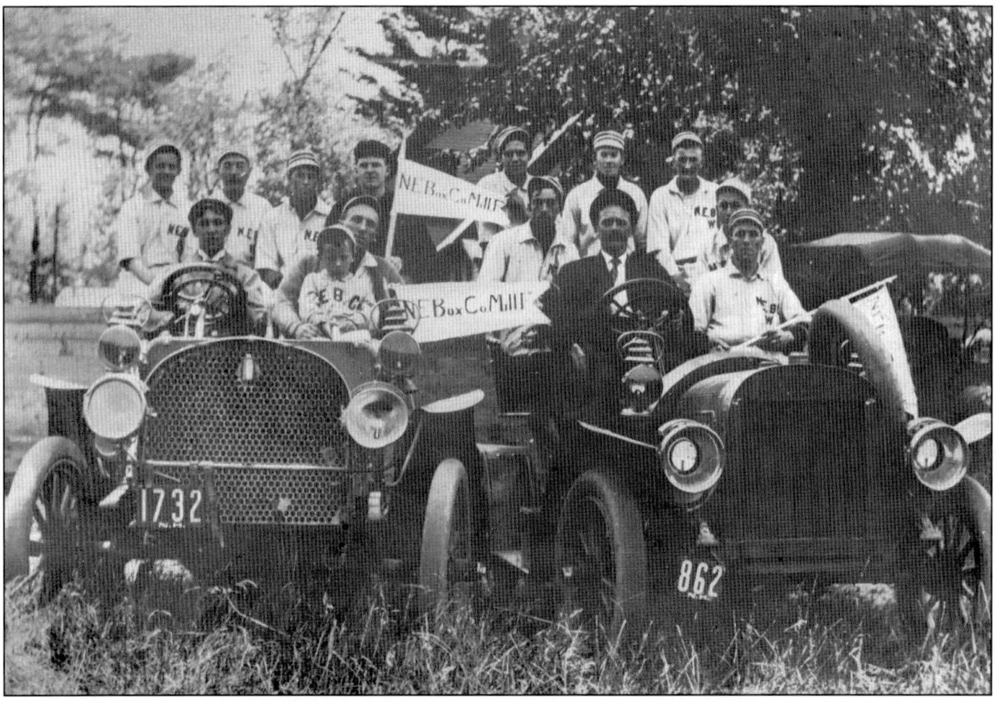

This is a c. 1910 team fielded by the New England Box Company. The players are not all identified, but those pictured include (in no particular order): John Minnat, Bill Curtis, Grover Thompson, Bob Powers, Charlie Drugg, Dean Foster, Harry Quigley, Dave Patten, Eddie Walsh, and Ed Costello.

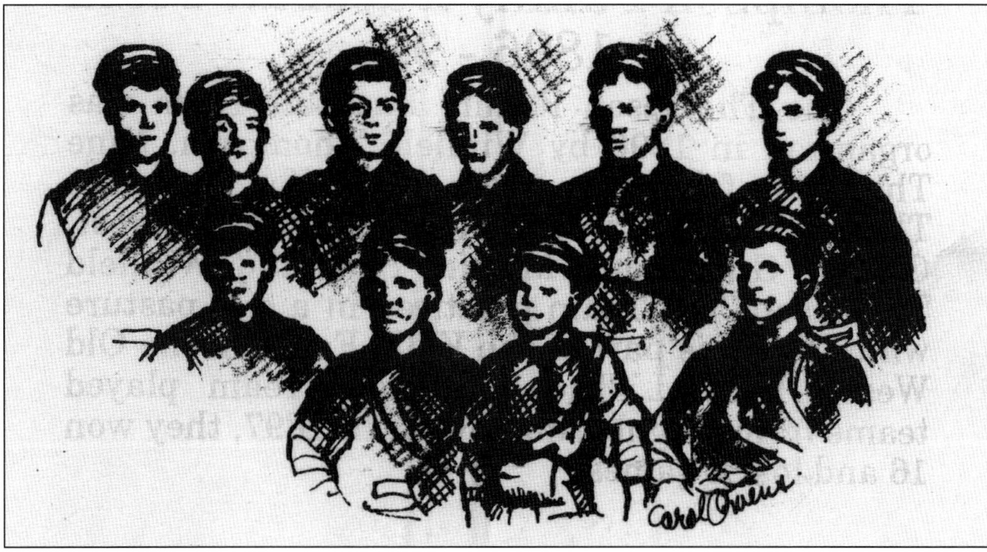

This sketch shows the Thompson Family Baseball Team, a group that included nine Thompson family members—Arch, Edward, Forest, Grover, Guy, John, Melvin, Sam, and Winfield. The team, which was organized in 1896 by Winfield Thompson, practiced in a cow pasture off of Old Westport Road that later became part of the Kelly farm.

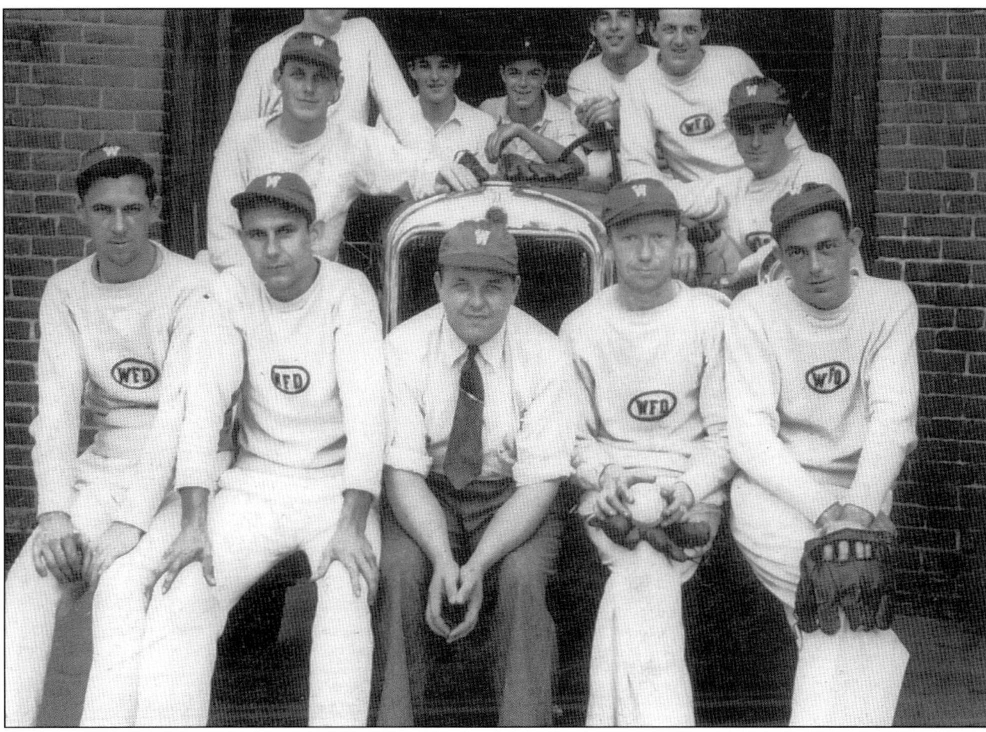

The Winchester Fire Department fielded a softball team for many years. This team probably played in the early 1940s. They are, from left to right, (first row) Louis Sosnoski, Eddie Erunski, Howard Barrett, Alex Erunski, and Eldon Thompson; (second row) Russell Barrett, Frank Zwolinski, Thurston Thompson, Thurlon Thompson, Leonard Tacy, Maxwell Thompson, and Lynn Thompson.

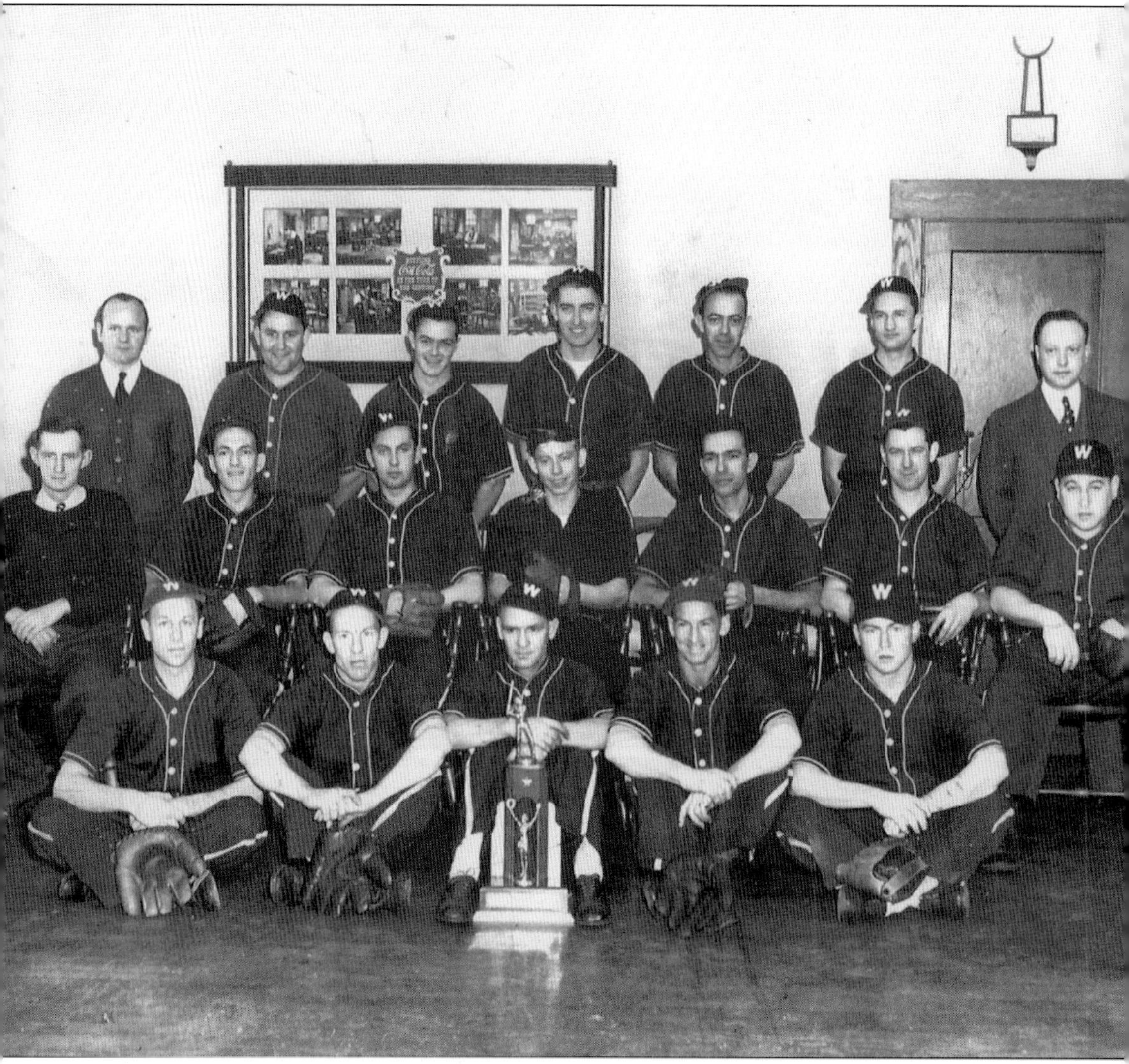

The A.C. Lawrence Tannery established a softball dynasty after World War II. They fielded softball teams that won the state championship three years in a row, in 1946, 1947, and 1948. This photograph is of the 1946 team. They are, from left to right, (first row) James Pulaski, William "Babe" Byrne, Kendall Baker, Bert "Red" Kempton, and James Durling; (second row) Harry Brayman, Joe Zabielski, Walter Snow, Joe Pitcher, John Zabielski, Stephen Sosnoski, and Edgar Durling; (third row) Stanley Naramore, Claire "Bob" Tacy, Thurlon "Lefty" Thompson, Francis Barden, Eldon Thompson, Eddie "Ike" Kingsman, and Harry Sabath.

Eight

Disasters

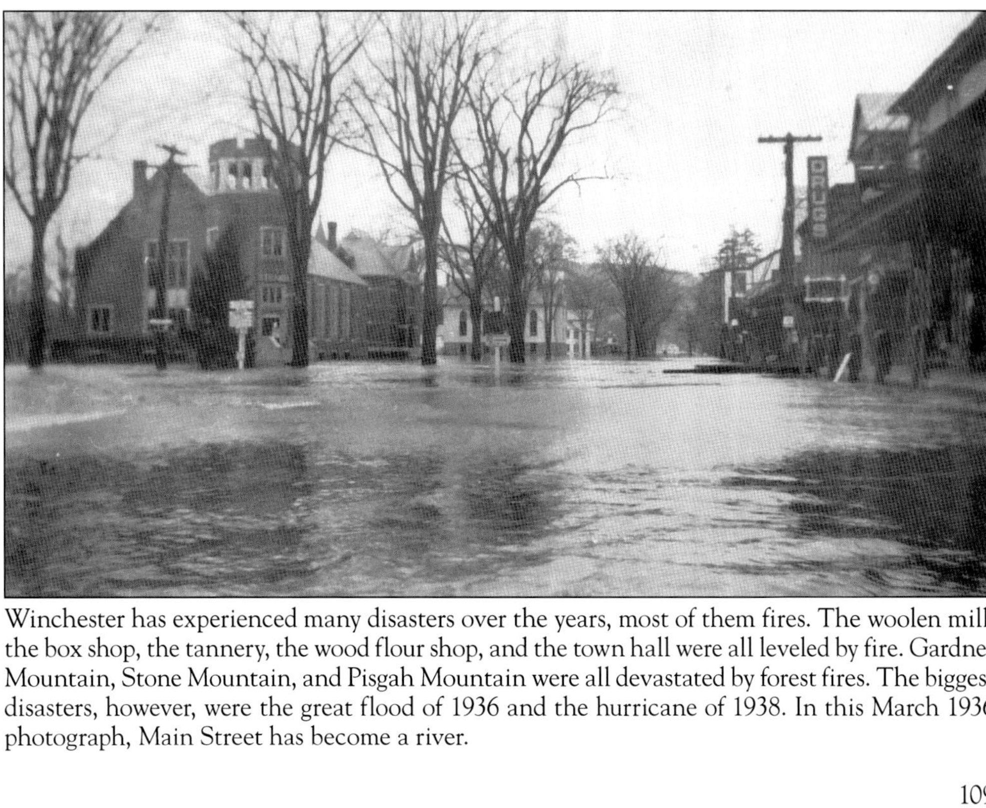

Winchester has experienced many disasters over the years, most of them fires. The woolen mill, the box shop, the tannery, the wood flour shop, and the town hall were all leveled by fire. Gardner Mountain, Stone Mountain, and Pisgah Mountain were all devastated by forest fires. The biggest disasters, however, were the great flood of 1936 and the hurricane of 1938. In this March 1936 photograph, Main Street has become a river.

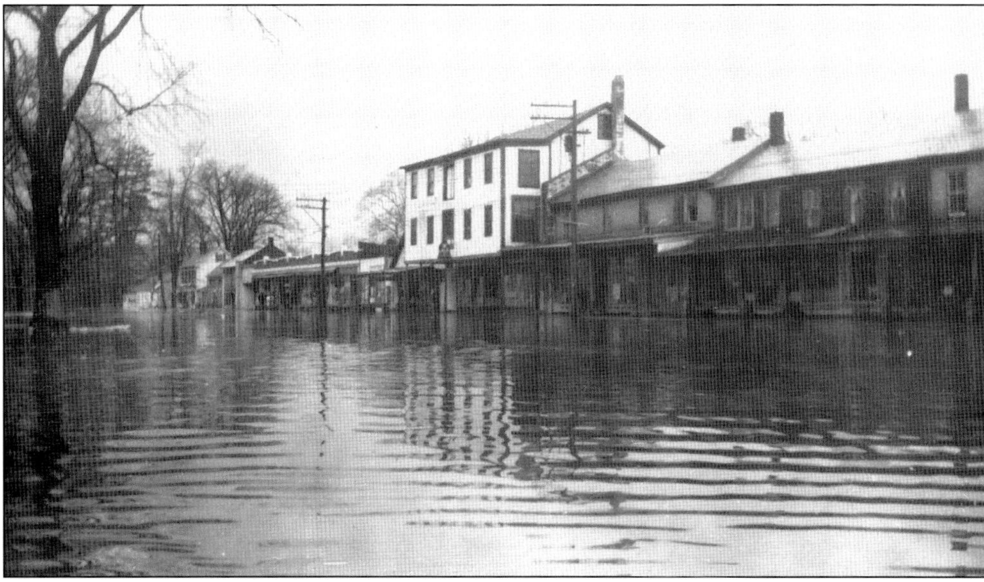

The winter of 1935–1936 was a hard one with lots of snow and frigid temperatures. A week into March, that suddenly changed when a warm front came through and created snowmelt. It then rained and rained . . . and rained. By March 19, 1936, there had been over 10 inches of rain and snowmelt in New England. Rivers and brooks were all over their banks. The Ashuelot River ran down Main Street. None of the stores where spared. Trade came to a standstill while everyone waited for the waters to recede. Nearly 200 lives were lost in New England, but Winchester was fortunate to lose none of its citizens.

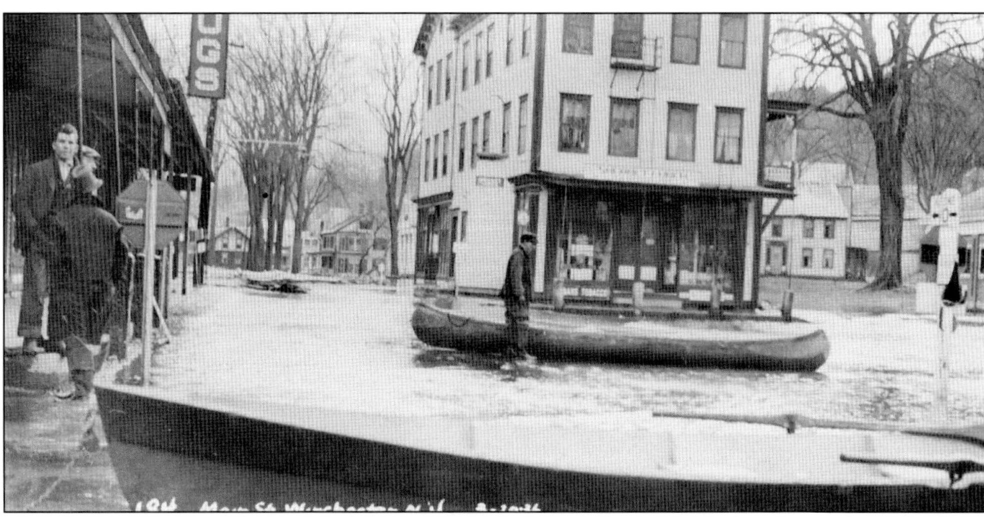

The Congregational Church (now the United Church of Winchester), located on the corner of Main and Parker Streets, still has the high-water mark from the 1936 flood on its granite foundation; it was the foundation that saved the sanctuary from being damaged.

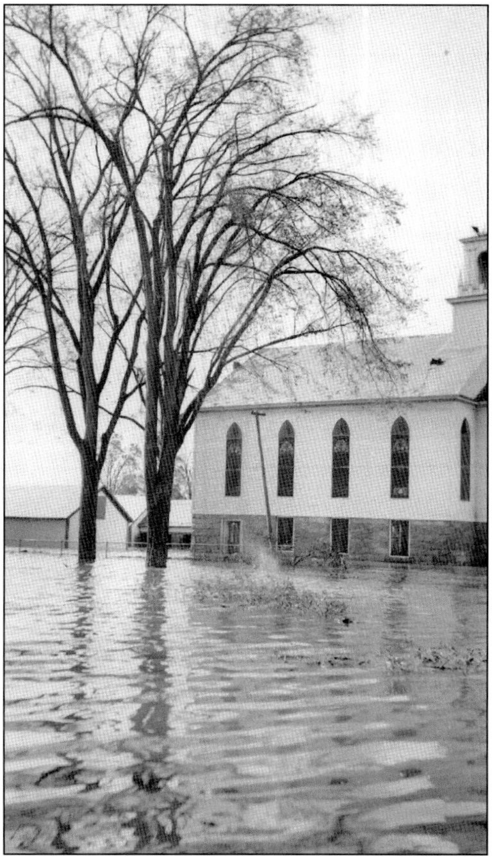

This photograph looking from Parker Street toward Main Street shows how far the Ashuelot River expanded. Behind the houses on the south side of the street, the river met the flooded Mirey Brook and turned the field behind the Alexander estate (the present-day location of the ball fields) into a lake.

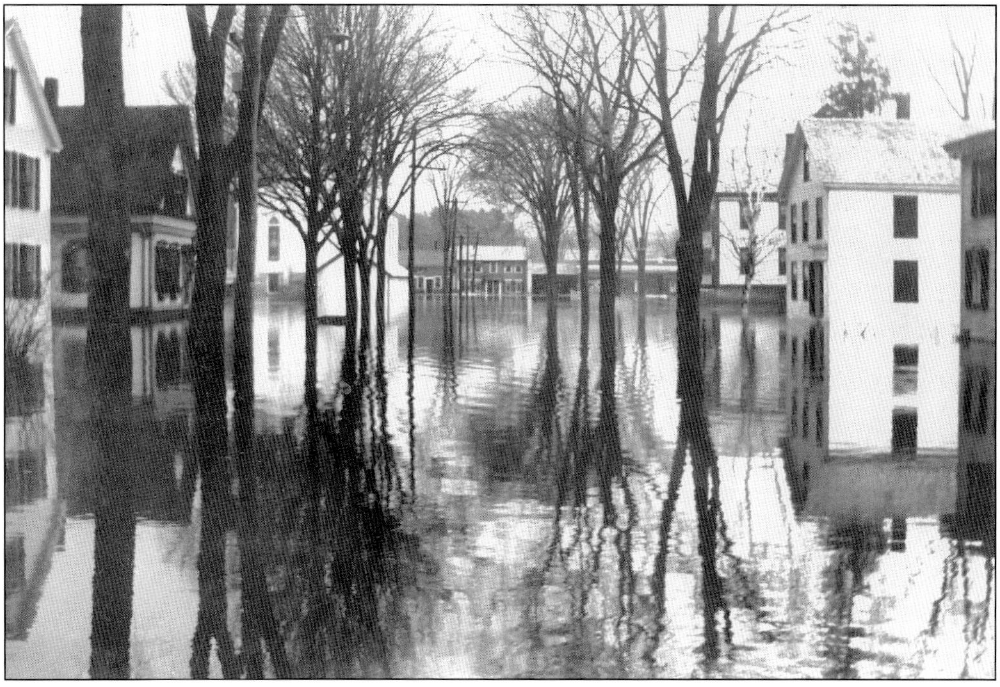

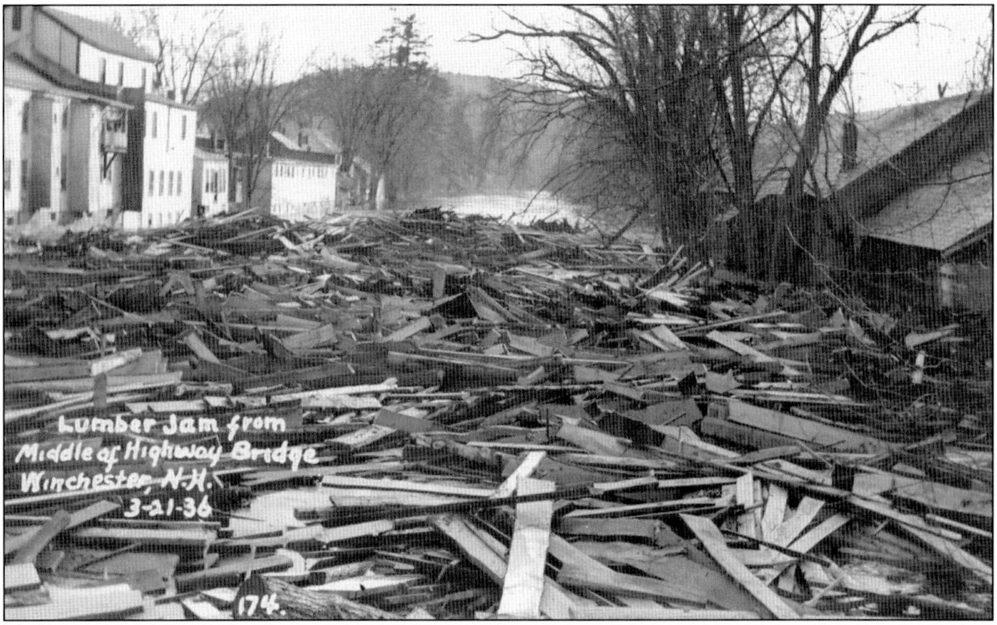

The biggest threat came from the lumber that was washed away from the New England Box Company. Looking south from the Elm Street Bridge shows an impressive pile of lumber clogging the Ashuelot River. People standing on the bridge could feel it moving as the water pushed the lumber into it. The bridge held, but cleaning up the lumber took months.

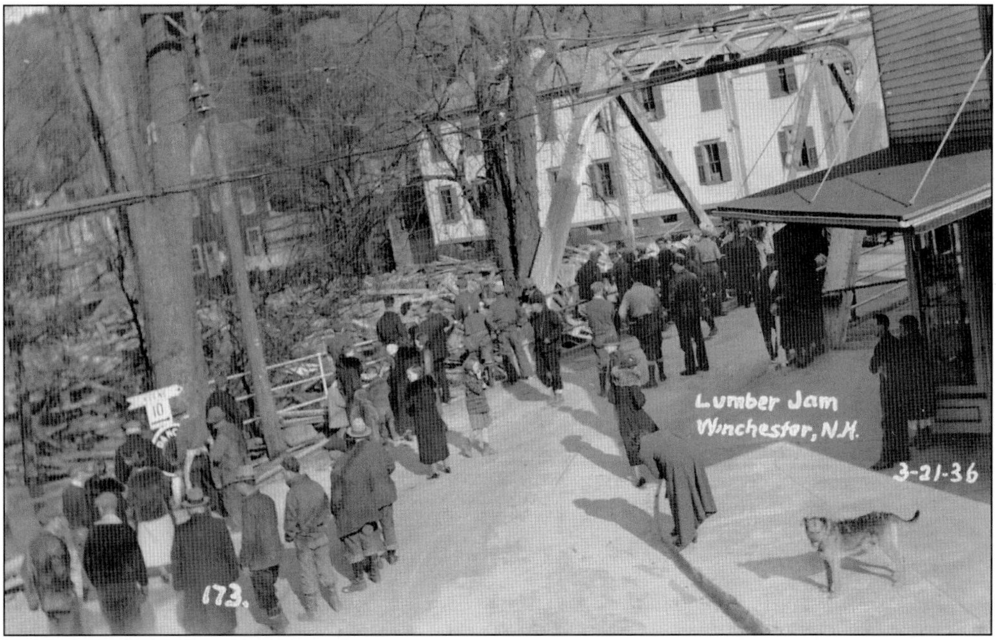

The "lumber jam" attracted many onlookers in the days following the flood. This view from the north end of Ashuelot Street shows the Cook Block at right and the Drugstore Block across the river. Note the Route 10 sign near the left side of the image; in 1936, Route 10 went across the bridge and down Ashuelot Street.

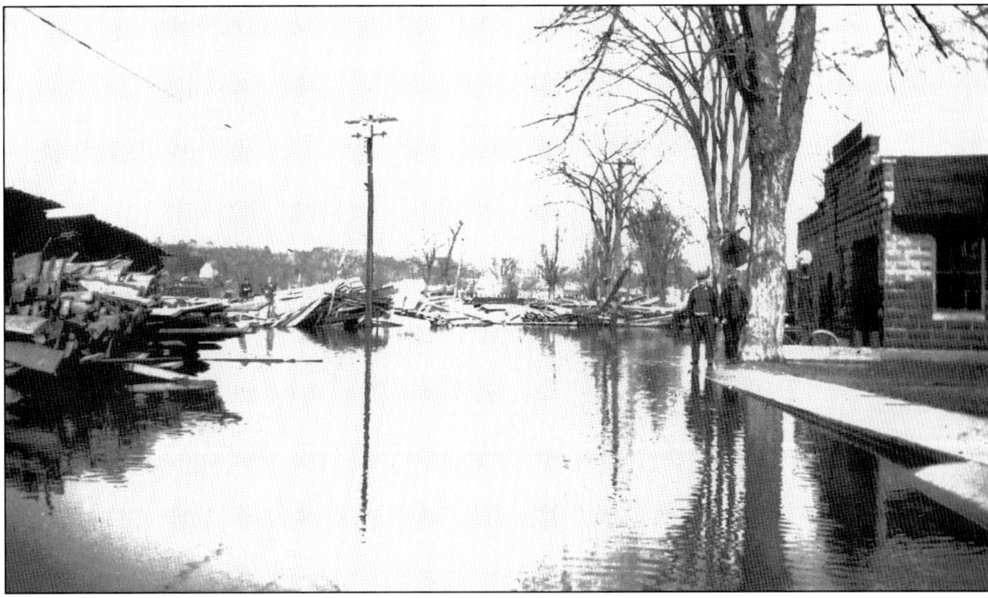

This photograph shows floating lumber blocking Keene Road near the corner of Maple Street. The New England Box Company had lumber staked on both sides of the Ashuelot River as far north as the tannery. "Staking" was a term used to describe lumber being stacked and stored for future use.

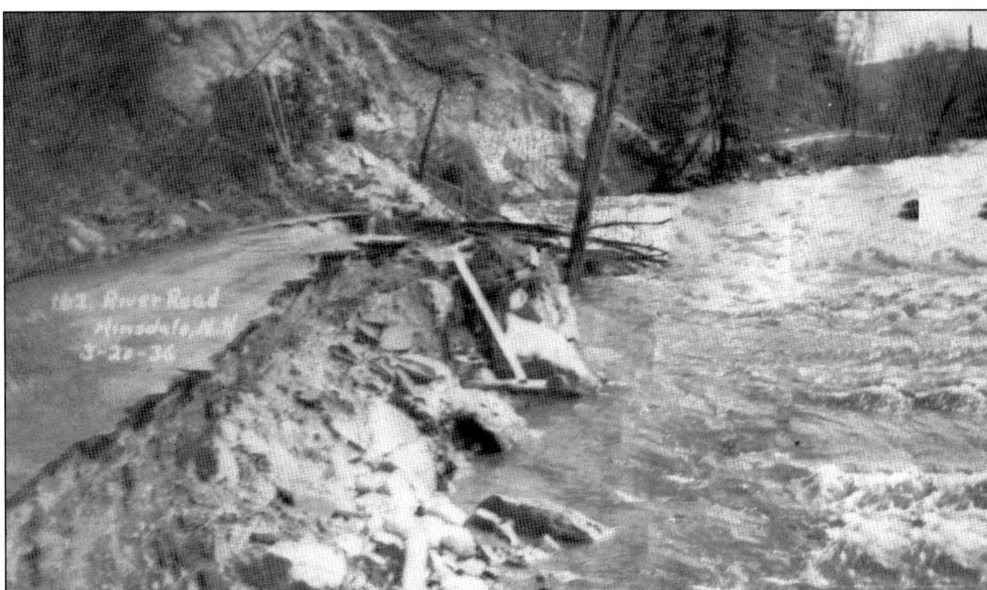

In Ashuelot, the Ashuelot River washed out the road to Hinsdale near the Ashuelot Paper Mill. After the flood of 1936, a major flood control project was undertaken all over the northeast. Dams were built upstream to help control the water and minimize future flooding.

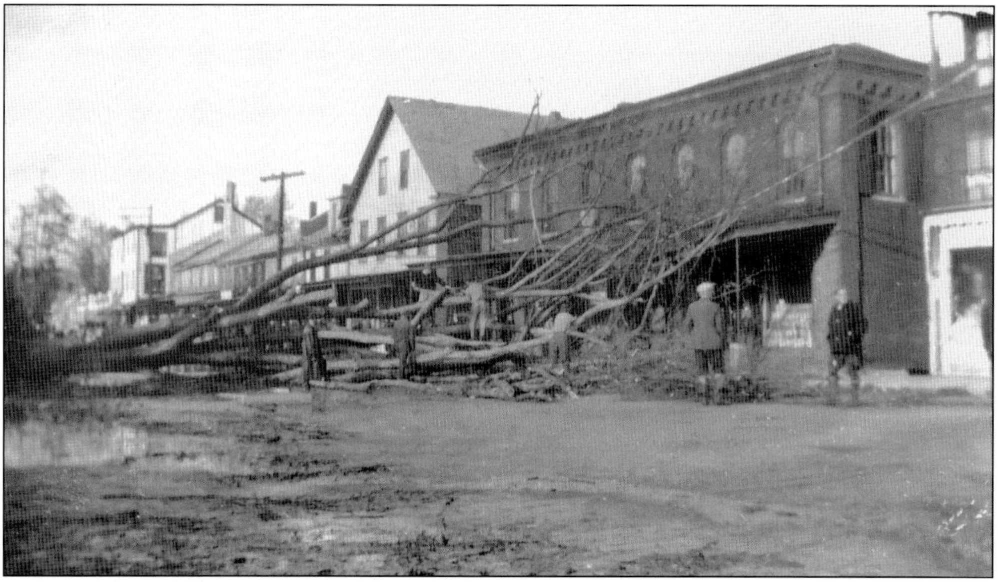

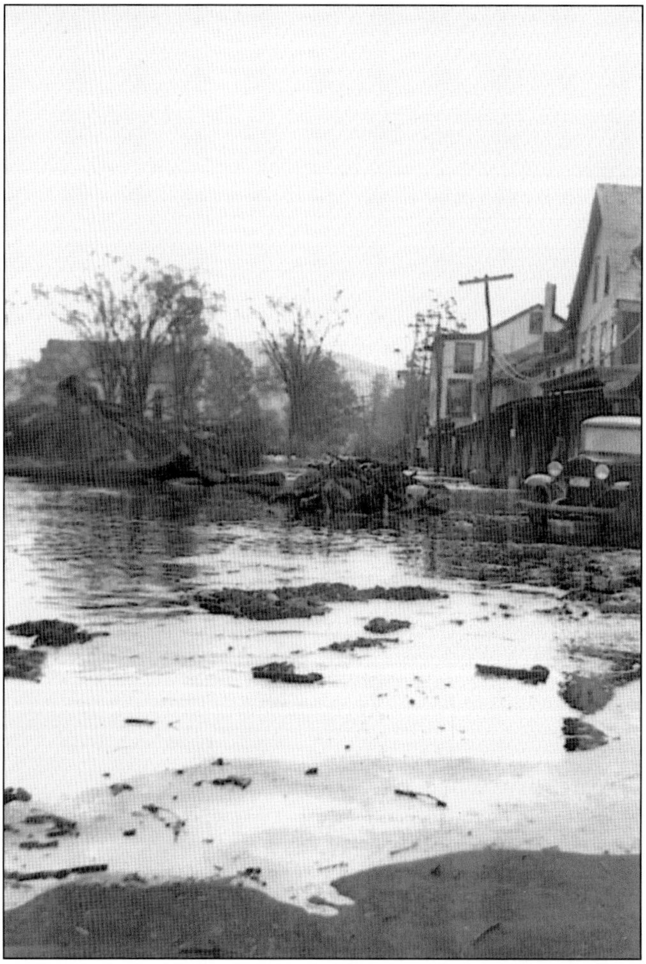

The hurricane of 1938 came without warning. It had been raining for five days, and flooding was already causing many problems, including a washout that severed the Ashuelot Railroad line between Hinsdale and Ashuelot. The wind began to pick up on the afternoon of Wednesday, September 21. It blew and howled as people huddled inside and the sky grew dark. By 9:00 that evening, it was over, but the extent of the damage was not evident until the next morning. Main Street was littered with debris and made impassable by fallen elm trees.

This photograph makes it clear that a boat was needed in order to negotiate Route 10 north to Keene. The Ashuelot River was over its banks, completely submerging the road just beyond the Strand Hotel.

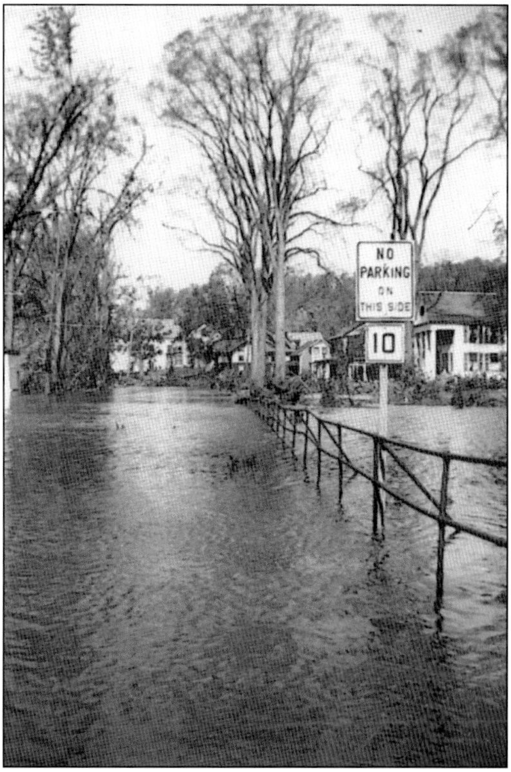

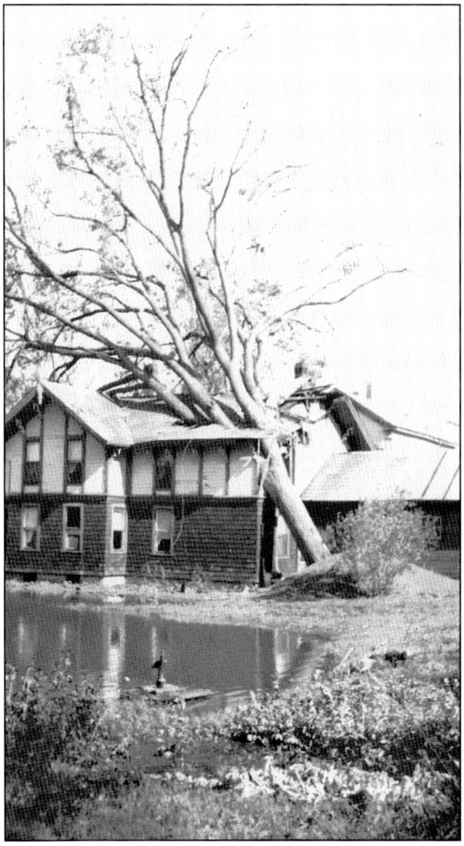

This house sustained serious damage, but it was repaired and still stands just south of the southern intersection of Mechanic Street and Keene Road. This house is also visible directly in the center of the photograph above.

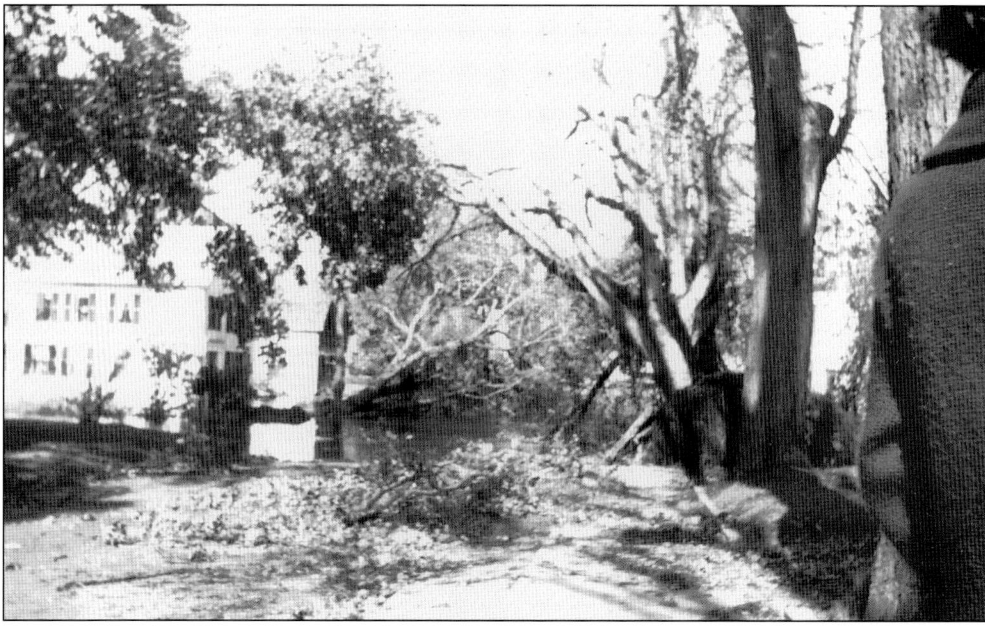

Tree-lined Parker Street fared even worse than Main Street; the western end of the street was obscured by the fallen trees. This photograph looks toward the east down Parker Street. The two visible houses, the first two houses after the Emergency Services Building, are still standing.

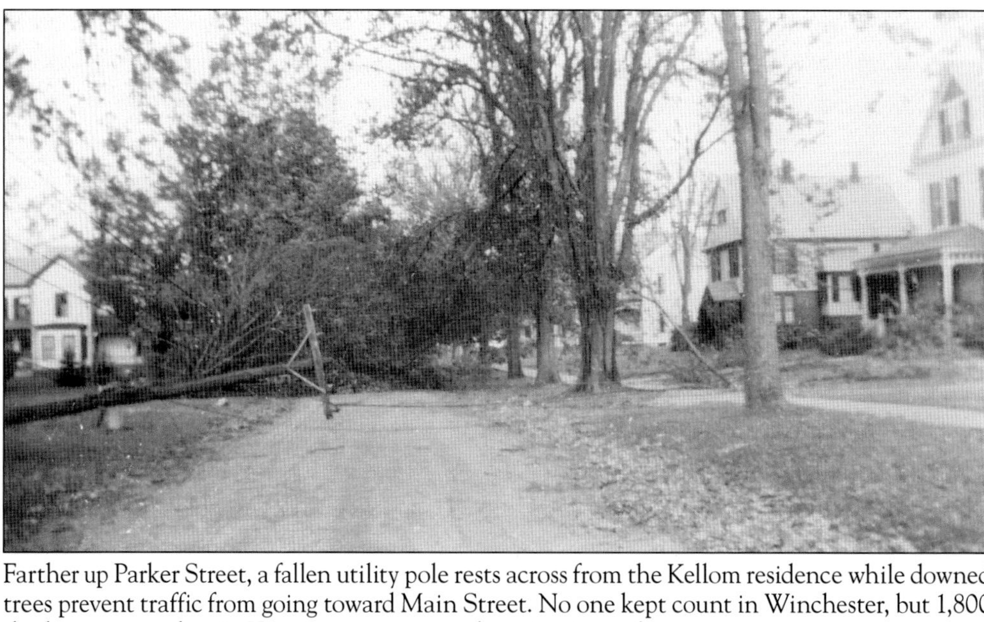

Farther up Parker Street, a fallen utility pole rests across from the Kellom residence while downed trees prevent traffic from going toward Main Street. No one kept count in Winchester, but 1,800 shade trees were lost in Keene, not counting those in city parks.

The photograph at right shows the current Gusan home, the house next door to the Kellom residence, draped in branches. It took days to clean up the trees and restore power, but, fortunately, none of the houses on Parker Street sustained serious damage.

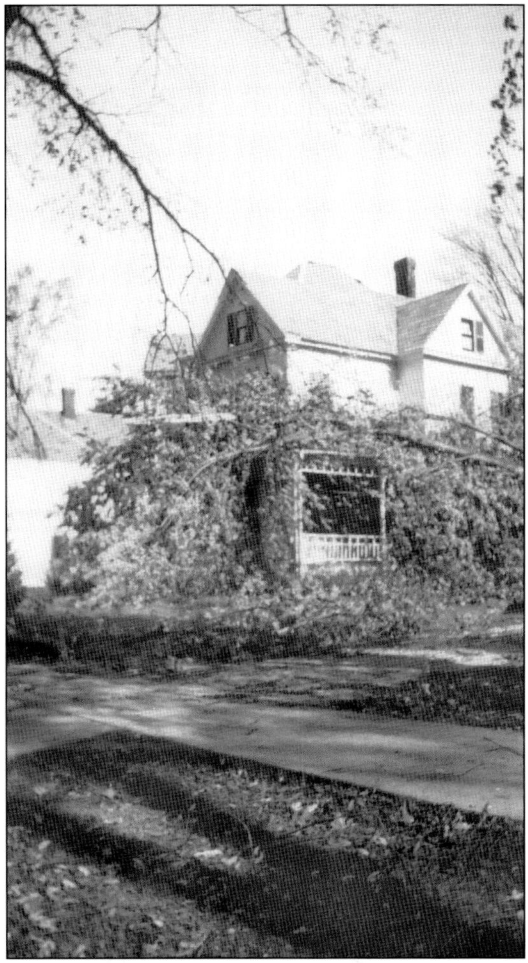

This photograph shows Ashuelot Street underwater and littered with debris. The Cook Block is at left and the fire station is at right. Though the sturdy elm trees remained standing, they were stripped of their leaves.

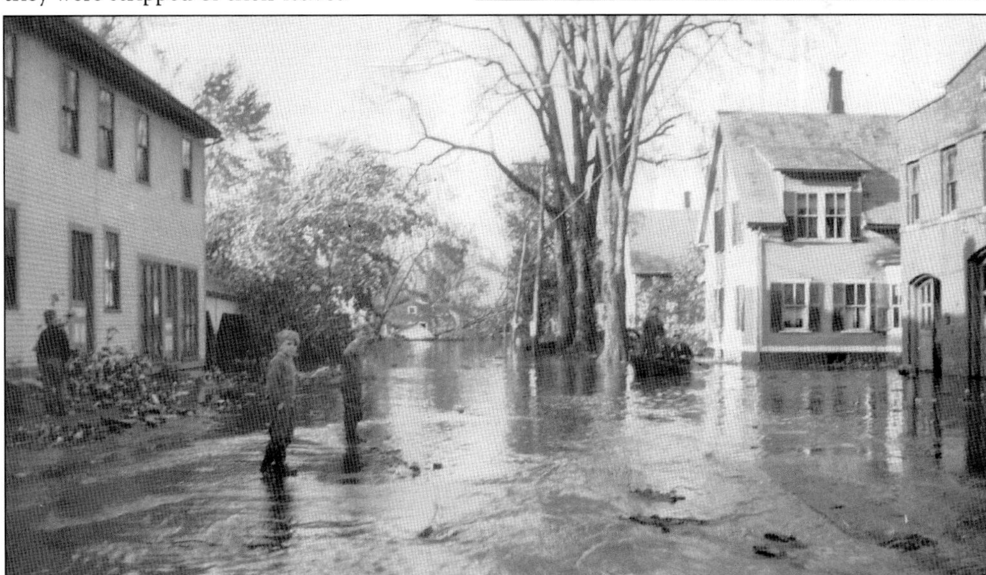

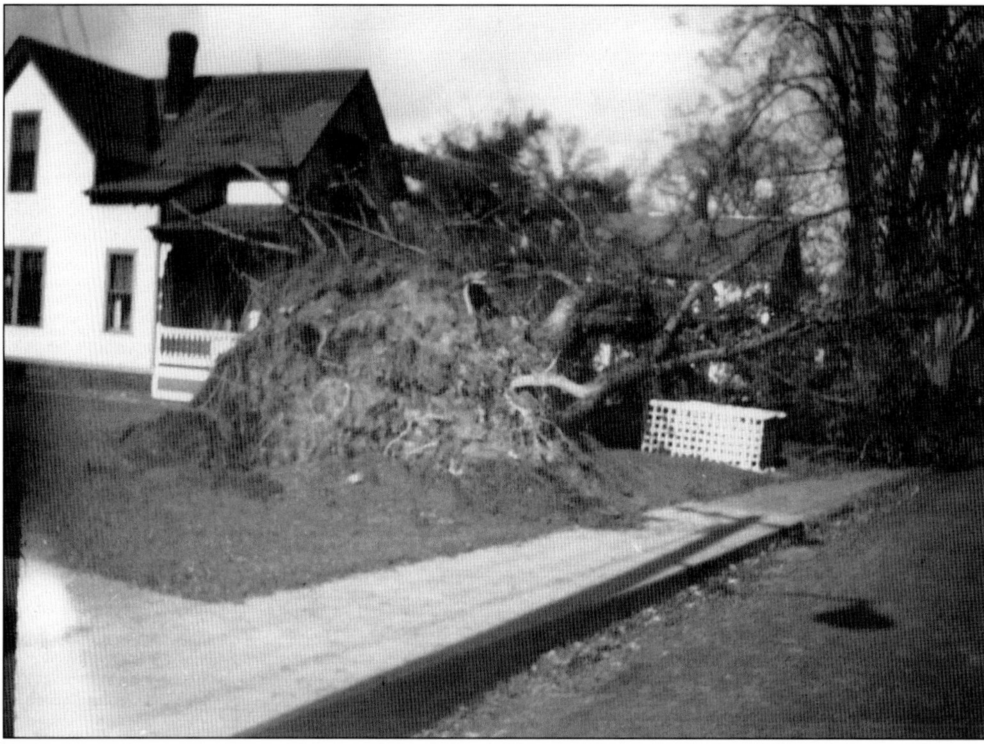

Richmond Street had less damage than Parker Street. This photograph shows the Thompson house inundated with fallen trees, but escaping serious damage. The house, which is on Richmond Street just east of Union Street, is now the Grant residence.

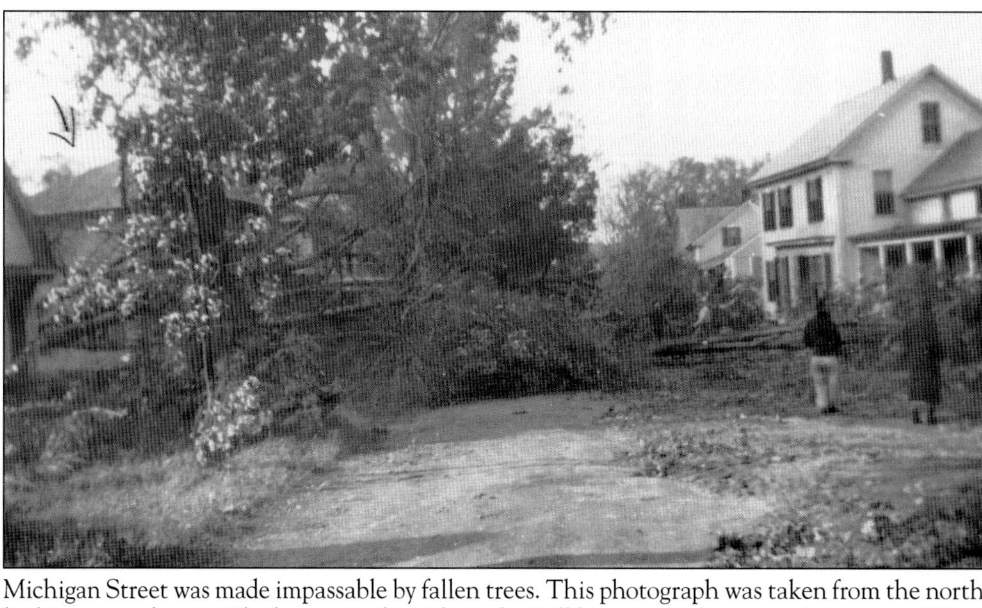

Michigan Street was made impassable by fallen trees. This photograph was taken from the north, looking toward town. The house on the right is the Ryll house, which was on the corner of Cross Street (now called Parkhurst Way).

The Evergreen Cemetery, located on Richmond Road, lost many trees. Winchester's oldest and largest cemetery is the burial place of many of the town's early residents, including Josiah Willard II, Ansel Dickinson, Persis Albee, and Jane Grace Alexander.

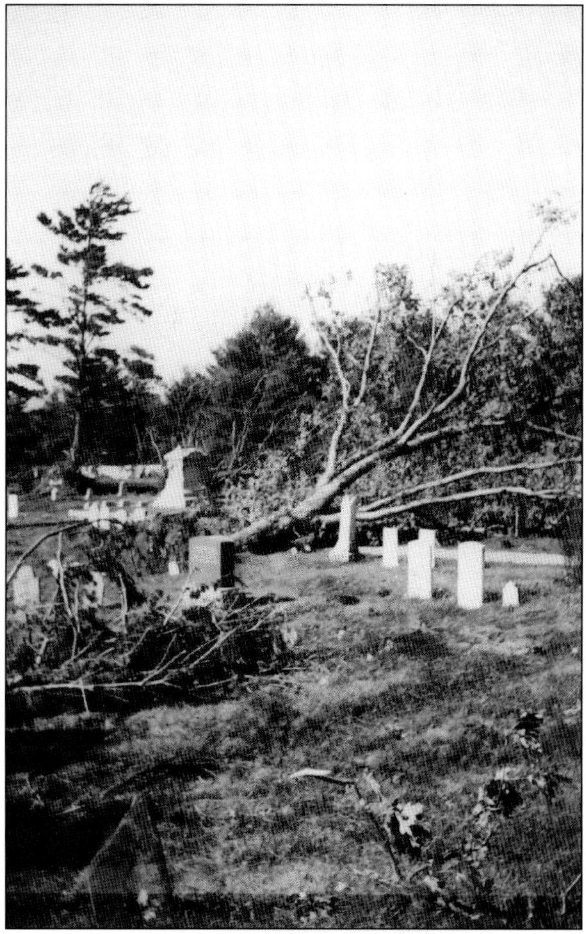

No part of town escaped damage, but unfortunately most of the destruction was not preserved in photographs. However, we do have this photograph is of the Felch house sitting on a knoll between Main Street and the river in the Lower Ashuelot Village.

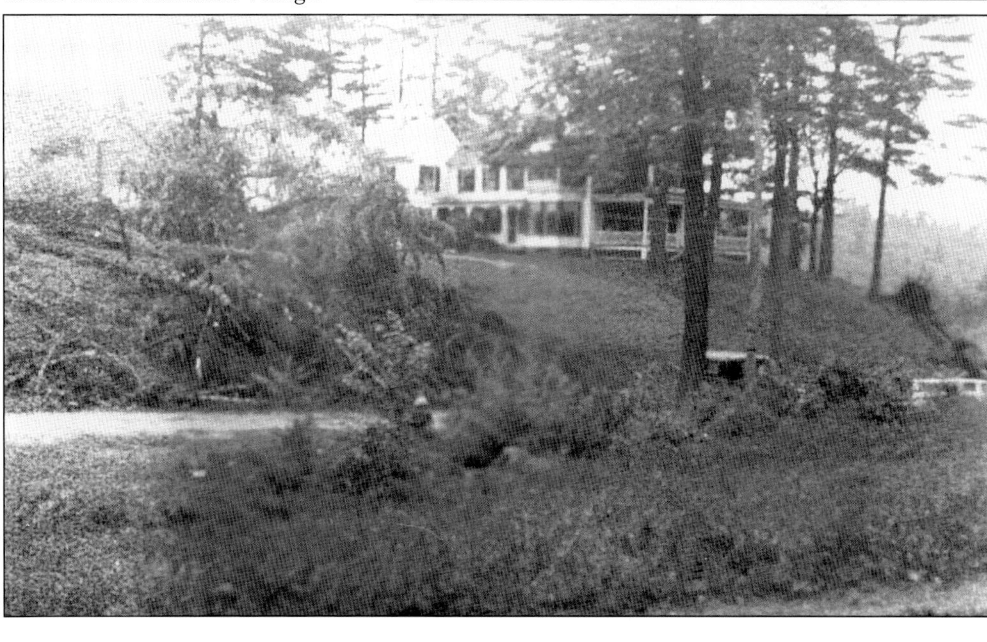

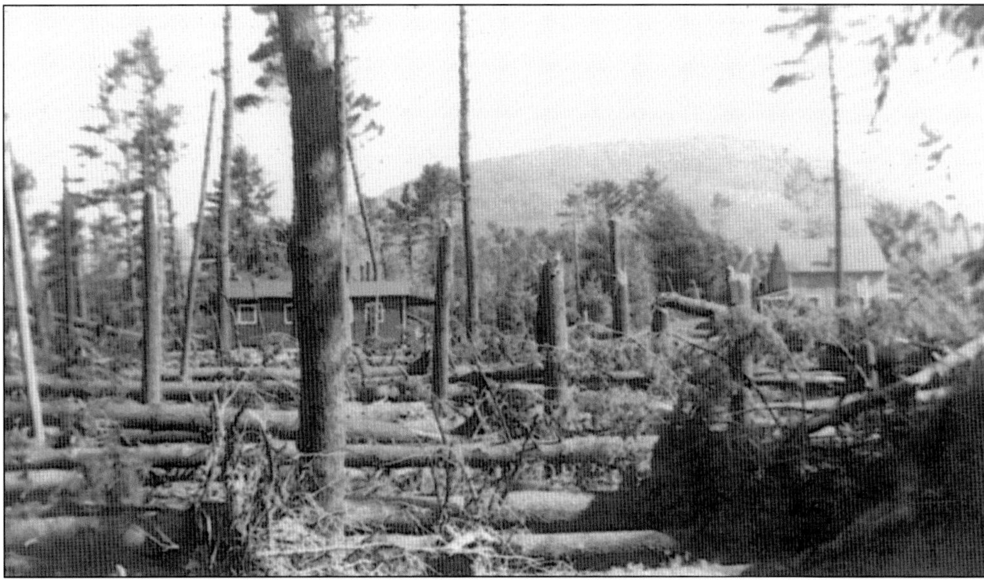

The pine grove at Forest Lake was flattened by the 1938 hurricane. The New England Box Company cleared many of the trees from the grove and around town and stored them in the lake. It took several years for the New England Box Company to harvest all of the trees. It took less time for James Phillips, owner of the pine grove, to replant it with saplings.

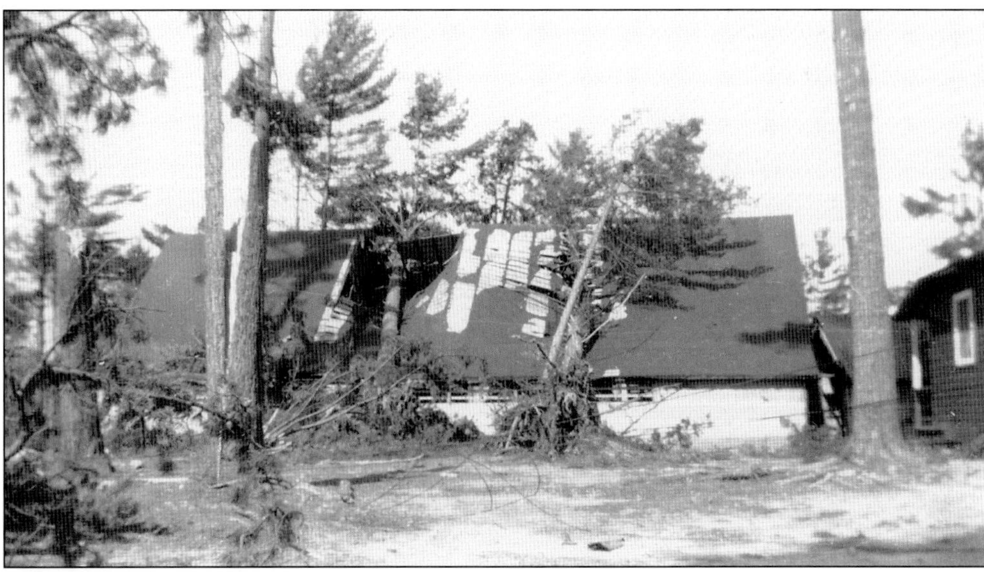

The hurricane wreaked havoc at Forest Lake. This photograph shows the pavilion at Forest Lake badly damaged by fallen pine trees. The pavilion, a popular social spot, was quickly rebuilt and improved. Many of the cottages were damaged, several beyond repair. Some owners chose to rebuild on the eastern shore, which signaled the beginning of development on that side of the lake.

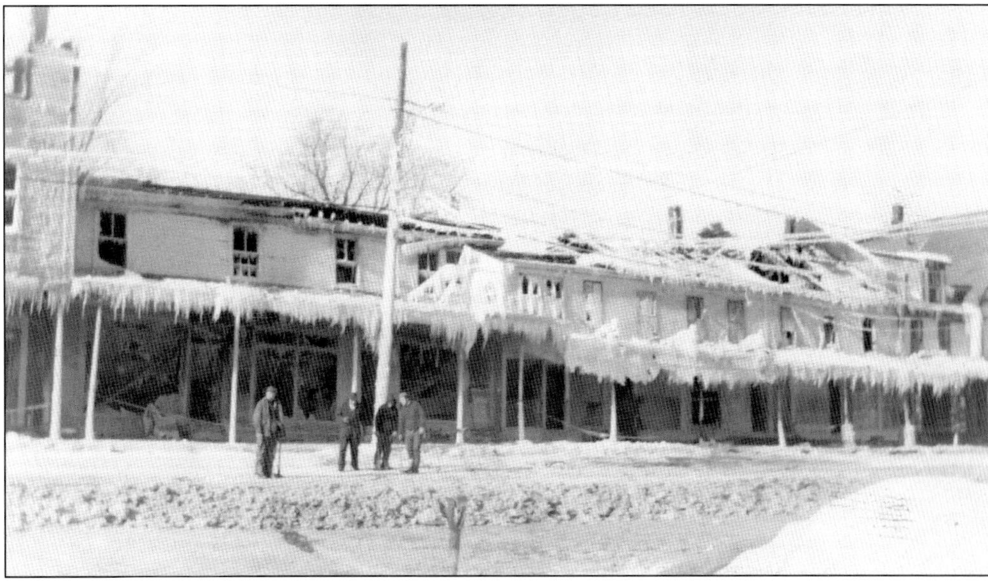

One night in January 1971, with the temperature sinking to 28 degrees below zero (a temperature that has not been reached since in Winchester), the alarm was sounded for a fire on Main Street. The fire began in an antiques store and spread south through a crack in the firewall to the three-story frame building housing Amarosa's Hardware Store. Units responded from surrounding towns as far away as Keene and Brattleboro. At the height of the blaze, 40 firefighting vehicles were involved.

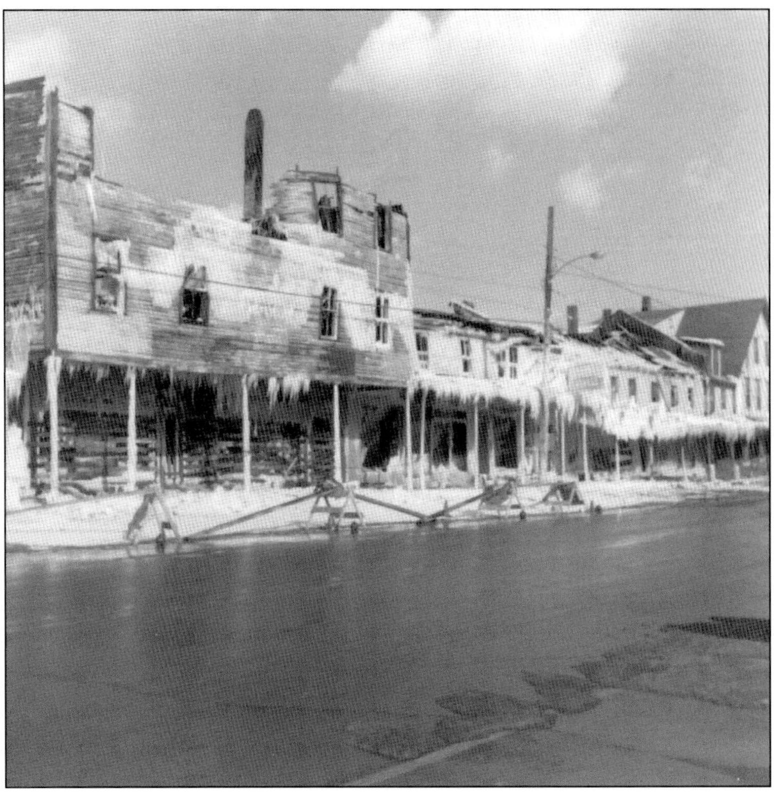

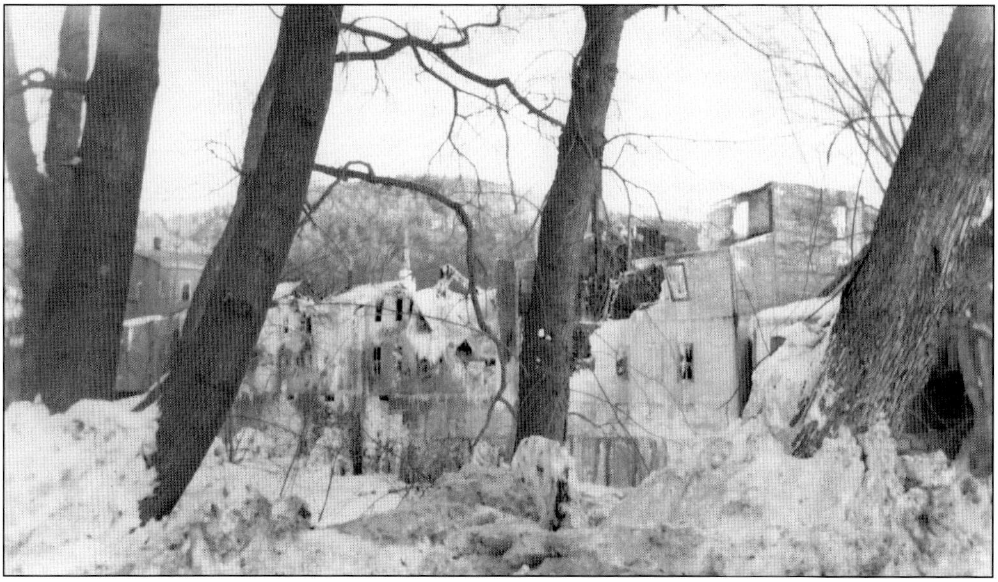

During the January 1971 blaze, firemen were hampered by the extreme cold, which caused the water to freeze into dangerous ice. They rotated shifts, sending firemen back to the station to warm up until they could return to fight some more. The authors were there that night, helping to keep hot coffee and snacks available for the men at the fire station on Ashuelot Street. The next day, the extent of the damage was evident. A stretch of stores, from Amarosa's Hardware to the barbershop, was gone. The fire had jumped several firewalls, but dedicated volunteer and professional firemen finally help stop it. No lives were lost, and the only injury was minor, but several businesses, homes, and historic buildings were gone forever.

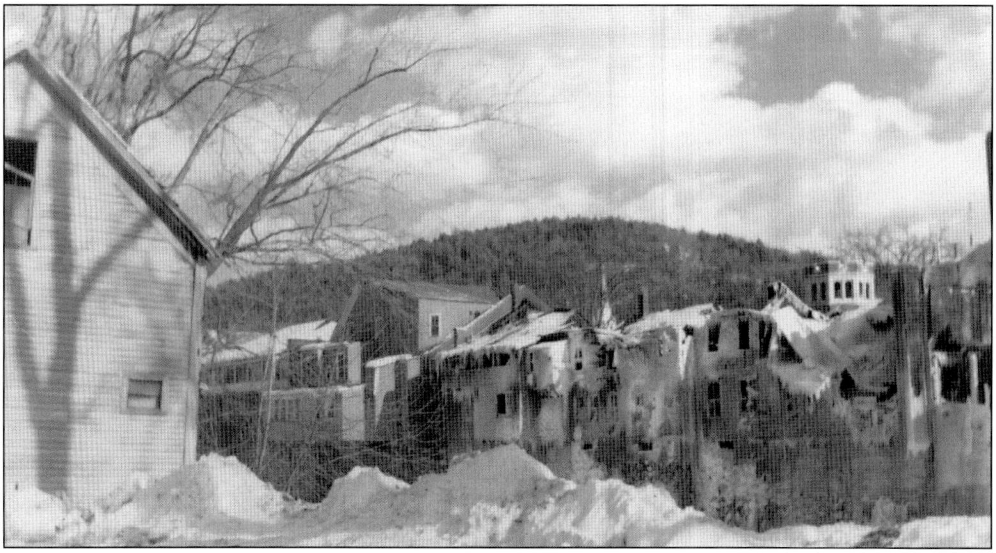

Nine

Covered Bridges

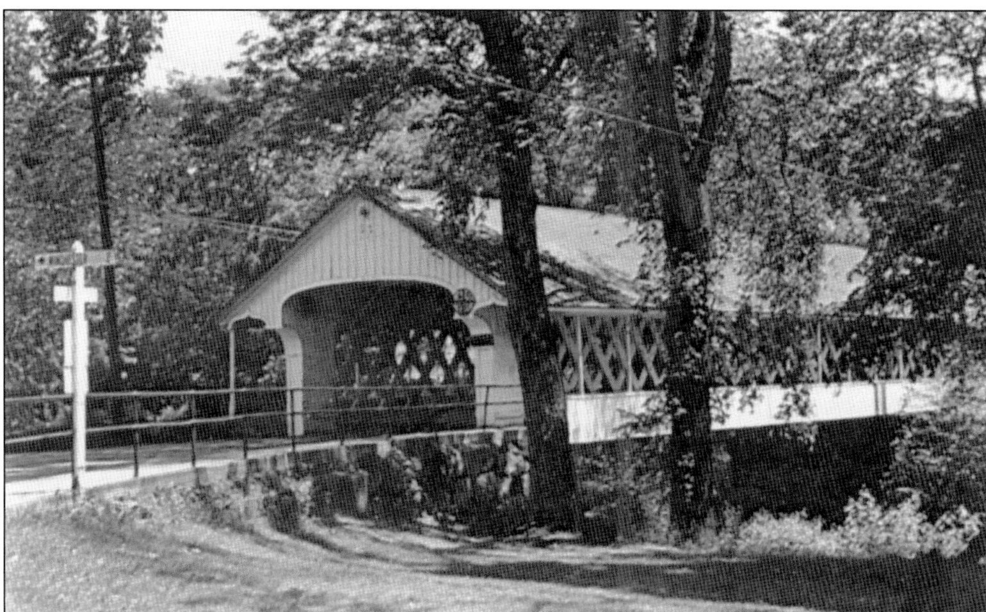

Covered bridges were built for longevity. The roofs protected the roadbed from the weather, minimizing upkeep. At one time, Winchester had five covered bridges, all, like the Ashuelot Bridge pictured here, of Town Truss construction. Ithiel Town invented this sturdy design that is easily identified by the latticework sidewalls. Only two of Winchester's covered bridges remain; the other three, though they had sturdy roofs that protected them from the elements, were destroyed by people.

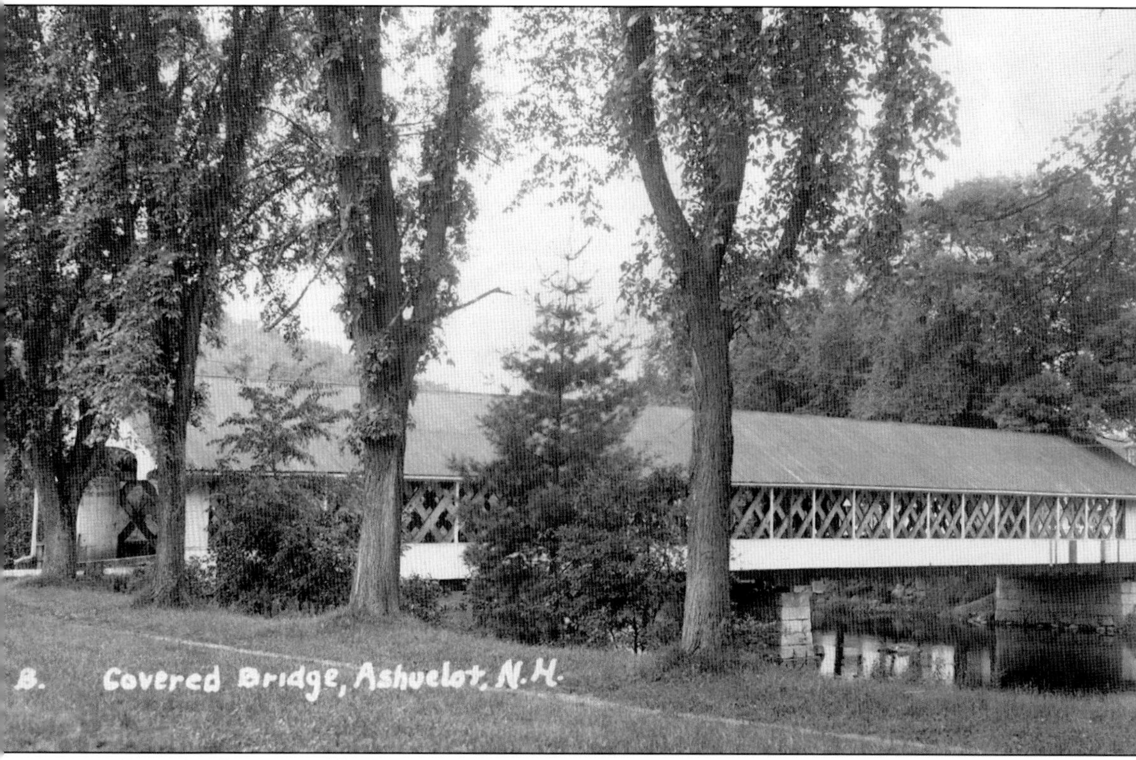

The Ashuelot covered bridge is Bridge No. 1 on the New Hampshire Covered Bridge Trail. It has been called the most photographed covered bridge in the country, and that is easy to believe. In 1864, the beautiful bridge replaced a less substantial crossing on the Ashuelot River, principally to afford access between the Ashuelot Railroad station and the woolen mill. This is the bridge Hugh Sheridan walked across each day to preside over his woolen mill. This is the bridge that Ashuelot School students crossed each day going to and from the bus stop. It is 160 feet long with a center support and walkways on both sides. Extensive repairs in 1999 put the bridge in good enough shape to last another century; old timbers were replaced, and new trunnels were fashioned on-site. Trunnels are the wooden pegs that fasten the timbers together. They are actually "tree nails," but the old-time pronunciation has turned them into trunnels.

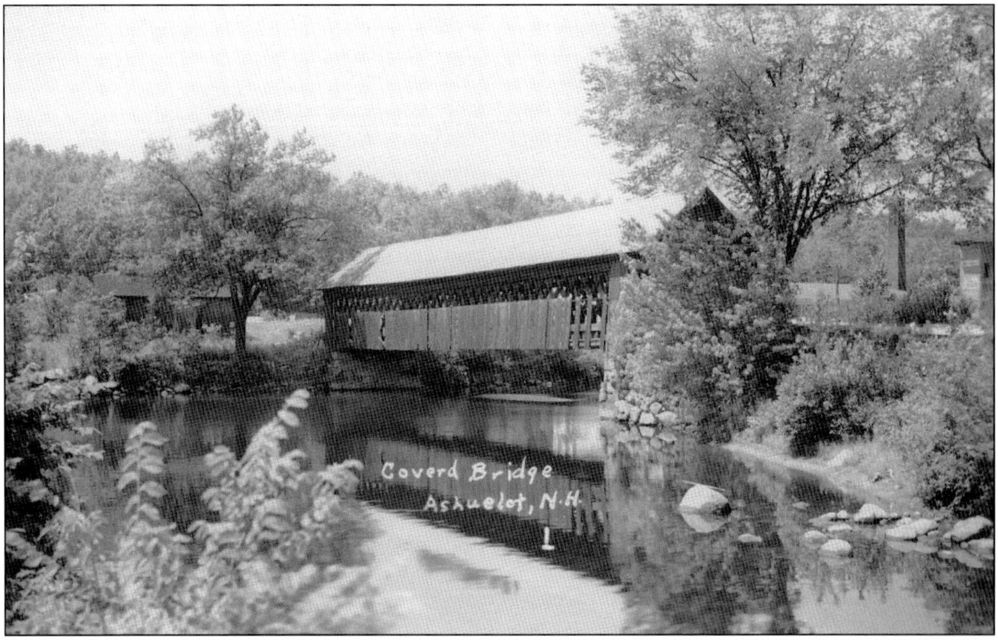

The bridge in Lower Ashuelot, sometimes called the Sawmill Bridge, allowed access to the mills and Ashuelot Railroad flag station on the south side of the Ashuelot River. In 1888, the town approved $2,000 to build it, and in 1946, the town approved $14,000 to tear the bridge down and build one that could accommodate modern commercial traffic.

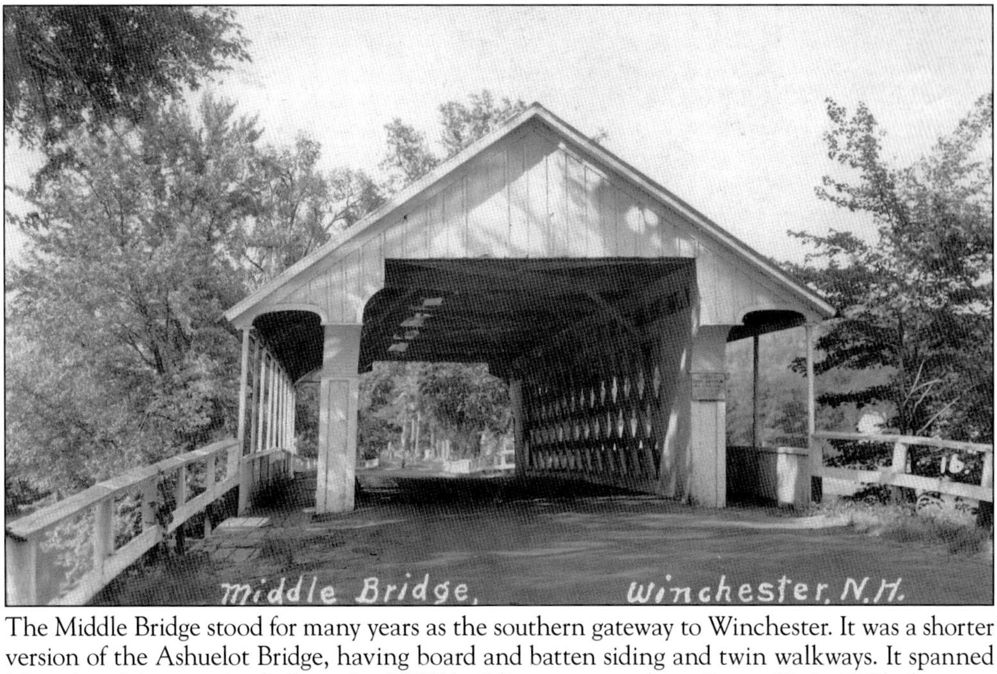

The Middle Bridge stood for many years as the southern gateway to Winchester. It was a shorter version of the Ashuelot Bridge, having board and batten siding and twin walkways. It spanned Mirey brook just south of where the VFW building now stands on Route 10. In 1940, the town appropriated $6,000 as its half of the cost of replacing it with a new span more suitable for the age of automobiles.

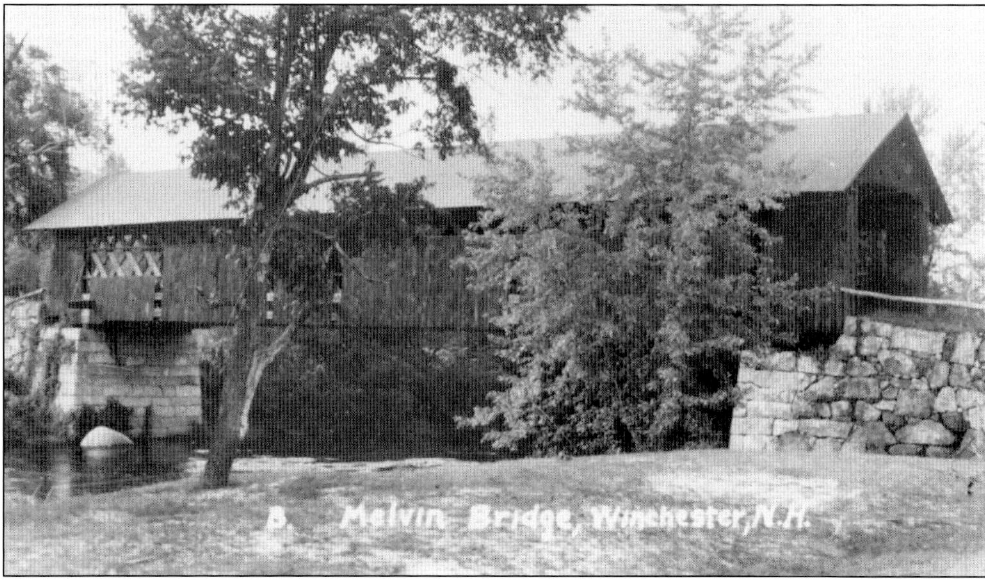

The Melvin Bridge allowed traffic from Pond Village at the Forest Lake outlet to cross the Ashuelot River to the intersection of Old Westport and Old Spofford Roads. Many a jitneyload of visitors was carted from the flag stop near the intersection to Forest Lake for a day or more of fun. The bridge survived a 1955 fire that was contained to the floor, but in November 1965, it was a victim of arson and was a total loss.

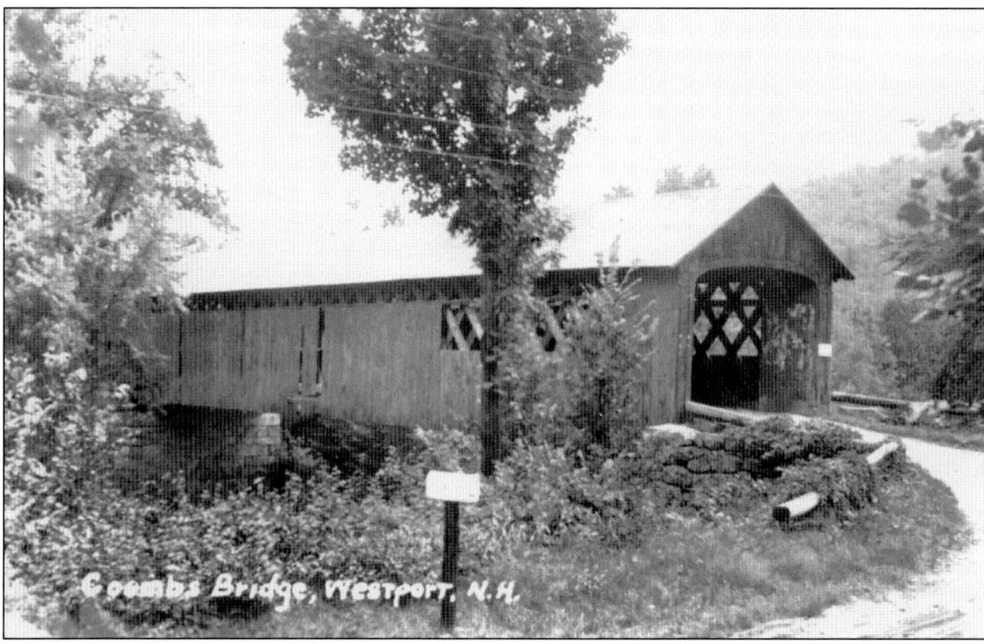

The Coombs Bridge crosses the Ashuelot River at the north end of town, allowing access from Route 10 to the Old Westport Road. It was built around 1847 and, with no walkways and remaining unpainted, looks much like the Melvin Bridge, but at 118 feet, it is 13 feet longer. For many years, the school bus would approach the bridge, then unload the students so that they could walk across the bridge; the bus would then drive across and reclaim the passengers on the other side. After the bridge was extensively renovated in 1997, the bus could cross with students on board.

BIBLIOGRAPHY

Atkins, Edith W., ed. *The Return of the Winchester Star*, vol. 4, no. 10. Winchester, NH: June 1983.

———. *Walking Back Through Time: Fifty Historical Sketches of Winchester, NH*. Palmer, MA: Turley Publications, 1997.

Buell, Janet, and the Write Sisters. *Women of Granite: 25 New Hampshire Women You Should Know*. Bedford, NH: Apprentice Shop Books, LLC, 2008.

Child, Hamilton, ed. *Gazetteer of Cheshire County, N.H. 1736–1885: Part First*. Syracuse, NY: Hamilton Child, 1885.

Pierce, George W. "Winchester: Earlington, Arlington, Winchester." Unknown publisher, 1896.

Poole, Carol L., ed. *The Return of the Winchester Star*, vol. 3, no. 10. Winchester, NH: June 1982

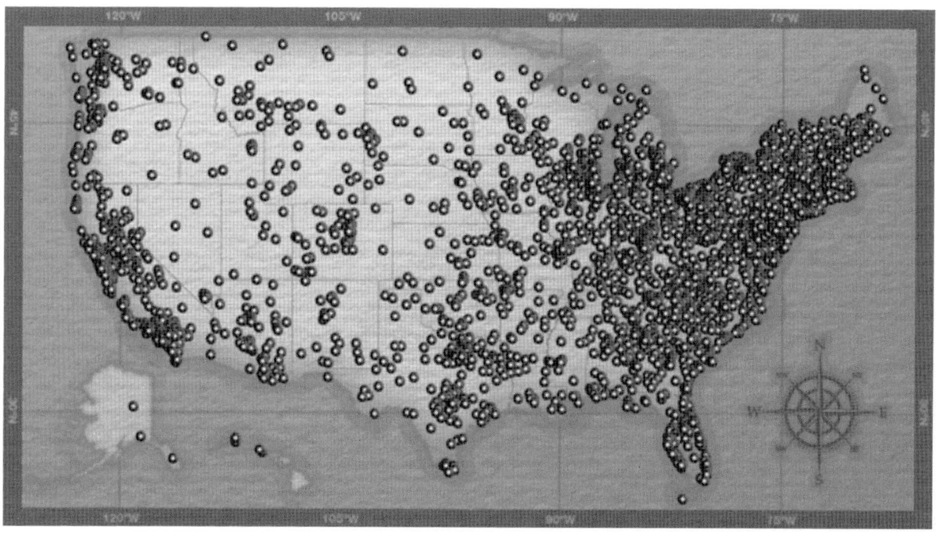